Cities, Suburbs, and Property Taxes

Cities, Suburbs, and Property Taxes

Norman Walzer
Western Illinois University
Glenn W. Fisher
Wichita State University

Oelgeschlager, Gunn & Hain, Publishers, Inc.
Cambridge, Massachusetts

International Standard Book Number: 0-89946-110-7

Library of Congress Catalog Card Number: 81-14175

Printed in West Germany

Library of Congress Cataloging in Publication Data

Walzer, Norman.
Cities, suburbs, and property taxes.

Includes index.
1. Municipal finance—United States. 2. Municipal finance—Illinois. I. Fisher, Glenn W. II. Title.
HJ9145.W34 352.1′0973 81-14175
ISBN 0-89946-110-7 AACR2

Contents

List of Figures

List of Tables

Preface

The present climate of property tax limits, cutbacks in federal aid, and runaway inflation has markedly increased attention paid to local public finance. Public officials are faced with pressures for additional services, higher wages, and compliance with a wide array of federal regulations at the same time that they must struggle to find additional resources or even to keep existing revenue sources.

In 1968, Glenn W. Fisher and Robert P. Fairbanks published *Illinois Municipal Finance*, which described the methods of financing cities in Illinois. In the subsequent decade or so, local finance has changed markedly. Home rule freed local officials from countless hours of legal research to find precedents for desired actions. Many new revenue sources came into use, allowing municipal officials to become involved in a broader array of services than formerly was the case. Municipal finance has become a very sophisticated and complicated topic. However, the availability of detailed information on methods used to finance cities has not kept pace with these new developments.

In 1977, the Institute of Government and Public Affairs, University of Illinois at Urbana, offered Norman Walzer an opportunity to research municipal finance in Illinois and collaborate with Professor Fisher in the writing of this book. At that time Fisher used part of a sabbatical leave from Wichita State University to work on the manuscript. Both authors would like to thank the universities for support.

Many persons contributed to this book. We both have spent many years learning about local government finance from state and municipal officials in Illinois and other states. In addition, we have drawn heavily on the rapidly expanding local public finance literature emanating from academic and governmental sources. It is impossible to name all who have helped us with various phases of this book or all the government officials who have responded to surveys and otherwise been available to answer questions.

Several persons and groups should be individually recognized for their assistance in this effort. Both authors worked with the Illinois Cities and Villages Municipal Problems Commission for many years and have learned immensely from the contacts with local public officials as part of this experience. The Illinois Municipal League staff has always been willing to provide assistance and answer questions to clarify issues. Various parts of the manuscript were read by William L. Day, Larry Frang, Samuel K. Gove, Ann Lousin, Pierre de Viśe, Pat Watt, and Richard E. Zody. Assistance with the computer and statistical analysis was provided by John Carroll and Vickie S. Winters. As usual, these people should be accorded no responsibility for our willingness to implement their suggestions.

N. W.
G. W. F.

Chapter 1

Introduction

In the past 100 years the U.S. economy has shifted from being mainly rural to being highly industrialized and urban. In 1870, 25.7 percent of the U.S. population lived in urban places, whereas a century later, 73.7 percent were classified as urban. The trend toward concentrated urban living not only has changed American lifestyles, but also has created a need for completely different public services and raised a much more complicated set of social problems. Changes in the private sector are easily recognized by higher income levels, better housing, and improved transportation facilities. Changes in the public sector in response to these private sector developments have been slower.

GROWTH OF GOVERNMENT

Much has been written about the changing prosperity in the United States and its effect on residents. What is not as clearly recognized is the role of the public sector in accommodating these developmental changes. While economies of scale in private production have permitted employment to grow and standards of living to improve, certain of these improvements would not have been possible without the public capital and infrastructure provided by government. These services have been financed through compulsory contributions by residents, in the form of taxes or charges for services. The lack of direct relationship between payment of taxes and receipt of public services has always caused taxes to be unpopular.

Whenever additional public services are deemed necessary, a method of financing has to be found. This usually means that a new tax is created or that an existing tax is increased. In other instances, a completely new revenue source may be instituted. When existing taxes cannot be increased and other revenue sources are not apparent, the program can sometimes be financed by a new government. Each of these financing decisions is carried out independently, often without regard for previous actions or without serious attention to its impact on the existing method of financing public services.

The outcome of these decisions has been a patchwork arrangement of overlapping and competing local governments. The Census Bureau estimates that there were 79,913 units of government in the United States in 1977. As large as this number might appear, it is considerably lower than the 116,807 units of operation twenty-five years earlier. But, whereas the number had been decreasing prior to 1972, an additional 1,644 units of government were formed between 1972 and 1977.

The governments providing services are of many different types. Specialized, single-purpose units were created to accomplish a particular task; many have been retained even though they have outlived their usefulness. There are also more than 39,000 general purpose governments providing a wide range of services. Each government has an elected or appointed governing board operating independently of other units at the same level and providing services that the board deems appropriate, often with minimum coordination and cooperation.

To finance public services, taxpayers have had to pay out an increasing share of their income as taxes and user charges. The federal income tax is structured so that in periods of high inflation and substantial money wage increases, taxpayers face higher marginal rates even though in real terms they have not gained. In other instances, increases in housing prices have caused property taxes to rise faster than increases in income. Some consumers have thus been placed in the uncomfortable position of paying higher taxes when their incomes will purchase less.

The combination of rising taxes and complex governmental structure has frustrated taxpayers. Often they are unaware of all the government-provided services and are further irritated that their complaints about taxes are rendered ineffective by the complexity of government structure. Government officials are also frustrated. Often they feel that they are blamed for actions over which they have no control. City officials tend to be most visible and are often criticized for the actions of all local governments.

TAXPAYER LIMITATIONS

The public's growing dissatisfaction with rising taxes in the face of shrinking real incomes culminated in California in June 1978 with the passage of Proposition 13, a constitutional amendment significantly reducing the average citizen's property tax bill and making the substitution of other taxes at the local or state levels difficult. The consequences of this vote were immediately felt in city halls and state capitols throughout the nation, as residents in many other states moved to institute limits on taxes and expenditures.

While the California experience may be unique due to the progressive income tax and the rapid increase in housing values in that state, there can be little question that taxpayers were voting for tax relief without fully understanding its long-term effects. The Jarvis-Gann Amendment limited the maximum amount of any ad valorem tax on real property to 1 percent of the full cash value of the property. The amendment stipulates that the 1975-76 full cash value cannot be increased more than 2 percent per year unless there is a change of ownership. The obvious outcome is that owners of recently purchased or newly constructed property face higher tax bills than do long-time owners of comparable property. The feeling of frustration with the property tax will probably be compounded.

The need to divide the maximum 1 percent tax levy among the units of local government has also resulted in a larger fiscal role for county government, while additional state aid has resulted in increased state control of local government affairs.

Not only has Proposition 13 changed the nature of the property tax and promoted government centralization, it has also limited the financial powers of the state. The constitutional amendment requires that any new taxes imposed or any rate increase legislation passed by the state legislature receive a two-thirds vote. No new taxes on real property or transaction taxes on the sale of real property may be levied. Local governments may impose nonproperty taxes only when such a move is approved by two-thirds of the qualified voters.

Events in California illustrate that the method of financing local services can be drastically altered through citizen action programs. Those programs have brought about a much larger role for state and county governments. Ultimately, the revenue source over which residents have the greatest control (property taxes) has been reduced in importance. Local officials have been limited in their flexibility in financing services, and the effective voice of citizens in the types of services that are to be provided has been reduced.

Precisely why residents have taken such an indiscriminate approach to limiting government spending rather than attacking particularly outmoded or inefficient units is subject to debate. Analysts offer many reasons for the success of Proposition 13 and other such movements. Frustration with the rising costs of living and the slowdown of income growth usually head the list.

There are other important reasons for the success of the tax limitation movements, however. Perhaps most important is a general lack of knowledge about how governments are financed and the types of services they provide. Decision making in local government is complex, involving numerous participants, many acting on a part-time basis, and each with his or her own objectives and favorite programs. Cities have always provided basic services such as public safety, street maintenance, environmental control, and health care. In recent years, the city government has also played a greater role in promoting the economic development of the city. Industrial revenue bonds are issued to attract industry to the city, and housing revenue bonds are issued to provide adequate housing to middle- and lower-income residents at reduced interest rates. Many of these and similar projects require that tax dollars be used either to support the program or for general administrative activities.

COMPLEXITY OF MUNICIPAL FINANCE

Unfortunately, the average citizen is often unaware of services provided until a particular service is discontinued or an unexpected need arises. The fact that better and more services require higher taxes is sometimes not fully understood.

One can argue over whose responsibility it is for the public to be informed about the use of its tax dollars and whether a better-informed public would react differently to tax issues. Local officials lament the fact that a budget hearing or a hearing on the proposed uses of revenue-sharing funds is attended by only a dozen or so residents, most of whom are interested in showing support for a favorite program. The average citizen apparently does not believe that it is worthwhile to become involved in local finance.

On the other hand, interested residents face formidable obstacles in determining exactly how money are spent or even how much. Municipal budgeting practices are designed for auditing rather than for showing the costs of programs clearly. Citizens without extensive accounting backgrounds face considerable frustration when they find that expenditures for police protection are contained in several separate places within the budget, for example. And to complicate the situation even more, methods of reporting expenditures differ among cities, thus making comparisons difficult without extensive analyses.

The news media are often of little help. While scandals among local officials make front-page news and dramatic stories involving police or fire departments may be featured from time to time, the routine government services that make a city livable receive little attention.

Given its complex nature, there is little likelihood that a majority of urban residents will ever thoroughly understand municipal finance. The time necessary to study the budget and related documents is not worth the effort when one considers the limited opportunities to affect tax rates and expenditure policies.

Regardless of the reasons that the public is not better informed, it is quite clear that the task of assembling relevant information about the financing of services in cities with differing responsibilities and contrasting economic bases is formidable. Although detailed data on expenditures, revenues, debt, and related characteristics are available from state agencies or from the Bureau of the Census, the information is often not presented in a consistent format. Information on expenditures and revenues of overlapping districts or services provided is often not easily accessible. These limitations combine to make meaningful comparisons of cities possible only with considerable effort and knowledge about local government finance.

PURPOSE OF THIS ANALYSIS

This book is designed to help fill a gap in the literature on municipal finance. Much has been written about narrowly defined issues, such as solid waste removal or the financing of police services using carefully thought out and innovative approaches. However, each study is undertaken on a limited sample of cities for which a detailed set of information is available. The studies are not consistent in the samples used nor in the approaches followed, and they usually involve fairly specific areas of municipal finance.

Existing studies have also suffered from the inadequate attention paid to alternative arrangements for service provision. In some states education is provided by cities, while in Illinois it is provided by a separate unit of government. Each state handles the financing of pensions differently, as well as the collecting and distributing of state-shared revenues. Some cities must operate within a fairly tightly controlled set of tax limits, while others have broad home rule powers.

An interested citizen, an elected public official, or a student of public administration experiences major difficulty finding a comprehensive analysis of factors underlying municipal finance in a relatively nontechnical presentation. While technical analyses of services and revenues are available, frequently the methodology is unfamiliar to the casual reader or scholars from many disciplines. In these cases, the usefulness of the research findings may be limited.

In undertaking a detailed and comprehensive analysis of the financing of municipal services, it is possible to make the analysis so specific to a certain group of cities, or to a particular state, that the results are not meaningful outside the sample. This hazard cannot be completely avoided, but its limitations can be substantially reduced by selecting a representative sample of cities and by using a classification system that allows city types to be identified with others across the nation.

In this study, we use Illinois cities with populations of 25,000 and more as the sample. A digression into the financing of cities with populations over 1 million has been undertaken in order to study Chicago. This disgression was necessitated by the importance of Chicago as the hub of a large Standard Metropolitan Statistical Area (SMSA) in Illinois and because of its relationship with surrounding cities.

Cities in Illinois were selected for several reasons. First, Illinois has among the broadest home rule powers of any state. These powers, possessed by all cities with populations of 25,000 or over, free local decision makers from tax rate limits and debt ceilings. Second, Illinois is a large, industrial state with lagging growth patterns similar to states in the Midwest and Northeast. Given the interrelationships between local economies and conditions throughout the state, the experiences of cities in Illinois should be comparable to those of cities in Ohio, Michigan, New York, and other states.

A third reason for selecting Illinois cities is the wide variety of city types represented. Approximately one-half of the sample is located in the Chicago Standard Metropolitan Area, with economies at least partially determined by events in the nation's third-largest central city. Like New York, Detroit, and other large cities, Chicago has experienced outmigration and a declining economic base. To the extent that relationships between the central cities and the surrounding cities can be established, these findings should provide insight into experiences in suburban cities in other large SMSAs.

Cities in Illinois also exhibit a wide range of economic characteristics. In the Chicago SMSA are cities which rank first, third, and fifth in terms of 1969 median family income among cities. Also within Illinois is a city ranking 883rd. Since the same state statutory requirements and constitutional restrictions pertain to all cities (excluding Chicago), an excellent opportunity is provided to study responses to financial needs with similar external constraints and maximum local decision-making powers.

Finally, Illinois clearly exhibits the suburbanization process so prevalent following the Second World War. The surburban cities in the Chicago SMSA experienced large population growth following the construction of interstate highways linking urban centers. This surburbanization process left in its wake cities with a wide range of economic bases and population characteristics. The suburbanization process has subsequently slowed and cities have entered an era of limited growth. Suburban cities in Illinois exemplify this pattern, with implications for future problems becoming apparent.

To summarize, this study offers insight into financial practices of middle-size cities with widely divergent characteristics, service needs, and economic bases. Although each city is subject to the same constitutional and statutory constraints, each possesses broad home rule powers in terms of taxing authority and program implementation.

For purposes of this study, Illinois cities have been subdivided into those economically linked with Chicago and those that are economically independent. As one might expect, arbitrary judgments had to be made regarding this subdivision in some cases, but for the most part the cities are easily classified.

This method of subdivision was chosen because of its relevance for cities nationwide, as well as its appropriateness for studying the Illinois sample. The suburbanization process has left us with relatively wealthy cities surrounding large central cities. The presence of poverty in the midst of plenty has spawned many studies regarding the role of suburban cities in the financing of central city services used by commuters. What is not always recognized is that suburban cities are very diverse in economic base, employment patterns, and social characteristics. As a result of these variations, suburban cities use considerably different methods to finance services —particularly regarding the importance of property taxes.

Economically independent cities face a different set of issues, including slower population growth, developments on the outer fringe threatening the tax base in the central business district, and a generally lower socioeconomic class of residents. These characteristics are likely to exist nationwide. Whereas these middle-size central cities have not received the attention paid to a New York, a Detroit, or a Chicago, they display many similar, though less pronounced, characteristics.

ORGANIZATION OF THE BOOK

Because this book is intended as a source of general information about municipal finance in an urbanized, industrial state, particular attention has been given to including information about the institutional setting within which municipal financial decisions are made. Thus, within each chapter, we describe legal requirements and accounting practices that might affect the resulting data.

Particular attention is paid to the property tax as it operates in the financing of municipal services. This revenue source has been declining in relative importance in recent years, but it still represents a major revenue item in most municipal budgets and has taken on an increased significance with the formation of taxpayer movements to limit its growth. The property tax is probably one of the least understood of the municipal revenues, mainly because of its complicated method of administration and long collection cycle. In the present antitax climate, some of the strong features of the property tax have been overlooked. Because of its importance, a complete chapter has been devoted to the operation of the property tax.

We also pay considerable attention to the growth in intergovernmental revenues. The shift from categorical grants—favoring cities with a better-qualified staff—to a greater emphasis on block grants and assistance to financially distressed cities may have triggered some subtle changes in the financing of city services. At the very least, the Illinois cities reveal basic differences in their methods of finance when grouped into suburbs and independent cities.

From a discussion of available revenue sources and their use, the study proceeds to examine the resulting outcomes, namely expenditures for services. The types of services provided and their level of quality are of major concern to residents. Considerable attention is paid to comparisons among cities and by city types, thus permitting the reader to see how cities with different socioeconomic characteristics or in different regions respond in providing public services. Particular attention is given to employment and wages paid to public employees so that expenditures by the city can be better understood.

Throughout the analysis, we consider the importance of services provided by other governments. When possible, we include expenditure and revenue data for these governments in the tables to provide the "full cost" of urban services. The inclusion of these expenditures can make substantive differences in the comparisons of municipal finance. One also finds distinct patterns, by city type, in the reliance on other governments for certain services. These differences have important implications for the recent growth in property tax collections.

The data base for subsequent analyses is the 1977 Census of Governments. This information is supplemented by detailed property tax data obtained from the State of Illinois and by personal interviews with officials in approximately one-third of the cities included in the study. Socioeconomic characteristics of the cities are included when deemed important, but since most of this information is from the 1970 Census of Population, its use is limited. In some cases, however, there is little reason to expect the cities to have changed in relative terms, and the information is still useful.

Throughout the comparisons, we have used statistical tests of significant differences. These tests compare the difference between the sample averages in light of the variations found within the city types. With these tests it is possible to determine whether the differences are due simply to chance or whether they reveal more meaningful variations between the cities. Unfortunately, this test does not identify the factors contributing to the disparity between city groups, and a further unraveling of these relationships requires a more powerful technique such as multiple correlation and regression analysis. On several occasions we have used multiple-regression analyses to identify factors related to variations in expenditure levels or tax effort (taxes collected as a percentage of personal income). Throughout the analyses, we have tried to provide assistance to readers unfamiliar with the statistical techniques and to keep the discussions nontechnical.

Because this book is written for casual readers, practitioners in local finance, and public administration students, it has been difficult to maintain an even presentation. Certainly, an experienced practitioner in local finance will find the detailed explanation of the property tax and the discussions of intergovernmental revenues commonplace. However, for an elected municipal official new to the job and interested in obtaining an overall picture of the way cities are financed, these should be very useful sections. To meet the requirements of the intended audiences, the institutional sections are largely self-contained and could be omitted without creating significant difficulties in understanding later analyses.

For the benefit of those with a special interest in Illinois and for those who might be interested in replicating the analyses that we have performed, detailed data regarding Illinois local finance has been included in the appendixes.

In the following chapters the reader will obtain a broad picture of the costs of providing city services and the types of revenues used. An understanding of the suburbanization process and resulting changes in the financing of services can also be obtained. For certain, the reader will be impressed with the complexities of financing cities and in this regard will better appreciate the flexibility in the local decision-making process needed for city officials to provide services efficiently.

Chapter 2

Urbanization, Suburbanization, and Government Finance

Although Americans tend to extol the virtues of rural living and to equate the "good life" with pastoral settings, there is little doubt that the vitality of a modern economy is closely related to the economic health of its cities. Not only does most economic production take place in cities, it can also be persuasively argued that cities provide the setting for much of the innovation that has allowed rapid economic progress in both urban and rural areas.[1] In fact, one might argue that if cities had not provided the capital and public programs to improve the productivity of residents, the rate of economic growth would have been substantially lower. At the very least, cities provide a setting without which economic production would be more costly.

Cities also become the places in which those individuals in greatest need of care are concentrated: immigrants, the lower socioeconomic classes, those entering the mainstream of our culture, and those leaving it. Unfortunately, the concentration of poor residents in cities creates problems and raises social costs, thus encouraging those who are able to flee the heart of the city and to avoid responsibility for such problems to do so. These demographic trends have complicated both the politics and the finances of cities and may have encouraged practices impeding the economic growth of the country.

Local governments are continually adapting to meet ever-changing needs. Unfortunately, the process of change can be very slow and is frequently initiated only in the presence of a crisis. The problems that lead to such crises have existed in one form or another for centuries and may never be solved. Rather, they surface time and time again, serving as the stimuli for change.[2]

THE PROCESS OF URBANIZATION

A study of municipal finance should begin with an examination of the urbanization process in the United States. Therefore, we will highlight important events representing changes in the role of the cities and factors contributing to the present-day problems.[3]

Prior to the Industrial Revolution, the food and fiber produced or processed in rural villages and the surrounding hinterland constituted the bulk of the nation's productive economic activity. Cities were trading centers and residents were employed in handicraft industries, but these activities were frequently overshadowed by either the governmental-military or the religious functions of the city. With the advent of the Industrial Revolution, the nature of cities changed. The use of powered machinery and the increasing specialization of labor within the production process meant that large labor pools had to be assembled. Initially, company towns were established, and many of the "public services" were provided by the factory owners. With growing industrialization, specialization increased and new industries began to locate in the city. This geographic concentration of industries resulted in a need to share ancillary activities in order to attract still more businesses to the cities.

This entire process resulted from both internal and external economies of scale. In technical terms, private economies of scale (internal) refer to cost savings resulting from a plant or firm becoming larger and thus increasing the division of labor. External economies reflect cost savings arising from the presence of other producing units. Other cost savings have been termed agglomeration economies and include public services (urbanization economies), such as wastewater treatment and electricity production. Supplemental activities provided in the private sector, such as legal or accounting services, can be obtained at lower cost in larger areas.

External economies of scale are also exemplified by more efficient labor markets operating within a larger urban area. A firm may not have to train its labor force if residents interested in changing jobs already possess the necessary skills. Likewise, in larger cities the school system may be better equipped to provide a vocational training program meeting the needs of local industries. However, it is not uncommon to find a positive relationship between city size and average wages. Some of the cost savings, therefore, may be offset, by higher wages.[4]

Private economies of scale resulting from urbanization appear to be accompanied by public diseconomies. Although there is not much solid evidence of "diseconomies" in the provision of public services, very large cities do tend to spend more on public services per person than smaller cities when average expenditures are compared by city size.[5] As evidence presented later will indicate, though, it is not always size, per se, that is related to higher expenditures.[6] Other social factors, such as congestion, social conflict, and the presence of population groups with special needs, must also be considered.

A brief examination of historical trends demonstrates the relatively rapid change that the United States has undergone. Table 2-1, for instance, shows that in 1870 about 26 percent of the U.S. population resided in urban areas. This was an increase of more than twenty percentage points from the 5.1 percent in 1790, eighty

Table 2-1. Percentage of Population Classified as Urban

Year	*U.S.*	*Illinois*
1790	5.1%	N/A
1840	10.8	2.1%
1870	25.7	23.5
1900	39.7	54.3
1910	45.7	61.7
1920	51.2	67.9
1930	56.2	73.6
1940	56.5	73.6
1950	64.0[a]	77.6[a]
1960	69.9[b]	80.7
1970	73.5[b]	83.0

Source: Historical Statistics of the United States: Colonial Times to 1970, (Washington: U.S. Government Printing Office), Part J, Series A 57-72 and A 195-209.

N/A = not available.

[a]Based on revised definitions of urban areas. The percentage using the earlier definition would have been 74.5 percent.

[b]Includes contiguous United States.

years earlier. By 1920, approximately half of the population resided in areas classified as urban, and the percentage had increased to nearly three-quarters by 1970.[7]

Illinois did not differ substantially from the nation in 1870, but by 1970 it was considerably more urban, with 83 percent of its residents in urban areas. Chicago, of course, accounted for a major portion of these urban residents.

The rate of urbanization has varied between the 1790s and the present, however. By the mid-1800s the Industrial Revolution was well under way and economies of scale favored urban growth. From 1910 to 1920, the First World War stimulated urban growth as the nation prepared for the war effort. Between 1910 and 1930, urban residents as a percent of the population increased by nearly eleven percentage points. During the 1930s, however, the urbanization process slowed considerably, without doubt because of the slow economic growth during the depression era. The urbanization process again gained support during the 1940s with the war effort and economic recovery. The rapid growth of urban areas continued during the 1950s and extended into the early 1970s.

THE PROCESS OF SUBURBANIZATION

Shortly after the turn of the century, suburban rings in metropolitan areas began increasing more rapidly than the central cities themselves. Greater use of automobiles and motor trucks permitted residents more flexibility in residental choice and facilitated the outward movement of economic activity from the central core of the metropolitan areas toward the suburbs.

Following the economic recovery from the depression and the Second World War, the suburbanization process increased. A major factor promoting the dispersal pattern was the federal financing of highways from the central cities. Highways provided access to a larger labor supply, expanded the retail markets, and promoted suburban residental development. High-income residents sought less densely settled, smaller cities with greater homogeneity of population. Federal housing policies and income tax allowances for interest payments and property taxes encouraged the construction of single-family "development" housing. Relatively low gasoline prices also contributed to this suburbanization, as did the prospect of lower taxes and better municipal services.

Whatever the reasons for growth—and they may differ by city—the evidence is quite clear that suburbs have been growing more rapidly than the central cities. Table 2-2 compares the percentage of the U.S. population residing in Standard Metropolitan Statistical Areas (SMSAs) from 1950 through 1976.[8] In 1950, 62.5 percent of the total population lived in SMSAs, and by 1976 the proportion had increased to 67.8 percent. Within the SMSAs, central cities accounted for 56.8 percent of the SMSA population in 1950. By 1976, this figure had decreased to 42.6 percent.

The composition of the population in metropolitan areas has changed also. In 1950, 63 percent of the white population lived in metropolitan areas, and during the next quarter-century the percentage increased to two-thirds. An even greater increase was found in the proportion of blacks in SMSAs—with 59.1 percent in 1950 compared with 75.6 percent in 1976.

While 56.8 percent of the metropolitan population lived in central cities in 1950, by 1976 the central city population represented only

Table 2-2. Suburbanization Trends, United States, 1950-1976

	Percent			
	1950	*1960*	*1970*	*1976*
Total Population[a]	100.0	100.0	100.0	100.0
Nonmetro areas	37.5	33.3	31.4	32.2
SMSAs—total	62.5	66.7	68.6	67.8
Central cities[b]	56.8	50.1	45.8	42.6
Outside central cities[b]	43.2	49.9	54.2	57.4
White Population	89.3	88.6	87.5	86.8
Nonmetro areas	37.0	33.8	32.2	33.5
SMSAs—total	63.0	66.2	67.8	66.5
Central cities[b]	55.0	47.0	41.0	37.2
Outside central cities[b]	45.0	53.0	59.0	62.8
Black Population	9.9	10.5	11.1	11.5
Nonmetro areas	40.9	32.4	25.7	24.4
SMSAs—total	59.1	67.6	74.3	75.6
Central cities[b]	74.7	78.3	78.4	76.5
Outside central cities[b]	25.3	21.7	21.6	23.5

Source: U.S. Bureau of the Census, *Statistical Abstract of the United States: 1973,* 94th ed. (Washington, D.C., 1973), Table 16. U.S. Bureau of the Census, *Statistical Abstract of the United States: 1977,* 98th ed. (Washington, D.C., 1977), Table 15.

[a]Although total population is used as the first category, population has been subdivided only into white and black. These two categories do not add up to 100.0%, as other minorities have not been included.

[b]These figures are a breakdown of "SMSAs—total", not the entire population.

42.6 percent. Outmigration by white residents is clear. In 1950, 55 percent of metropolitan area whites lived in the central cities, but by 1976 only 37.2 percent resided there. A similar pattern is not evident for blacks. In 1950, 74.7 percent lived in the central city and in 1976 the comparable figure was 76.5 percent.[9]

Population shifts to the suburbs are well recognized. Also important is the effect of such shifts on municipal finance. Considerable attention has been focused on the fiscal plight of large central cities such as New York, Detroit, and Newark. Until recently, however, relatively little attention has been paid to the impact of these population shifts on the financing of the middle-size suburban cities.

The outmigration of middle- and upper-income residents to the suburbs allowed these cities to serve as "bedroom" communities, providing limited services and relying on the central city as an employment center. Housing was relatively new and the population was wealthy. Public services, therefore, could be provided without a heavy reliance on a broad industrial base.

This is not to say that all suburbs serve as bedroom communities for the wealthy. Suburbs are differentiated in many ways—including by race or nationality of residents, by city organization or physical appearance, and by availability of transportation or access to the central city. With population shifts came movements in economic activity with an outward migration of business activity from the central city. Land was cheaper, the labor force was better trained, and access by motor vehicle was improved on the outskirts of the city. While the outmigration of economic activity further aggravated the central cities' fiscal problems, it also changed the complexion of many suburbs.

Today the suburbs are a diverse group, with some experiencing growth and others suffering population declines. The economic bases differ also. Some suburbs provide housing and few public services while others contain a broad employment base and a full range of services. The latter group includes cities that were initially freestanding or independent, but which have been engulfed by suburban growth. As a general rule, however, suburban cities are younger, wealthier, and have experienced more recent population growth than the central cities.

CONSEQUENCES OF SUBURBANIZATION

The suburbanization process has created several problems in the financing of municipal services. First, with the outmigration of the wealthy to the suburbs, local officials in central cities are experiencing more difficulty financing needed services. In fact, one reason residents left the central city was to escape the relatively high property taxes there and simultaneously to obtain better services. Second, because some suburbs are not large employment centers, their residents who work in the central cities impose a cost on central city residents for services that the suburbanites enjoy but do not support with taxes. Although this increased burden on the central city contributes to its fiscal problems, the question of whether suburban residents exploit the central city remains subject to debate. In particular, one must realize that without suburban residents working in the central city, businesses might find the labor pool inadequate and leave. Since suburban residents are usually better skilled and more productive, their presence in the central city can cause the average wage rate paid to central city residents to be higher.[10] Also, certain taxes are paid by nonresidents, and the presence of these visitors may increase property values within the city. In fact, central cities have attempted to recover revenues by shifting to taxes based on the number of workers, to employment-based income taxes, and to an increased use of charges for services. There have also been attempts to finance services through other governments, such as a special district, the county, or perhaps the state.

More comprehensive approaches to the problems created by outmigration include the creation of a metropolitan government. Consolidation of the city and county governments has been attempted in several places, but the process is complicated by the presence of many independent governments, which can be expected to fight to maintain their existence. The Chicago SMSA, for example, contains 1,214 governments, each providing services and collecting taxes. Within Cook County, the central county containing the city of Chicago, there are 520 separate governments.

There have been other successful attempts to share the wealth of the suburban areas. In Minneapolis–St. Paul, for instance, a specific portion of the increase in the tax base is allocated among other government units in the area. Thus, even though employment growth takes place in the outer ring of the SMSA, the inner city shares the increase. The effect of this program has been to narrow tax base differences. For example, the commercial-industrial valuation per capita among cities larger than 9,000 in the Minneapolis–St. Paul area ranged from a low of $341 to a high of $2,091 in 1975. If the law had not been in effect, the range probably would have been from $230 to $2,368 per capita.[11]

Although the central city problems created by suburbanization have received much attention, officials in the suburbs have also encountered difficulties in financing public services. A major difficulty facing these officials is coordinating services. Sometimes the areas are too small to provide certain services efficiently. Suburbs, like central cities, are also called upon to provide services benefiting nonresidents as well as residents. Often as a suburb grows, it annexes areas already served by a special district that provides fire, park, sanitary, or other services. In this situation, it is not unusual to find two residents in the same city paying substantially different property taxes on comparable property while receiving basically similar services. There is no question that the system of overlapping governments and difficulties of coordination take their toll on taxpayers. The tax bill is accompanied by a list of tax rates pertaining to each government in the county. However, taxpayers frequently are not sure which rate applies to their property and, without a careful study of the tax bill or knowledge about how it is prepared, they experience considerable frustration determining to which government their tax dollars are being paid. The introduction of computerized billing in recent years has lessened this problem.

CHANGING FUNCTIONS OF GOVERNMENT

The financing of public services has also been affected by the changing nature of government operations. With growing urbanization has come a marked increase in the importance of government in the economy. Government's role has changed from one of protecting life and property—or providing basic services—to one of active participation in economic decision making through regulation of economic activity, redistribution of income, and promotion of economic development.

While an increase in government activity has occurred at all levels, the major expenditure growth has taken place at the federal level. Table 2-3 reveals that in 1929 the total public sector expenditures were $10.2 billion, or 9.9 percent of the gross national product (GNP). By 1976, however, the total public sector expenditures were $575.1 billion, or 34.0 percent of the GNP. In 1929 federal expenditures accounted for 25.5 percent of total government expenditures; by 1976 the federal percentage had grown to 67.6 percent.[12] Domestic programs account for the major growth in federal government expenditures. Between 1969 and 1976, federal

Table 2-3. Government Expenditure (Own Funds) Trends

Year	Total Public Sector	Federal[a] Total	Federal[a] Defense	Federal[a] Domestic	State	Local
		In billions of dollars				
1929	$ 10.2	$ 2.6	$ 1.1	$ 1.5	$ 2.1	$ 5.5
1939	17.4	8.9	1.5	7.4	3.7	4.8
1959	131.0	91.0	53.6	37.4	18.7	21.3
1969	285.6	188.4	95.5	92.9	49.6	47.6
1976	575.1	388.9	121.5	267.4	103.0	83.2
1979[b]	758.8	509.0	154.5	354.5	139.3	110.5
		As a Percent of GNP				
1929	9.9%	2.5%	1.1	1.5	2.0	5.3
1939	19.2	9.8	1.7	8.1	4.1	5.3
1959	26.9	18.7	11.0	7.7	3.8	4.4
1969	30.5	20.1	10.2	9.9	5.3	5.1
1976	34.0	23.0	7.2	15.8	6.1	4.9
1979[b]	32.0	21.5	6.5	15.0	5.9	4.7
		Percentage Distribution				
1929	100.0	25.5	10.8	14.7	20.6	53.9
1939	100.0	51.5	37.1	42.5	21.3	27.6
1959	100.0	69.5	40.9	28.5	14.3	16.3
1969	100.0	66.0	33.4	32.5	17.4	16.7
1976	100.0	67.6	21.1	46.5	17.9	14.5
1979[b]	100.0	67.1	20.4	46.7	18.4	14.5

Source: Significant Features of Fiscal Federalism, 1979-80 ed. (Washington, D.C.: Advisory Commission on Intergovernmental Relations, 1980), Table 1.

[a] Includes Social Security and all federal aid to state and local governments.

[b] Preliminary data.

domestic expenditures nearly tripled. These expenditures, though, include federal aid to the states and local governments, so that many of the services financed by these federal expenditures are actually provided by state and local governments.

The data in Table 2-3 showing government expenditures as a percentage of gross national product also demonstrate that the federal government accounts for most of the growth in the relative size of the public sector. Included in this growth is a large payment by the federal government to state and local governments. In 1950 federal aid represented 10 percent of state and local expenditures. By 1977 this figure had increased to 27 percent.[13] More recently this percentage has been declining.

The expenditures of local governments from their own funds have decreased steadily as a percentage of total public sector expenditure. In 1929 local government expenditures from own funds represented 53.9 percent of government expenditure but by 1979 had declined to 14.5 percent.

It appears the proportion of GNP represented by the public sector may well have peaked in 1975. In that year government expenditures represented 35 percent of GNP, in 1976 they represented 34 percent, and in 1979 the estimate was 32.0 percent.[14]

The reasons for growth and shifts in the public sector are varied. Following the depression of the 1930s, the role of government in stabilizing the economic system was expanded. Government's greater intervention into the private sector resulted from residents living in more densely populated areas, the introduction of additional dangerous and toxic substances resulting from the production process, and a growing complexity of the economy. With the advent of improved living standards, society responded more to meeting the needs of its less fortunate members by attempting to provide adequate nourishment, housing, and medical assistance through myriad government programs.

Not all the causes underlying the expansion of the public sector fall outside the structure of the government decision-making process and the political system, however. Expansion of government programs creates departments and agencies employing individuals with expertise and concern about specific societal problems. These employees are able to anticipate unmet needs and to develop programs that serve to increase the agency's budget and activities. They are also able to mobilize groups of clientele to bring influence to bear when support is needed for new or expanded programs. The net result is that new programs often create demands for expenditures in related areas.[15]

Growth in the public sector has also been facilitated by the federal income tax. This tax, with progressive rates and fixed personal exemptions, is income-elastic. In periods of rising personal income, tax collections rise at a faster rate than personal income. This has meant a rapid and, until recently, largely unnoticed increase in the portion of personal income that must be paid in taxes. Even a number of federal tax rate decreases in the postwar years have not prevented this expansion in the public sector. The income tax growth has facilitated federal expenditure increases and, through intergovernmental aid programs, has stimulated state and local expenditures.

At the municipal government level, demands for additional services of a higher quality are being imposed. As the standard of living increases, residents want better protection for their property and personal safety. A greater concern for the rights of citizens has produced court mandates regarding procedures to be followed in police work and prosecution. Environmental safety legislation has caused cities to upgrade their waste disposal facilities. City governments are also being asked to support economic development of the community with additional services, tax concessions, or construction projects.

Even this brief discussion of changes in the scope of government makes clear that the financing of cities is not only very complicated but also crucial to maintaining the quality of life that Americans have come to expect. Cities finance services from many revenue sources and provide services affecting the lives of residents in the surrounding areas well as in the cities. Since taxpayers in recent years have exhibited a greater interest in exerting direct control over a major revenue source, the property tax, it is especially important that they understand the decision-making process in city government and that they be aware of the services their tax dollars provide.

ILLINOIS AS A SETTING FOR STUDYING MUNICIPAL FINANCE

Whereas decisions affecting the levels of service are made locally, many factors affect the decision-making process. Needs for services are determined by population changes and characteristics, which in turn are related to the economic health of the state or a broader region. The responses city officials make to local issues are limited by the powers provided by the state statutes or constitution. The manner in which revenues are collected and converted into services is related to the structure of local governments. Before we can embark on an analysis of city characteristics, it is useful to understand these external constraints. A detailed understanding of Illinois as a state also demonstrates the applicability of our findings to cities in other states.

Population and Income

Illinois is both a wealthy urban state and a rich agricultural state. Chicago is the center of the third largest metropolitan area in the United States. The "Windy City" experienced spectacular growth in the latter half of the last century and quickly became the nation's most important railroad center, as well as an important center for manufacturing, agricultural processing, and finance.

Illinois has a relatively high per capita income and ranked seventh among states in 1978 with an average income level of $8,745 per resident, compared with a national average of $7,810. In 1960 and 1970 Illinois ranked eighth among states and in 1976 ranked second. Without question, a major factor underlying this relatively high income is the fact that the state is highly urban.

An average income level, though high, can sometimes disguise inequalities in its distribution. Particularly in large metropolitan areas, pockets of poverty can create needs for additional services in areas least able to afford them. In 1969, 10.2 percent of Illinois residents were below the officially established poverty line. During the same period, the national average was 12.6 percent.[16] More will be said later about the location of poverty within Illinois.

Although Illinois ranks high in per capita income, there is evidence that the rate of growth in income has been lower than for the nation as a whole. Between 1960 and 1970, the percentage change in personal income in the United States was 56.7 percent, while in Illinois it was 45.7 percent. Between 1970 and 1978, personal income in the United States rose 32.1 percent, but in Illinois the increase was 22.3 percent.[17] The percentage of national income earned by Illinois residents has clearly been declining.

The population in Illinois has also grown more slowly than in the nation as a whole. Between 1950 and 1960, the national growth rate was 1.7 percent annually, and during the 1960s the increase slowed to 1.3 percent. The annual increase in Illinois during the 1950s was 1.4 percent and during the 1960s, 1.0 percent. This lagging growth continued into the 1970s, when the population increase in Illinois was 0.1 percent compared with an increase of 0.9 percent for the nation.[18]

While the state population during the 1970s remained stable, the population distribution within the state did not. During the 1960s the metropolitan population in Illinois grew by 12.2 percent, while the nonmetropolitan population increased by only 1.4 percent. From 1970 to 1975, the nonmetropolitan increase was also 1.4 percent, while the metropolitan population increase was 0.7 percent.[19] Thus, the growth patterns of metropolitan areas have changed, and the 1970s may have represented a changing trend in the population distribution within the state.

Employment Distribution

Table 2-4 shows the employment distribution by industry within Illinois. The final column is an index computed so that the U.S. percentage equals 100. For example, the 73.0 for agriculture means

Table 2-4. Percentage Industrial Distribution of Employed Persons, 1970

Persons Age 16 and Over	*Illinois*	*U.S.*	*Index*
Agriculture	2.7%	3.7%	73.0%
Mining	0.5	0.8	62.5
Construction	5.1	6.0	85.0
Manufacturing	30.3	25.9	117.0
Railroads, trucking, other transport	4.4	3.6	122.2
Communications, utilities, sanitation	2.9	3.1	93.5
Wholesale trade	5.0	4.1	122.0
Retail trade	16.1	15.9	101.3
Banking, credit, other finance	1.8	1.7	105.9
Insurance, real estate	3.5	3.3	106.1
Business services, repair services	3.2	3.1	103.2
Entertainment and recreation	0.7	0.8	87.5
Private household, other personal services	3.7	4.6	80.4
Hospitals and health services	5.2	5.5	94.5
All education	7.3	8.0	91.3
Professional, religious, welfare services	4.0	4.1	97.6
Public administration	4.4	5.5	80.0

Source: Robert N. Schoeplein "Illinois and the United States: Some Economic Parallels," *Illinois Government Research*, No. 42, March 1976. Final column showing Illinois percentage as percent of U.S. percentage computed by the authors.

Note: Seven of the illustrated industries are consolidated from a more detailed presentation in Table 5 of the *Illinois Economy: A Microcosm of the United States?* Because different states are involved, no weights can be calculated for multiple industries.

that the percentage of workers employed in agriculture in Illinois (2.7 percent of the employment in Illinois) is 73.0 percent of the national percentage (3.7 percent). The Illinois economy has a greater concentration in manufacturing, transportation, wholesale trade, retail trade, banking, insurance, and business services than the nation as a whole. The manufacturing category is the largest in terms of numbers employed: nearly one in three workers are employed in manufacturing industries in Illinois, compared with one in four nationwide.

The lagging population growth in Illinois is consistent with the recent experience in employment changes. From 1970 to 1975 private nonfarm employment in Illinois decreased 1.1 percent, compared with a nationwide increase of 5.6 percent. Illinois experienced a 10-percent decrease in manufacturing employment during the same period; national manufacturing employment decreased by 5.6 percent.

There has been much speculation about the reasons for the

relative employment declines in Illinois. Much of the discussion has centered on the snowbelt-sunbelt controversy, but other possibilities—such as the impact of recent changes in workers' compensation insurance rates and enforcement of the environmental protection legislation—have also been proposed.[20]

A study by Toal, which examined 1958 through the second quarter of 1977, revealed several additional findings.[21] First, employment changes in Illinois do not mirror changes in the national economy. Rather than simply lagging behind the national growth in employment since 1970, Illinois's employment growth, Toal found, has lagged behind the national rate for the past twenty years. Second, employment growth has straggled because Illinois industries have grown more slowly than their national counterparts (regional share effect), not because of a concentration of industries that have slow national growth rates (industry mix effect).[22] Most Illinois industries exhibited slower growth rates.

The trends revealed by Toal are consistent with a general tendency for economic growth to proceed more rapidly in the less industrial states with lower wages and pleasant climates. This general shift is common in the postindustrial era.[23] A lesser reliance on the products of heavy manufacturing, the greater importance of knowledge as a form of capital, the development of lighter material, more flexible transportation, and the development of air conditioning have contributed to the trend. How far this trend toward straggling employment growth in industrial states will continue before reversing itself is difficult to predict. However, it will certainly have an impact on the economies of cities in Illinois, and it will definitely affect the decisions made by local governments.

Public-Sector Characteristics

Growth in the private sector is partly related to a state's taxing and expenditure policies. Businesses must pay for public services provided by state or local governments, and these costs can represent a significant portion of operating costs. In FY 1977, Illinois ranked fourteenth in state and local per capita tax burdens at $860 per capita, compared with a U.S. average of $813. In recent years, the tax burden in Illinois has declined slightly compared with other states—from thirteenth in 1973 to fourteenth in 1977.[24]

Table 2-5 shows the percentage of general revenue obtained from local sources, from the state, and from the national government. The U.S. average is shown to indicate how closely Illinois

Table 2-5. Sources of Revenue by Level of Government in 1977 (As Percentage of Total Revenue)

	General Revenue (Own Sources)		State Revenue		Federal Revenue	
Government	*U.S.*	*Ill.*	*U.S.*	*Ill.*	*U.S.*	*Ill.*
Counties	54.7%	61.7%	34.5%	23.5%	9.0%	10.5%
Municipalities	60.4	69.3	23.4	13.5	14.6	14.9
Townships	70.3	61.4	20.4	23.0	7.5	15.4
Special districts	60.1	58.7	7.0	4.5	23.6	23.2
School districts	49.6	56.0	46.8	42.9	1.5	0.7
All local governments	57.0	62.3	33.7	29.3	9.2	8.4

Source: U.S. Bureau of the Census, *Governmental Finances in 1976-77* (Washington, D.C.: Government Printing Office, 1978), Series GF 77, No. 5, Table 24.

Note: Percentages do not total 100.0 because of intergovernmental transfers.

corresponds with other states. On the average, 69.3 percent of the revenue generated by Illinois municipalities is derived from own sources—mainly from sales and property taxes—whereas nationwide the average was 60.4 percent. Municipalities in Illinois derive a substantially greater proportion of their revenues from own sources than any other government type within the state. It should be noted that in Illinois the sales tax is a local option tax included in the own-source category even though the tax is collected by the state for municipalities. The income tax, on the other hand, is a state tax, part of which is distributed to municipalities.

The percentage of municipal government revenues provided by the state is considerably lower in Illinois than in other states, with 13.5 percent of municipal general revenue coming from the state government, compared with a national average of 23.4 percent. Municipal governments in Illinois compare favorably with their counterparts in federal revenue, however. For example, in 1977, 14.9 percent of the municipal revenue in Illinois was obtained from the federal government, compared with an average of 14.6 percent in other states. For all local governments, the 8.4 percent of revenue received from the federal government in Illinois was close to the 9.2 percent nationwide.

One common method for examining the public sector is to determine the revenue that could be obtained if a representative tax system, based on experiences in other states, were applied to the tax bases in the state.[25] The result is termed fiscal capacity. A comparison of the fiscal capacity with the actual revenue obtained is a measure of the government's tax effort.

In 1975, the tax capacity of all state and local governments in Illinois was estimated at $734.84 per resident, ranking it sixth among states, or 114 percent of the national average. The actual amounts collected, on the other hand, were $714.45 per capita, or 97 percent of the U.S. average. In 1975, Illinois tied with Mississippi and New Hampshire, ranking seventeenth among the states in tax effort. Although time-series data are limited, it appears that from 1960 through 1975 the trend in the state–local government relative tax effort in Illinois increased. In 1960, for example, the tax effort index was 88, increasing to 100 in 1972 (with slight decreases in 1967 and 1969), and back to 97 in 1975.[26]

Local Government Structure

Citizens obtain services from many governments and, in some instances, receive similar services from more than one government. At the very least, a resident's ability to determine how tax dollars are being spent is inversely related to the number of governments involved. Illinois has the dubious reputation of having more governments than any other state. The impact of overlapping governments and fragmentation is not well understood, even though it has been examined numerous times. Since we will discuss this impact later, we will provide here a description of the types and numbers of governments.

In 1977 there were 6,620 local government units in Illinois, substantially more than the 5,247 units in Pennsylvania, the state with the second highest number. Table 2–6 lists the types and number of governments in Illinois for two previous "Census of Government" years.

Counties are the largest geographical units of local government. Each area of the state is included within a county, the boundaries of which have not changed for many years. Eighty-five of the Illinois counties are subdivided into townships. The township counties, other than Cook County (which contains Chicago), are governed by a county board consisting of from five to twenty-nine members elected at large or by districts. Special provisions for Cook County stipulate that ten of the sixteen commissioners shall be elected from the city of Chicago and the remainder from the county outside Chicago.

In townships, an elected supervisor is the chief administrative officer. The primary functions of townships are to assess property for taxation, maintain township roads, and provide general assistance for the needy. However, townships do provide other services. Township governments often overlap municipal governments and

Table 2-6. Number of Local Governments in Illinois

Type of Government	*1962*	*1972*	*1977*
Counties	102	102	102
Municipalities	1,251	1,267	1,274
Townships	1,433	1,432	1,436
School districts	1,540	1,177	1,063
Special districts	2,126	2,407	2,745
Fire protection	620	705	770
Highways	13	23	23
Health	18	21	22
Hospitals	37	36	33
Housing and urban renewal	107	103	97
Libraries	16	49	91
Drainage	852	787	877
Flood control	18	26	33
Irrigation, water conservations	4	9	4
Soil conservation	99	98	90
Parks and recreation	179	282	321
Sewage	76	128	151
Water supply	34	50	68
Utilities other than water	1	6	10
Cemeteries	19	40	88
Sewerage and water supply	4	5	15
Other	29	39	52
Total	6,453	6,386	6,620

Source: U.S. Bureau of the Census, *1977 Census of Governments,* Vol. 1, No. 1 (Washington, D.C.: Government Printing Office, 1978), Table 1.

some cities have township boundaries coterminous with the municipal limits. These municipalities are covered by special provisions under which an expansion of the municipal boundaries automatically enlarges the township boundaries.

The U.S. Census Bureau classifies Illinois school districts into twelve different types.[27] All are governed by elected boards except the special charter districts and except the Chicago School District and Chicago Community College District, whose boards are appointed by the mayor with the approval of the city council. In the Chicago suburbs, high school and elementary school districts are often separate units of government. Counties, or multicounty regions, have replaced the former county boards of school trustees. Illinois law provides for certain local boards and officials to manage school funds and lands and to deal with district boundary changes.

As indicated in Table 2-6, the number of school districts in Illinois substantially decreased between 1962 and 1977, but this reduction was more than offset by an increase in the number of special districts. Some special districts do not have powers of taxation, but rather depend on fees or special assessments for revenue. Some are governed by elected boards and others by appointed boards. Most are quite small. In fact, almost 91 percent employ fewer than five full-time personnel and 77.5 percent reported having no full-time employees at all and 73.8 percent claimed no debt.

In contrast to the multitude of small special districts are several large districts in the Chicago area, including the Regional Transportation Authority (covering a six-county area), the Chicago Transit Authority, the Metropolitan Sanitary District of Greater Chicago, the Chicago Park District, and the Cook County Forest Preserve District. All have substantial budgets and many employees.

Special districts are often criticized as sources of waste and confusion, but they do permit an opportunity for citizen participation in government and for spreading the costs of services to residents outside the city limits. Past research has not shown that special districts increase spending, but it is clear that providing services through single-purpose governments can cause a greater reliance on property taxes.[28]

For taxpayers and students of municipal finance, the presence of special districts makes a comparison of expenditure and revenue data difficult. In some cities, parks, sewage treatment, and fire protection are provided by city employees and the expenditures are shown in the city budget. In other cities, single-purpose districts provide these services, and determining the full cost of a service requires compilation of finance information from several governments.

The overlapping government issue is especially complicated in metropolitan areas. The Chicago Standard Metropolitan Area contained 1,214 local governments in 1977. The central portion of the SMSA (Cook County) contained 520 units, and the outlying areas contained 694. By comparison, the Census Bureau indicates that the New York SMSA contained 362 local governments (3 in the central portion and 359 in the outlying areas). Although the ratio of governments to population is lower in the suburban areas, the chances of a municipal area being served by several similar special districts is greater. What starts as a logical system of providing services can become a complex system of overlapping governments as cities increase in size and begin providing services similar to those of special districts.

METROPOLITAN AREAS IN ILLINOIS

While cities are legal entities created by the legislature operating within the powers accorded by the constitution (including home rule) and the statutes, they are sometimes part of a larger economic area, the Standard Metropolitan Statistical Area.[29] Since cities inside an SMSA are in close proximity, actions by a government in one city can affect residents in another. Some impacts may be economic; for example, a new employer in one city can foster population growth in surrounding areas. Alternatively, higher expenditures for police protection in one city can shift crimes to a neighboring area.

There are seven SMSAs entirely within Illinois, and two include Illinois counties even though their central portions are in neighborboring states. The Chicago SMSA is also in the Chicago-Northwestern Indiana Standard Consolidated Area (SCA), which includes the Gary-Hammond-East Chicago SMSA.

Table 2-7 shows the Illinois counties included in SMSAs, their estimated 1975 populations, and the number of governments in each county. The Chicago SMSA, including six counties and 261 municipalities, is by far the largest; it comprised 62.6 percent of the total state population in 1975. The smallest SMSA is Kankakee, containing 96,228 residents and sixteen municipalities.[30] In all, 80.0 percent of the Illinois population resided in SMSAs in 1975.

The SMSAs contain many units of local government. For example, in 1977 in the Chicago SMSA are forty-four municipalities larger than 25,000. Even in the smallest SMSA there were 101 local governments. The Decatur SMSA, with 126,439 population, had virtually the same number of governments as did the Rockford SMSA, which has more than twice the population. Nationally, there is a tendency for the number of units of government per 10,000 population to decrease with the size of the SMSA.[31] This tendency also appears in Illinois, but the pattern is not consistent. In 1977 the Chicago SMSA contained one government unit for each 5,159 population, while the Bloomington-Normal SMSA contained one unit for each 922 residents. Within Cook County, the central county of the Chicago SMSA, there was one governmental unit for each 9,692 population, but in the suburban counties there was one government unit for each 2,040 residents.

Table 2-8 illustrates the wide divergence in population characteristics of the SMSAs in Illinois. Between 1960 and 1975, the growth rate ranged from 24.5 percent in the Bloomington-Normal

Table 2-7. Population and Number of Governments in SMSAs

		Number of Governments (1977)		
SMSA	*Population (1975)*	*Total*	*Municipalities*	*Mun. Larger than 25,000*
Bloomington-Normal				
*McLean County	114,284	114	21	2
Champaign-Urbana				
*Champaign County	162,304	166	23	2
Chicago				
*Cook County	5,369,328	520	121	30
DuPage County	553,670	170	29	6
Kane County	262,675	85	20	3
Lake County	407,373	185	43	3
McHenry	125,981	100	24	—
Will County	296,224	154	24	2
Total	7,015,251	1,214	261	44
Decatur				
*Macon County	126,439	86	11	1
Kankakee				
*Kankakee	96,228	101	16	1
Peoria				
*Peoria County	199,023	89	14	1
Tazewell County	125,189	106	16	1
Woodford County	29,727	65	15	—
Total	353,939	260	45	2
Rockford				
Boone	26,592	23	3	—
*Winnebago	245,040	69	10	1
Total	271,632	92	13	1
Springfield				
*Sangamon County	169,753	100	25	1
Menard County	10,761	18	5	—
Total	180,514	118	30	1
**Davenport (Iowa)-Rock Island-Moline				
Henry County	55,802	89	15	—
Rock Island	165,313	78	15	2
Total (Illinois portion)	221,115	167	30	2
**St. Louis (Missouri)				
Madison County	249,685	130	26	2
St. Clair County	280,946	126	28	2
Clinton County	29,557	65	12	—
Monroe County	18,977	24	6	—
Total (Illinois portion)	579,165	345	72	4

Source: U.S. Bureau of the Census, *1977 Census of Governments*, Vol. 1, No. 1 (Washington, D.C.: Government Printing Office, 1978), pp. 157–61, 170, 204.

*Indicates central portion of SMSA.

**Central portion in state other than Illinois. Data are for Illinois counties only.

SMSA to 4.5 percent in the Kankakee SMSA. The nonwhite population varied from a high of 18.7 percent in the Chicago SMSA to 2.3 percent in Bloomington-Normal. The percentage of residents over sixty-five years of age ranged from 12.0 percent in Springfield to 6.7 percent in Champaign-Urbana.

In general, the Chicago SMSA characteristics most closely approximate those for the state as a whole during the study year. This, of course, is not surprising; it largely results from the fact that the Chicago SMSA population is such a major portion of the state population. The figures do point out, however, that variations are apt to be greatest among small SMSAs. The relatively small percentage of aged persons in the Champaign-Urbana area, for instance, results from the concentration of students attending the University of Illinois.

PROFILE OF ILLINOIS CITIES

In studies of urban public finance, metropolitan areas are frequently the primary unit of analysis. Because an SMSA approximates the "economic" city, this approach facilitates an analysis of economic and demographic trends. However, public finance decisions are made by officials in each city, and it therefore is

Table 2-8. Population Characteristics of Illinois Standard Metropolitan Statistical Areas

SMSA	*Percent of Families Below Poverty Level 1970*	*Percent Population Change*		*Percent Negro and Other Races (1970)*	*Percent over 65 (1975)*
		1960–1975	*1970–1975*		
Illinois	7.7%	10.2%	0.8%	13.6%	10.3%
Bloomington-Normal	6.2	24.5	9.5	2.3	9.6
Champaign-Urbana	7.2	23.3	–0.6	7.9	6.7
Chicago	6.8	12.2	0.5	18.7	9.2
Davenport-Rock Island-Moline (Iowa-Ill.)	6.7	13.5	2.1	3.7	10.5
Decatur	6.8	5.7	1.1	8.1	11.2
Kankakee	8.2	4.5	–1.4	11.4	11.2
Peoria	5.7	9.1	3.5	4.7	7.0
Rockford	6.4	18.2	–0.2	6.2	9.5
St. Louis (Mo.-Ill.)	8.1	12.3	3.0	16.4	10.9
Springfield	6.7	10.1	5.2	5.1	12.0

Source: U.S. Bureau of the Census, *County and City Data Book, 1977* (Washington, D.C.: Government Printing Office, 1978), Table 3.

necessary to examine each city government as a distinct entity. In this study, the primary units of analysis are municipalities with populations of more than 25,000 in 1975.

There were sixty-five Illinois cities with a population of over 25,000 in 1975. In that year, 53.7 percent of the state population lived in these cities. Slightly more than one-half were in Chicago. The movement of population to smaller cities is shown by the decline of the percentage of the state population living in Chicago: from 35.2 percent in 1960 to 27.7 percent in 1975. Most of this change represents an increase in the population of cities in the 25,000–200,000 class. In 1960, only 19.3 percent of the state population lived in these cities, but by 1975 the figure had increased to 26.0 percent.[32]

Our analysis focuses on sixty-one Illinois municipal governments larger than 25,000 for which 1977 Census of Governments expenditure and revenue data are available (Table 2–9). These cities exhibit a wide range of socioeconomic characteristics. Many of them are located in the Chicago SMSA and thus are economically integrated with Chicago. Some are centers of smaller downstate SMSAs, while others are middle size cities lacking the size necessary to qualify as the central city of an SMSA.

Many of these cities have been studied intensely before, so a considerable amount of public finance information is available.[33] This group of cities constitutes a "sample" that not only is interesting in its own right but also, due to its diversity, can be useful for understanding experiences in cities of similar size nationwide.

The municipalities listed in Table 2–9 are grouped into four separate classes. The first category consists of twenty-three independent or free-standing cities most of which are located outside the suburban areas of Chicago and St. Louis. Some are central cities in small SMSAs, and others are not in an SMSA. This category includes several municipalities located in the Chicago SMSA that seem to be physically and economically distinct from Chicago. Both Bloomington–Normal and Champaign–Urbana are twin cities comprising the central portion of an SMSA. Although the independent cities are surrounded by small satellite cities that might be characterized as suburbs, the independent cities more closely approximate the concept of a complete "economic" city than do the suburban cities.

The locations of these independent cities and those classified as suburban St. Louis are shown in Figure 2–1. The four cities classified as "suburban St. Louis" are probably not typical suburban cities. Most of the St. Louis SMSA lies in Missouri, and a large share of the affluent residents normally residing in the suburbs live in Missouri rather than in Illinois. East St. Louis, which is separated from downtown St. Louis by the Mississippi River, is an old and deteriorated railroad and manufacturing center. Alton, Belleville, and Granite City are more prosperous, are physically separated from St. Louis, and have many characteristics of independent cities. Because of the unusual characteristics of these cities, the importance of the Missouri cities comprising the SMSA, and the small size of the group, the cities in this category are excluded from some of the statistical analyses in this volume.

The category "suburban Chicago" consists of cities that are suburbs of Chicago (Figure 2-2). All are in the Chicago SMSA and represent a sampling of cities normally considered big-city suburbs. Chicago, of course, is in a category by itself. At certain points in the analysis it is compared with other major cities in the United States.

The descriptive data in Table 2-9 serve as the basis for a preliminary analysis of city characteristics in each category. The average population size and the variation in the populations of the independent cities are larger than those of the suburban cities. The six largest cities in Illinois, excluding Chicago, are in the independent group, but the suburban cities have grown much more rapidly in the fifteen-year period from 1960 to 1975. The average growth of the suburban group was 70.6 percent, whereas the independent cities grew 23.4 percent on the average.

The image of suburban cities as places of residence for high-income people is confirmed by the per capita income figures. This group averaged $6,720 per resident, compared with $5,050 for the independent cities. The differences between the two city types is statistically significant. What is even more interesting, however, is the wide diversity within the suburban cities. Highland Park, a north-shore suburb, had an average income of $10,594 per capita in 1975. On the other hand, Harvey, a southern suburb, had an average income of $4,366 per resident. Chicago Heights, Harvey, and Maywood, the three cities with a relatively high percentage of nonwhites, also had the three lowest per capita incomes among the suburbs.

The relative affluence of the average suburb is highlighted by a comparison with the city of Chicago, whose residents had an average income of $4,984 per capita. This difference is expected in light of the outmigration of relatively prosperous residents to

Table 2-9. Selected Characteristics of Study Cities

City Type	Population (1975)	Population Growth, 1960–1975 (percent)	Reached Half of Present Population (year)	Density (1975)	Percent[a] Nonwhite	Per Capita Income (1975)
Independent Cities						
Aurora	76,955	20.8%	1930	3,420	7.1%	$5,330
Bloomington	41,509	14.4	1900	3,294	4.1	5,448
Carpentersville	25,446	46.0	1960	5,414	0.5	4,347
Champaign	58,398	17.8	1950	6,083	10.5	5,180
Danville	41,603	-0.6	1910	3,059	12.9	5,117
Decatur	89,604	14.9	1930	2,683	11.1	5,388
De Kalb	30,468	64.8	1960	7,812	2.7	4,110
Elgin	59,754	20.8	1930	3,213	5.2	5,429
Freeport	26,390	-0.9	1900	2,900	8.1	4,658
Galesburg	34,891	-6.3	1900	2,604	5.3	5,002
Joliet	74,401	11.4	1920	3,367	12.3	5,238
Kankakee	27,961	1.1	1910	3,329	13.8	5,044
Moline	44,568	4.4	1910	3,482	1.5	6,006
Normal	33,336	149.6	1970	5,556	2.1	4,408
North Chicago	42,639	85.9	1960	7,106	8.1	3,559
Pekin	32,254	14.6	1930	3,291	Z	5,652
Peoria	125,983	22.1	1910	3,298	11.9	5,878
Quincy	43,784	-0.02	1870	3,421	3.3	4,447
Rockford	145,459	14.8	1930	4,029	8.6	5,282
Rock Island	49,031	-5.5	1920	3,429	10.3	5,503
Springfield	87,418	5.0	1910	2,476	8.4	5,739
Urbana	34,418	26.1	1950	6,038	10.9	6,038
Waukegan	65,133	16.9	1930	3,340	13.5	3,340
Average	56,148	23.4	1926	4,028	7.8	5,050
(S.D.)	(31,665)	(35.2)		(1,505)	(4.2)	(729)
Suburban Chicago						
Addison	27,111	302.2	1970	4,236	0.9	5,458
Arlington Heights	70,019	151.2	1970	4,731	0.9	7,184
Berwyn	49,618	-8.5	1930	12,723	Z	6,289
Bolingbrook	27,477	N/A	1970	3,087	4.3	5,514
Calumet City	37,974	51.9	1960	5,754	2.4	5,907
Chicago Heights	39,527	15.1	1930	5,068	17.4	4,978
Cicero	63,444	-8.2	1920	10,939	Z	5,433
Des Plaines	55,828	60.0	1960	4,691	0.9	6,280
Dolton	26,531	41.5	1960	5,202	1.3	5,549
Downers Grove	38,597	82.5	1960	2,992	0.2	7,046
Elmhurst	45,020	21.7	1960	4,641	0.3	7,042
Elmwood Park	26,137	9.5	1940	13,068	Z	6,542
Evanston	76,665	-3.3	1930	10,222	16.0	7,267
Glenview	30,550	68.5	1960	3,250	1.3	8,606
Harvey	32,933	13.3	1940	5,399	30.9	4,366

Table 2-9. *(continued)*

City Type	*Population (1975)*	*Population Growth, 1960–1975 (percent)*	*Reached Half of Present Population (year)*	*Density (1975)*	*Percent Nonwhite*	*Per Capita Income (1975)*
Highland Park	31,810	24.6	1950	2,623	1.8	10,594
Lansing	28,779	59.0	1960	5,756	0.1	6,051
Lombard	35,012	55.2	1960	2,806	0.6	6,202
Maywood	27,861	1.9	1930	5,066	42.8	4,537
Morton Grove	26,095	27.1	1960	5,219	*Z*	7,082
Mount Prospect	49,140	159.9	1970	4,129	*Z*	6,788
Naperville	29,819	130.6	1970	2,509	0.2	7,092
Niles	30,237	48.3	1960	5,039	0.5	6,392
Northbrook	28,855	148.0	1970	2,186	1.6	9,078
Oak Lawn	62,317	126.9	1970	7,508	*Z*	6,152
Oak Park	59,773	−2.2	1920	12,718	0.2	7,085
Palatine	30,450	164.7	1970	4,115	1.0	6,090
Park Forest	29,844	−0.5	1960	6,589	2.3	6,158
Park Ridge	42,957	31.5	1960	5,303	0.1	8,042
Schaumburg	39,882	404.5	1970	5,248	1.7	6,0[illegible]7
Skokie	67,674	14.0	1960	6,700	1.0	8,252
Wheaton	37,720	55.2	1960	4,336	2.8	6,688
Wilmette	32,383	14.6	1940	5,997	0.3	9,994
Average	40,547	70.6	1955	5,806	4.9	6,720
(S.D.)	(14,665)	(91.8)		(2,979)	(10.3)	(1402)
Suburban St. Louis						
Alton	35,824	−16.8	1920	2,777	16.2	4,486
Belleville	43,762	17.4	1920	3,805	0.6	5,372
E. St. Louis	57,929	−29.1	1900	4,168	68.9	3,076
Granite City	39,790	−0.7	1930	4,627	*Z*	4,770
Average	44,326	−7.3	1918	2,903	28.6	4,426
(S.D.)	(9,630)	(20.2)		(2,065)	(35.8)	(973)
Chicago	3,099,391	−12.7	1900	13,911	32.7	4,984

Source: U.S. Bureau of the Census, *County and City Data Book, 1977* (Washington, D.C.: Government Printing Office, 1978), Table 4; *The Municipal Yearbook: 1978* (Washington, D.C.: International City Management Association, 1978), Table 1-1; U.S. Bureau of the Census, *Population Estimates and Projections, 1976* (Washington, D.C.: Government Printing Office, 1978).

Z = data not available.

[a] Most recent Census

the suburbs and the inmigration of minorities and disadvantaged populations seeking cheap housing in close proximity to unskilled jobs. Within Chicago, of course, one finds neighborhoods of very wealthy residents, causing the average income to hide considerable disparity.

Incomes in the St. Louis suburban cities, with the exception of

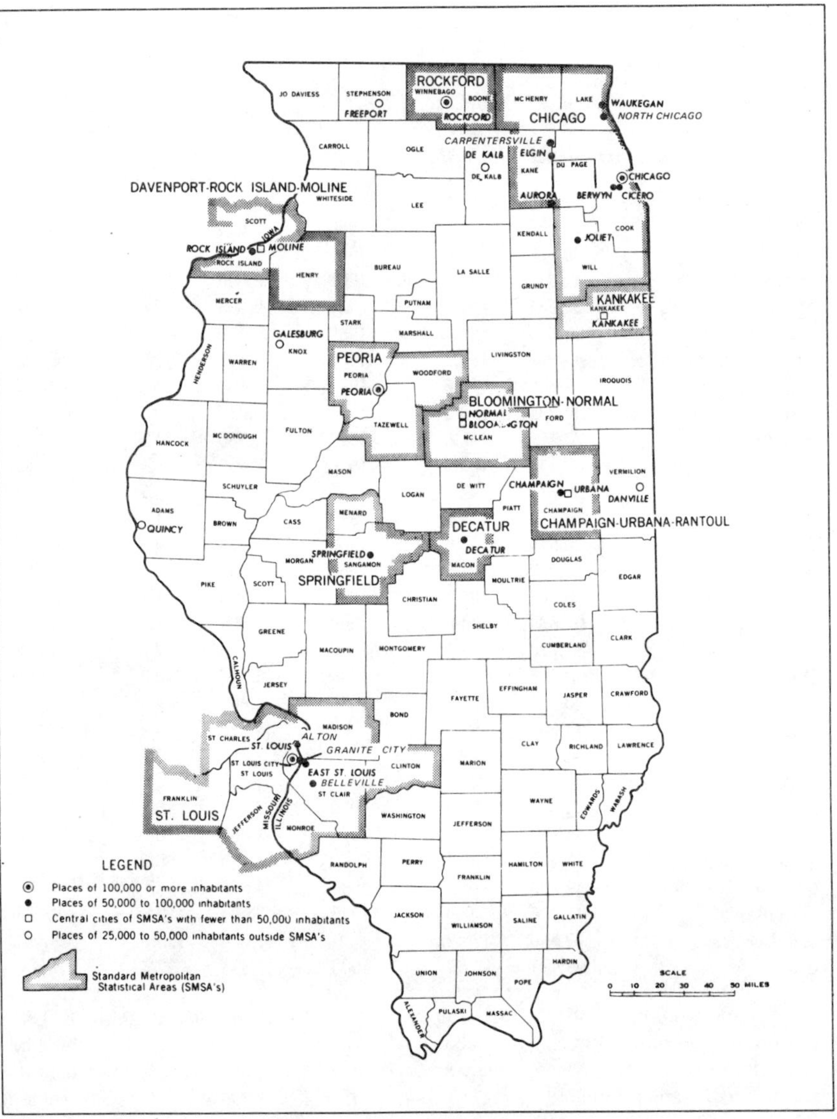

Source: Adapted from map provided by Northeastern Illinois Planning Commission

Figure 2-1. Map of Illinois, SMSAs outlined.
Location of all independent cities (including those in Chicago SMSA) and all suburban St. Louis cities shown.

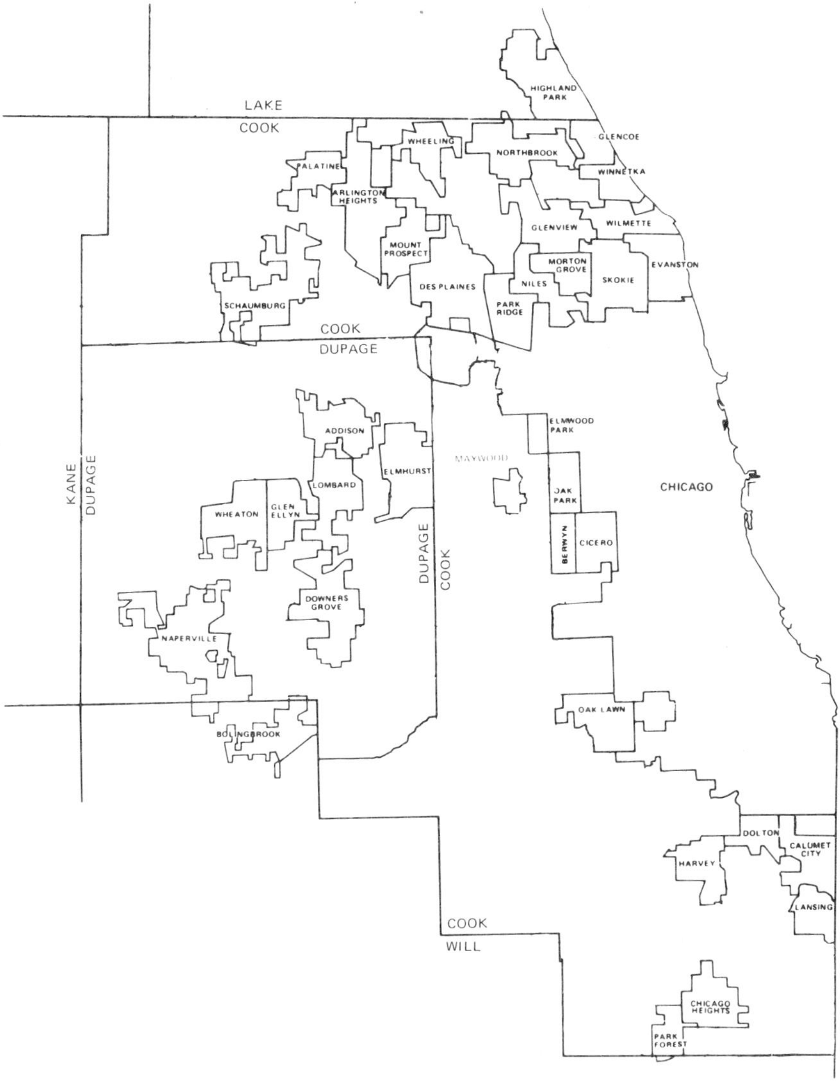

Source: U.S. Department of Commerce, Bureau of the Census

Figure 2-2. Map of Chicago SMSA, Counties outlined.
Location of all suburban Chicago cities shown.

Belleville, were below the independent cities and Chicago suburban cities. East St. Louis was clearly the poorest city in terms of per capita income and was substantially below Alton and Granite City. The percentage of nonwhite residents in East St. Louis was 68.9, far greater than any other city in the sample. In 1970, 28.5 percent of East St. Louis families had incomes below the poverty line.

An estimate of the city growth patterns over a longer period is provided in the column headed "Reached Half Present Population." The dates in this column represent the census year in which the population of the city first reached one-half of its 1975 population. This measure provides a strong clue to the time period in which the city experienced its major development. Quincy, a Mississippi River town, is by this measure the "oldest" city in the study group, having reached one-half its population in 1870. Chicago is one of several cities that reached its halfway point by 1900. The independent cities, on the average, are much older than the suburban group. The average halfway point for independent cities was 1926, while the average date for the Chicago suburban group was 1955. These figures, along with the fifteen-year growth rates, again emphasize the recent nature of the suburbanization process.

Table 2-9 also lists the population densities (persons per square mile) of the study cities. Within each city type (independent or Chicago suburban) there is a wide dispersion. However, the average density is greater in the suburbs than in the independent cities. Likewise the population density in Chicago is much higher than in any of the smaller cities. These relationships are partially explained by the price of land. Land is relatively cheaper in the suburbs than in Chicago, and residents are better able to live in single-family homes on larger lots in the suburbs. One might easily argue that this is a major attraction for residents moving from the central city. The lower density in the independent city probably also reflects lower land prices and the presence of manufacturing or commercial activities within the city limits. However, within the two groups of cities, the dispersion (as revealed by the standard deviation) is higher in the suburban group.

Cities are also compared in terms of minority populations. One might expect the independent cities to have more diverse populations if, as is often claimed, the suburbanization process partially involved whites fleeing from changing neighborhoods. The data in Table 2-9 indicate a substantial difference between the independent cities and the Chicago suburbs, with the average for each group being 7.8 percent and 4.9 percent, respectively. However, a closer examination of the data reveals even greater differences if selected suburbs are removed. Harvey and Maywood have relatively large concentrations of nonwhites, whereas the majority of the remaining Chicago suburbs have nonwhite populations of less than two percent. These data are not current, however, and without question there have been significant changes in the racial composition of the city populations as will become clear in the 1980 census.

INDEPENDENT CITIES

This suburban-independent city classification is simple, but it emphasizes some of the more important aspects of urban development and highlights important aspects of city financial problems. It may also provide clues to future development.

The profile of Illinois cities presented in Table 2-9 clearly shows significant differences between independent and suburban cities. Although there are variations within groups, there are also significant differences between the groups in such variables as per capita income, rate of growth, "age" of the city, population, density, and racial composition. In the remainder of this chapter we will look more closely at the way cities in the two groups have developed and offer additional information regarding each group.

The independent cities developed in response to economic circumstances different from those in the suburbs. Some developed as agricultural trading centers, some as manufacturing centers, and some to serve governmental or institutional needs. Often these origins are reflected in the present character of the city economy. This means that independent cities, like suburban cities, may be economically specialized, but unlike suburban cities, they are not heavily dependent on the existence of a neighboring city for their economic survival.

The simple set of statistics showing percentage of labor force employed as professionals-managers or in clerical-sales occupations in Table 2-10 hints at the diversity of the independent city economies. The above-average percentages in the professional-managerial and clerical occupations in Bloomington, Normal, Champaign, Urbana, and DeKalb reflect the presence of major universities and, in the case of Bloomington, the presence of a large insurance company and a major agricultural organization. Issues faced by university cities are somewhat different because of dependence on a state-supported "industry" and the presence of a great many college-age students. All five cities serve also as agricultural trading centers. In addition, Bloomington-Normal and Champaign-Urbana are economic cities politically divided into two separately incorporated "twin" cities. Each pair of cities is the center of an SMSA.

Among the nonuniversity cities there is relatively little variation in the percentage of employment in professional-managerial occupations except for North Chicago and Carpentersville. In North Chicago the presence of a large military base greatly affects the figures. Aurora, Elgin, North Chicago, and Waukegan are industrial centers located on the outer fringes of the Chicago SMSA. They are older cities with populations of average socioeconomic status or below. Certainly these cities are less well off than the remaining suburbs in the Chicago area; they are included in the SMSA mainly because the metropolitan area grew up around them after they had developed as independent cities.

Rock Island-Moline, Peoria, Rockford, Danville, and Decatur are manufacturing centers located in the center of an SMSA or a region lacking SMSA status only because of population size. These cities are a focal point for residents of the region, who rely on them for employment and shopping facilities. Each city carries out unique manufacturing and commercial activities, but all are similar in that they have good transportation facilities with access to an interstate highway.

Springfield is unique because it is the state capital, although manufacturing within the city also affects its economy. It provides the surrounding area with commercial activities, and its downtown serves tourists visiting historical landmarks. Springfield also has excellent transportation facilities.

Freeport, Galesburg, and possibly Pekin can be grouped together as smaller cities in rural areas, but with access to reasonably good highway facilities. Pekin is part of the Peoria SMSA and differs in its dependence on a central city, whereas Freeport and Galesburg are freestanding cities serving a largely rural region.

Quincy is unusual because of its location on the Mississippi River and lack of good highway access. It is located in a rural region that has been losing population. The city developed early and has suffered declines in manufacturing employment. In recent years, however, it has shown signs of economic revival.

As indicated in Table 2-9, population growth in the independent cities has been much slower than in the suburban cities. In fact, several of them have suffered substantial population loss. In this respect, their problems resemble those of Chicago: the population is outmigrating to outlying areas.

Independent cities also have a higher percentage of residents below the poverty line and a higher percentage of pre-1939 housing. In the average independent city, 6.4 percent of the families were below the poverty line in 1970; in the Chicago suburbs the average was 3.0 percent. Even the three suburban cities with the lowest per capita incomes were only slightly above the average of the independents. The high percentage of pre-1939 housing in the independent cities and the plumbing deficiency data shown in Table 2–10 also emphasize that many of the independent cities are old compared to suburban cities.

Independent cities occupy a key role in providing public services to surrounding areas. In many instances they are the largest cities in the county and often are county seats. To a considerable extent, residents of surrounding areas look to these cities for services and cultural activities supported by the city government or by not-for-profit organizations within the city.

SUBURBAN CITIES

To obtain a clear picture of the suburban cities, it is useful to examine the Chicago SMSA first and then to consider the economic base of the individual suburbs. This comparison illustrates the wide diversity in economic conditions among cities within a large SMSA—any large SMSA regardless of the state in which it is located.

The Chicago SMSA, with 7,015,251 residents, experienced a 12.2 percent population increase during the 1960s, with 0.1 percent being attributed to net migration. From 1970 to 1975, however, the six counties gained only 0.1 percent, with a 3.8-percent natural increase and a net outmigration of 3.7 percent.[34] Within the metropolitan area, Cook County (the central county containing the city of Chicago) and the nearby suburbs experienced a population loss of 2.3 percent during the first half of the 1970s. The population of each suburban county, on the other hand, increased: from 19.5 percent in Will County to 4.6 percent in Kane County.

The economic development and land use patterns in a metropolitan area depend on the time at which the development occurred and the physical features of the landscape. The time period is important because of transportation routes and modes. Older metro areas in the Northeast, for instance, are more densely populated because of an early reliance on steam transportation and horse-drawn vehicles. The metro areas in the Southwest and West, on

Table 2-10. Occupation, Housing, and Poverty: Independent Cities and Suburban St. Louis

	Percent Employed		*Percent Families in Poverty (1970)*	*Pre-1939 Housing (1970)*	*Plumbing Deficiency (1970)*
	Professional Manager	*Clerical Sales*			
Independent Cities					
Aurora	20.7	25.2	3.6	56	3.6
Bloomington	25.2	32.6	9.2	64	4.2
Carpentersville	16.0	23.4	3.9	—	—
Champaign	36.4	29.0	7.3	36	—
Danville	21.9	24.7	8.7	63	6.6
Decatur	22.7	25.3	7.7	50	4.6
DeKalb	29.1	29.2	4.8	42	2.3
Elgin	21.8	25.9	3.9	56	2.7
Freeport	20.4	25.7	5.4	68	3.4
Galesburg	21.8	25.3	7.6	65	5.1
Joliet	21.1	25.0	5.8	56	4.6
Kankakee	22.4	24.3	6.9	59	3.0
Moline	24.5	28.2	5.5	55	2.7
Normal	32.5	31.7	3.8	26	1.7
North Chicago	14.8	24.1	6.8	38	1.9
Pekin	18.9	26.3	4.8	40	2.7
Peoria	25.0	28.0	7.7	54	3.6
Quincy	21.1	26.9	9.6	69	4.9
Rockford	22.0	26.3	7.1	44	2.9
Rock Island	22.9	27.8	7.8	56	4.1
Springfield	26.2	36.3	6.9	58	3.1
Urbana	45.5	22.9	7.6	42	3.7
Waukegan	21.9	27.9	6.0	41	2.7
Average	24.1	27.0	6.4	52	3.5
(S.D.)	(6.6)	(3.2)	(1.7)	(11.6)	(1.2)
Suburban St. Louis					
Alton	18.9	23.2	9.5	59	3.9
Belleville	23.2	31.3	5.8	50	3.9
East St. Louis	12.8	24.8	28.5	55	7.8
Granite City	16.6	27.7	7.1	42	2.8
Average	17.9	26.8	12.7	51.5	4.6
(S.D.)	(4.4)	(3.6)	(10.6)	(7.3)	(2.2)

Source: U.S. Bureau of the Census, *General Social and Economic Characteristics, 1970* (Washington, D.C.: Government Printing Office, 1972), Tables 86 and 105; *Municipal Yearbook, 1978* (Washington, D.C.: International City Management Association, 1978, Table 1/1; U.S. Bureau of the Census, *County and City Data Book, 1977* (Washington, D.C.: Government Printing Office, 1978), Table 4.

the other hand, were developed after the introduction of the automobile and are much less densely settled. The physical features of the landscape are important because wealthier residents will select land with the greatest amenities and these areas will be developed early.

During the 1870s the railroad system in the Chicago area was well developed, and the suburbs were already linked with the central city.[35] As early as 1856, Chicago was serviced by ten trunk rail lines and as many as fifty-eight passenger trains and thirty-eight freight trains arrived and departed daily. Figure 2-3 shows the major rail routes in 1871.

An inspection of the early rail routes reveals that many large suburbs were linked with Chicago. Of particular importance are the north shore cities, such as Evanston, Wilmette, and Highland Park. Since wealthy residents have the income to live where they choose, it is common for the more desirable sections of the area to be developed first. In the Chicago area, the most attractive sites were along the north shore of Lake Michigan. This area was served early by rail transportation, thus providing an additional advantage for residents to live in the suburbs and commute to Chicago with a minimum of discomfort and inconvenience, given existing transportation modes.

Rail service also was established early in the northwesterly direction, linking Palatine and Des Plaines and allowing development in these areas. To the west of Chicago, cities such as Oak Park, River Forest, and Elmhurst were served by rail, as were Aurora, Naperville, and Cicero in the southwest.

With the development of the automobile, the importance of the rail passenger service declined and the advantages due to rail connections lessened. Post-World War II highway construction, fostered by federal subsidies, permitted suburban residents a greater choice of residence. The Chicago area is served by several major limited-access expressways. Suburbs in close proximity to one of these expressways have more attraction for commuters working in Chicago. The introduction of the major highway networks also made it easier for businesses to relocate or expand to the suburbs with cheaper land and a higher quality of labor. Recent improvements in air travel may stimulate the suburban cities even more, expecially those near airports.

The linkage between the suburban cities and Chicago is demonstrated more clearly in Table 2-11, which shows the percentage of suburban residents working in Chicago. By far the largest

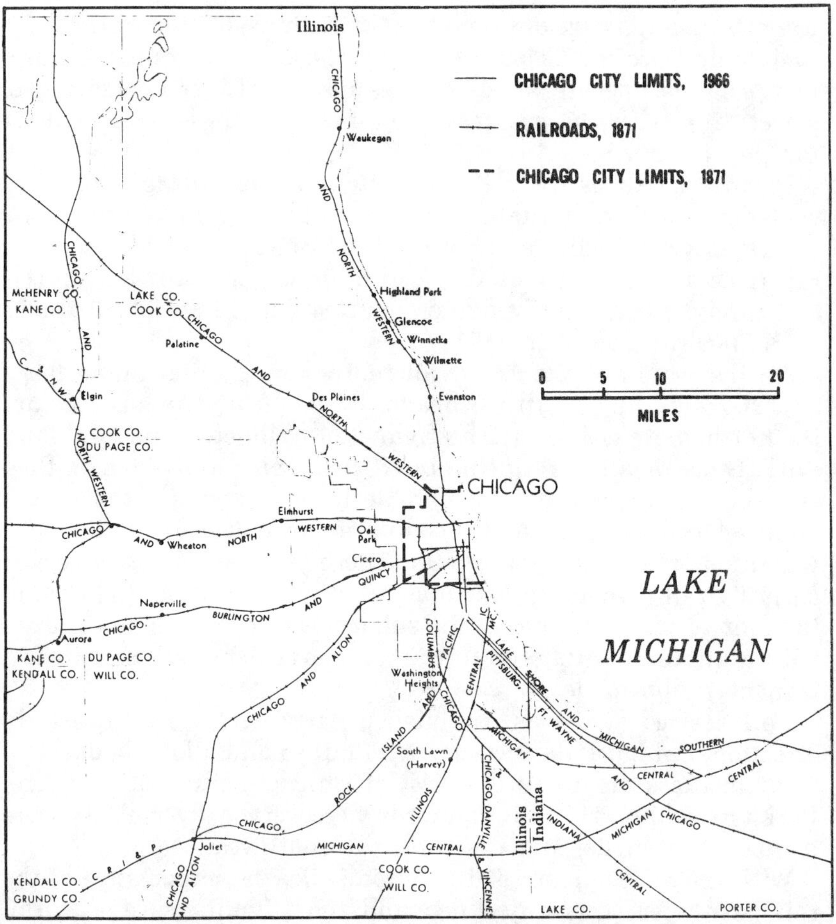

Source: *Reprinted, with adaptations, from Chicago: Growth of a Metropolis by Harold M. Mayer and Richard C. Wade by permission of the University of Chicago Press. Copyright 1969 by the Univesity of Chicago Press.*

Figure 2–3. Railroad systems in Chicago area, 1871.

Table 2-11. Commuting Characteristics, Suburban Cities, 1970

	Percent Working in			*Percent Commuting in*		
	Chicago CBD	*Rest of Chicago*	*Home County*	*Car*	*Bus/Streetcar/ Subway*	*Railroad*
Addison	3.8%	16.0%	44.7%	88.8%	0.3%	3.8%
Arlington Heights	8.1	17.5	66.6	78.5	0.5	14.3
Berwyn	7.3	33.6	54.0	68.9	16.7	5.2
Bolingbrook	2.4	25.0	26.9	92.6	0.4	2.3
Calumet City	5.9	26.3	34.0	83.6	5.1	4.0
Chicago Heights	4.3	8.7	80.9	81.2	2.8	5.8
Cicero	5.2	35.1	59.4	64.9	19.9	0.7
Des Plaines	4.2	21.3	70.7	83.3	1.6	6.4
Dolton	9.2	37.1	46.6	79.0	3.5	10.2
Downers Grove	8.2	15.8	52.8	76.8	0.2	14.8
Elmhurst	6.7	20.1	46.4	78.4	2.6	9.0
Elmwood Park	7.8	44.4	44.3	74.8	12.3	5.5
Evanston	10.8	21.7	64.1	57.4	22.0	4.6
Glenview	10.4	21.8	61.4	77.9	3.7	9.8
Harvey	5.8	22.1	66.4	77.2	4.2	10.4
Highland Park	10.5	20.9	49.7	69.1	0.6	15.4
Lansing	4.3	18.7	45.7	88.5	2.0	2.6
Lombard	5.9	18.4	47.8	81.9	1.0	10.5
Maywood	3.9	18.7	72.8	79.5	8.1	2.3
Morton Grove	6.4	28.8	62.4	82.3	5.9	3.6
Mt. Prospect	9.1	19.3	66.6	77.8	0.6	13.5
Naperville	9.0	11.8	58.2	72.2	0.1	14.4
Niles	4.4	30.7	60.2	86.0	4.6	2.3
Northbrook	9.2	23.3	53.7	79.0	1.0	13.8
Oak Lawn	7.4	43.8	44.2	82.5	5.8	4.7
Oak Park	16.2	36.4	42.8	57.8	30.7	0.7
Palatine	7.6	14.5	69.4	78.1	0.7	13.0
Park Forest	14.5	20.2	55.0	69.9	0.8	22.4
Park Ridge	8.9	34.4	52.7	76.3	4.0	10.9
Schaumberg	5.4	19.4	61.0	86.3	0.5	7.9
Skokie	8.5	37.0	50.6	79.7	11.8	1.4
Wheaton	6.9	12.0	66.1	73.2	0.4	11.9
Wilmette	13.1	29.3	51.9	69.7	7.8	11.8
Average	7.6	24.4	55.4	77.4	5.5	8.3
(S.D.)	(3.1)	(9.2)	(11.6)	(7.9)	(7.3)	(5.3)

Source: Suburban Factbook, 1973 (Chicago: Northeastern Illinois Planning Commission, 1973), Table 35.

percentage working in the Chicago central business district (CBD) was found in Oak Park, a middle-income city on the western edge of Chicago. Oak Park has excellent rail and highway access to the central business district and is architecturally attractive and historical. Over half the residents work in Chicago, and nearly

Table 2-12. Occupation, Housing, and Poverty in Chicago and Suburbs

	Percent Employed		Percent Families in Poverty (1970)	Pre-1939 Housing (1970)	Plumbing Deficiency (1970)
	Professional Manager	Clerical Sales			
Suburban Chicago					
Addison	24.4%	30.0%	2.4%	—	—
Arlington Heights	41.7	35.7	1.4	8	0.2
Berwyn	19.8	36.4	3.5	67	0.9
Bolingbrook	16.7	19.0		—	—
Calumet City	17.1	28.4	3.5	33	0.7
Chicago Heights	19.4	26.4	7.9	42	3.2
Cicero	13.9	30.8	4.1	71	1.6
Des Plaines	27.9	33.0	2.1	16	0.7
Dolton	22.2	32.5	3.6	12	0.5
Downers Grove	38.9	31.1	2.3	25	0.3
Elmhurst	33.8	35.1	1.9	32	1.0
Elmwood Park	23.0	35.8	4.4	38	0.5
Evanston	39.8	33.4	3.6	60	0.9
Glenview	43.6	34.0	2.1	—	—
Harvey	14.8	26.2	7.0	39	3.3
Highland Park	45.2	30.7	2.1	37	0.8
Lansing	23.2	29.3	3.3	16	0.6
Lombard	30.7	33.7	2.0	16	0.5
Maywood	18.2	26.0	6.0	72	1.1
Morton Grove	31.2	38.1	2.2	8	0.6
Mt. Prospect	37.2	35.8	1.7	5	0.6
Naperville	44.8	29.0	2.5	—	—
Niles	27.5	35.2	1.4	3	0.3
Northbrook	47.1	32.4	1.7	7	0.1
Oak Lawn	26.0	31.4	2.6	8	0.8
Oak Park	37.6	38.9	3.3	80	1.3
Palatine	37.2	33.1	2.1	11	0.3
Park Forest	45.4	32.0	2.5	—	0.2
Park Ridge	40.1	36.0	1.8	26	0.4
Schaumburg	33.7	29.6	2.8	—	—
Skokie	37.2	42.1	2.2	8	0.2
Wheaton	39.4	31.5	3.1	24	0.7
Wilmette	50.3	33.7	2.3	42	0.9
Average	31.8	32.3	3.0	30	0.8
(S.D.)	(10.6)	(4.4)	(1.5)	(23.1)	(0.8)
Chicago	17.8	30.1	10.6	67	3.5

Source: U.S. Bureau of the Census, *General Social and Economic Characteristics, 1970* (Washington, D.C.: Government Printing Office, 1972), Tables 86 and 105; *1978 Municipal Yearbook* (Washington, D.C.: International City Management Association, 1978), Table 1/1; *County and City Data Book, 1977* (Washington, D.C.: Government Printing Office, 1978), Table 4.

a third of them commute by rapid transit. The heavy employment in the Chicago central business district is consistent with the fact that 37.6 percent of the residents are employed in professional-managerial and 38.9 percent in clerical-sales occupations.

Evanston, Glenview, Highland Park, and Wilmette (high-income cities along the north shore of Lake Michigan) also are the homes of commuters to Chicago. In Evanston, immediately adjacent to Chicago on the north, a relatively high percentage of residents use the subway, streetcar, or bus. Wilmette bounds Evanston on the north, and Highland Park is considerably farther north with several cities in between. Accordingly, 11.8 percent of the Wilmette residents commute by rail, while 15.4 percent of those commuting from Highland Park do so. In both Highland Park and Wilmette nearly half the residents are employed in the professional-managerial category and approximately one-third have clerical-sales occupations.

Park Forest, a post-World War II city, is a somewhat unusual case, since it was developed privately as a totally planned city with a maximum population of 30,000. It is located approximately thirty miles southwest of the Chicago CBD. Although the commuting distance is considerable, well over a third of Park Forest's labor force worked in Chicago in 1970, and 14.5 percent commute to the CBD. The rail service linking Chicago with Park Forest helps explain the high percentage: 22.4 percent of the commuters ride the train to and from work. As indicated in Table 2-12, Park Forest ranked second among the cities in percentage of the work force employed in professional-managerial occupations as of 1970.

In several other cities, including Northbrook (47.1 percent), Park Ridge (40.1 percent), Arlington Heights (41.7 percent), Glenview (43.6 percent), and Naperville (44.8 percent), substantial proportions of the working populations are professionals or managers. Northbrook and Park Ridge are directly north of Chicago to the west of Evanston, Skokie, and Highland Park. These are relatively high-income cities with good rail access. Arlington Heights is a northwestern suburb approximately twenty-four miles from the Loop; Naperville is a suburb approximately thirty miles distant. Residents in both cities rely heavily on rail transportation. The cities are similar in income status, both being considerably above the suburban average.

At the other end of the spectrum, Berwyn (19.8 percent), Calumet City (17.1 percent), Cicero (13.9 percent), Harvey (14.8 percent), and Maywood (18.2 percent) are below average in terms of professional and managerial employment. They are also below average in per capita income. Berwyn, Cicero, and Maywood are immediately west of Chicago. Harvey and Calumet City are on the extreme southern edge of the city.

Within the sales-clerical employment category, Skokie heads the list. A wealthy northern suburb with a heavy Jewish concentration, 42.1 percent of Skokie's working population are in the sales-clerical category, compared to an average of 32.3 percent for the cities as a group. Skokie is only slightly removed from Chicago and is bordered by Morton Grove, Niles, and Park Ridge. It had the fourth highest per capita income among the cities in the present study, and ranked twenty-three in the nation among cities over 25,000 in 1974.

In the northwestern quadrant of the Chicago SMSA lies a group of contiguous middle-income cities, including Park Ridge ($8,042 per capita), Des Plaines ($6,280), Mount Prospect ($6,788), Arlington Heights ($7,184), and Palatine ($6,090). Park Ridge borders Chicago on the northwest, and Palatine is thirty miles from the Loop. With the exception of Des Plaines, each city is above average in the professional-manager employment category. As one might except, the greater distance from Chicago the percentage employed in the city declines steadily from 43.3 percent in Park Ridge to 22.1 percent in Palatine. In each instance commuters make extensive use of the rail service, although there is access to expressway facilities.

The data presented in Tables 2-9, 2-11, and 2-12 confirm the general impression of suburbs as high-income, rapidly growing areas with a high percentage of quality housing. Nevertheless, not all suburbs are alike. During the 1970s suburbs close to the central city experienced population declines. Prime examples are Evanston (-4.3 percent), Oak Park (-4.4 percent), Cicero (-5.4 percent), and Park Ridge (-0.8 percent). By contrast, suburbs on the outer rings gained population. Northbrook (13.5 percent), Palatine (16.9 percent), Addison (10.7 percent), Wheaton (21.1 percent), Naperville (29.2 percent), and Park Forest (7.5 percent) experienced substantial population growth between 1970 and 1975.

The suburbs as a group contain very low percentages of minority populations, although in certain instances cities had substantial concentrations. An outmigration of minority groups from Chicago has been under way, and close suburbs such as Oak Park have been experiencing racial change.

The suburban cities also differed considerably in population density. Evanston, Cicero, and Oak Park, for instance, are considerably more densely settled than the newer suburbs. This most likely reflects the period in which they were populated. In certain instances the cities have very little room for expansion, while others are not constrained. Housing costs are also an important factor as families choose a suburb. In the older suburbs with well-maintained homes, the housing costs may be beyond the reach of many prospective residents. In the near future, the costs of commuting by automobile will also take on increased importance, which should benefit cities with good transportation alternatives.

SUMMARY

Since the beginning of the Industrial Revolution, the functions of cities have changed greatly. The need to concentrate labor around production facilities originally transformed cities from religious and military centers with some merchandising functions into centers of production.

More recently, changed technology and transport have lessened the need to concentrate factory labor, but cities continue to be centers of management, finance, and innovation. One result of this change has been an acceleration of the suburbanization process. Residents of large central cities have found it possible and desirable to move out of the city into smaller suburban cities. This movement of population and the flexible motor transport that has made it possible have also encouraged many commercial and industrial enterprises to follow.

Accompanying these demographic changes has been a change in the relationship between the public and private sectors of the economy. Government has assumed a much greater responsibility for economic stabilization, for the provision of equal opportunity, and for the guarantee of some minimum level of health and welfare for all people. The greater concentration of population and specialization of activities that accompanies urbanization has also increased the need for various kinds of regulatory and police activities.

The federal government has, of necessity, played a leading role in these expanded activities, but local governments are still of great importance. Unfortunately, the local government structure has not changed rapidly. The large number of local governments that exist are a heritage of a much simpler period. As a result, an "economic" city whose boundaries are roughly approximated by a Standard Metropolitan Statistical Area may be divided into many "political" cities represented by the municipalities. These municipalities share the local government function with a number of neighboring or overlapping units of governments, such as counties, special districts, and townships. The result may be difficulty in coordinating services, competition for revenue, and conflicting development policies.

These trends are well illustrated in Illinois, where cities developed to meet a variety of economic needs. Many were primarily service centers for agricultural areas. Some became specialized manufacturing centers. In all cases, transportation was an important factor. Chicago, for instance, developed as an important rail center adjacent to Lake Michigan, and Quincy was an important river town with good rail connections 100 years ago.

Transport was also an important factor in determining land use within an urban area. In the Chicago area the development of passenger rail service permitted affluent persons to establish residences away from the crowded city. More recently, the development of motor transport has accelerated the dispersal of population and encouraged the dispersal of commercial and industrial activity.

The outcome of the process in Illinois has been to create a very large central city and many smaller cities that can be divided into two general classes. The older independent cities have a population that is more representative of the state or nation in terms of occupational and economic status. The housing stock is older and population growth has been moderate. Some of these cities, in fact, have experienced population declines and there is evidence that some, like Chicago, are losing population to smaller cities around them or to the open countryside. These cities, also like Chicago, remain the economic and cultural center of the area and are called on to provide a variety of services to their residents and to assume a major responsibility for the area's prosperity.

As a group, the suburban Chicago cities do conform to the common image of suburbs as residences for people who are affluent, white, and apt to be employed in managerial-professional or clerical occupations in the central city. However, there are many exceptions. Some are relatively low-income suburbs with a number of commerical and industrial establishments within their boundaries. Some of the older suburbs are also beginning to exhibit characteristics common to central cities, such as loss of population, increasing number of low-income and minority residents, and aging housing stock.

Local government services are provided to these urban areas by a large number of governmental units having boundaries that generally do not coincide with natural economic boundaries. Revenues are raised from a number of different sources—including the venerable property tax, which developed under conditions far different from those found today. This tax is the subject of the following chapter.

NOTES

1. For an easily readable account of this argument, see Jane Jacobs, *The Economic of Cities* (New York: Vintage Books, 1969).
2. The presence of present-day problems in ancient times is documented in L. Sprague de Camp, *Great Cities of the Ancient World* (New York: Doubleday, 1972).
3. Good accounts of U.S. urban development can be found in Zane L. Miller, *The Urbanization of Modern America: A Brief History* (New York: Harcourt, Brace, Jovanovich, 1973); Eric E. Lampard, "The Evolving System of Cities in the United States: Urbanization and Economic Development," *Issues in Urban Economics* (Baltimore: John Hopkins Press, 1968), pp. 81-140.
4. One writer has attributed New York's growth, as compared with Pittsburgh's, as partly a result of the size and number of firms. New York initially had many smaller firms that promoted the development of many specialized firms, whereas Pittsburg depended more on large firms providing most of their necessary services internally. See Benjamin Chinitz, "Contrasts in Agglomeration: New York and Pittsburgh," *American Economic Review,* Vol. 51, No. 2 (May 1961), pp. 279-289.
5. Segal, for example, argues that large SMSAs had a return to factors of production averaging from 8 percent above that for smaller SMSAs (those with less than 2 million population). He attributes the cost savings to economies in transportation and communication. It appears that these agglomeration economies more than offset the diseconomies such as congestion, etc., resulting from the larger city size. See David Segal, "Are There Returns to Scale in City Size?" *Review of Economies and Statistics,* Vol. 58, No. 3 (August 1976), pp. 339-350.
6. The concept of economies of scale in the public sector must be kept distinct from variations in expenditures per capita. Economies of scale mean that the per unit cost of producing the same service declines as the number of units produced increases. There is considerable evidence that large cities produce a different type of service than smaller cities and the same or a higher expenditure per capita may not actually reflect diseconomies in the typical production sense.
7. In 1950, the Bureau of the Census changed the urban definition, which tended to increase the percentage classification as urban.
8. The Census Bureau classifies a central city or twin cities with a population of 50,000 or more and the contiguous counties that are economically linked as Standard Metropolitan Statistical Areas (SMSAs).
9. A detailed discussion of these trends is provided in Norval D. Glenn, "Suburbanization in the United States Since World War II," in *The Urbanization of the Suburbs,* ed. by Louis H. Masotti and Jeffrey K. Hadden (Beverly Hills: Sage Publications, 1973), pp. 51-78.
10. For a detailed analysis of the fiscal impact on the central city from commuters, see Phillip E. Vincent, "The Fiscal Impact of Commuters," in *Fiscal Pressures on the Central City: The Impact of Commuters, Nonwhites, and Overlapping Governments,* (New York: Praeger Publishers, 1971), pp. 41-121.

11. For a discussion of the Minnesota metropolitan tax-base sharing act see Paul A. Gilje, "Sharing of Tax Growth—Redefinitions," *Governmental Finance* (November 1977), pp. 35-40, or Peter Nye, "Minnesota Helps Its Metropolis Share the Tax Base," *Nation's Cities* (November 1977), pp. 21-24.
12. The domestic programs include social security payments and all federal aid to state and local governments, including general revenue sharing.
13. *Significant Features of Fiscal Federalism,* 1979-80 ed. (Washington, D.C.: Advisory Commission on Intergovernmental Relations, 1980), M-123, p. 4.
14. Ibid.
15. Samuel H. Beer, "Political Overload and Federalism," *Polity,* Vol. 12, No. 1, (Fall 1979), pp. 5-17.
16. *Statistical Abstract of the United States: 1977* (Washington, D.C.: U.S. Government Printing Office, 1977), Table 735.
17. Ibid., Table 703.
18. Ibid., Table 10.
19. Ibid., Table 17.
20. The workers' compensation rate increases are summarized in John B. Parrish, *Organized Labor and Workmen's Compensation in Illinois: An Interim Study, 1974-1977* (Arlington, Va.: Foundation for the Advancement of the Public Trust, Inc., 1978).
21. William D. Toal, *Illinois Employment Cycles and Trends—A Comparative View,* (Springfield: State of Illinois Office of the Comptroller, 1977), Issues in Public Finance, Study No. 4.
22. The employment changes were examined using the shift-share framework popularized by Ashby during the 1960s. See Lowell B. Ashby, "The Geographical Redistribution of Employment: An Examination of the Elements of Change," *Survey of Current Business, Vol. 44 (1964), pp. 13-*20.
23. The sunbelt-snowbelt controversy has been receiving considerable attention, especially as states apply pressure on the federal government for policies to stem the loss of employment from the Northeast and Midwestern states. See C. L. Jusenius and L. C. Ledebur, *A Myth in the Making: the Southern Economic Challenge and the Northern Economic Decline* (Washington, D.C.: Office of Economic Research, Economic Development Administration, U.S. Department of Commerce, 1976); Economic Development Research Report: "The Second War Between the States," *Business Week,* (May 17, 1976), p. 92.
24. *State Tax Review,* Vol. 38, No. 42 (October 18, 1977).
25. For a technical discussion of the techniques involved in computing tax capacity and effort, see *Measuring the Fiscal Capacity and Effort of State and Local Areas,* Information Report (Washington, D.C.: Advisory Commission on Intergovernmental Relations, 1971); D. Kent Halstead, *Tax Wealth in Fifty States* (Washington, D.C.: National Institute of Education, 1978), esp. Ch. 4.
26. Halstead, *Tax Wealth in Fifty States,* p. 40.
27. A brief discussion of the types of governmental units in Illinois and other states is provided in U.S. Bureau of the Census, *Governmental Organization* (Washington, D.C.: Government Printing Office, 1978), pp. 333-513.
28. Norman Walzer, *Financing Local Services in Illinois* (Urbana: University of Illinois Agricultural Experiment Station, 1979).
29. A discussion of the criteria for defining SMSAs is available in *Standard Metropolitan Statistical Areas, 1975* (Washington, D.C.: Office of Management and Budget, 1975)
30. Municipalities crossing county lines are counted in the county having the largest share of its population.

31. See Thomas M. Scott, "Suburban Governmental Structures," in *The Suburbanization of the Suburbs,* ed. by Louis H. Masotti and Jeffrey K. Hadden (Beverly Hills: Sage Publications, 1973), p. 215.
32. U.S. Bureau of the Census, *1962 Census of Governments,* Vol. 1 (Washington, D.C.: U.S. Government Printing Office, 1963), p. 32; U.S. Bureau of the Census, *1977 Census of Governments,* Vol. 1, No. 1 (Washington, D.C.: U.S. Government Printing Office, 1978).
33. Glenn W. Fisher and Robert P. Fairbanks, *Illinois Municipal Finance* (Urbana: University of Illinois Press, 1968); Thomas P. Murphy and John Rehfuss, *Urban Politics in the Suburban Era* (Homewood, Ill.: The Dorsey Press, 1976); Harold M. Mayer and Richard C. Wade, *Chicago: Growth of a Metropolis* (Chicago: University of Chicago Press, 1969).
34. U.S. Bureau of the Census, *County and City Data Book,* 1977, Table 3.
35. An excellent pictorial history of the development of the Chicago area is provided in Mayer and Wade, *Chicago: Growth of a Metropolis.* The following section relies heavily on this source.

Chapter 3

Property Taxes

State governments create local governments and give them a variety of powers and responsibilities. While this is done, in part, for the administrative convenience of the state, it also permits residents in a particular locality to choose the types and levels of local services they receive. Local officials know, however, that residents are sharply limited in their choice of services. States limit the functions that local governments can perform and typically place explicit limits on their power to raise revenue. State governments—and increasingly the federal government—mandate services or expenditures that may or may not be accompanied by financial support.

In addition to legal constraints, municipalities are constrained by competition from other units of government. "Economic" cities grow and develop in response to market forces and geographic features, but governmental boundaries rarely follow the same contours. Overlapping and neighboring units of government may serve the same residents and, to the frustration of local officials, are often confused in taxpayers' minds. This latter fact causes particular anxiety for municipal officials, who are frequently held responsible for the policies of other local officials over which they have no control. Most Illinois residents would probably be surprised to learn, for instance, that school district revenues exceed municipal revenues by 79 percent and that property tax revenues raised by school districts are more than three times the revenues raised by municipalities.

Table 3-1 reveals that municipalities have the most balanced revenue structure of local governments in Illinois. In 1976-1977, cities received 26.0 percent of their revenue from property taxes, 27.8 percent from other taxes, and 30.7 percent from intergovernmental revenue sources. An additional 15.4 percent was obtained from charges and miscellaneous sources. This balance among the four major categories of revenue sources represents a significant change from earlier times. Once the property tax was the predominant source of revenue for local governments in the United States. Throughout this century, however, there has been a steady decline in its relative importance, while the reliance on other taxes, charges for services, and intergovernmental revenues has risen.

A broader perspective on the revenue sources used in financing services is available from Table 3-2, which compares Illinois cities with their counterparts nationwide in 1976-1977. For the study years, the property tax is only slightly more important in Illinois, whereas the greatest difference between the two groups is found in state revenues received. Illinois cities receive approximately the same percentage of revenue from the federal government as cities nationwide, but the state revenues represent a much smaller proportion.[1] Although the property tax represents approximately the same proportion of revenues, the average per capita collection is substantially lower in the Illinois cities. Table 3-2 shows that per capita revenues of Illinois cities are only 60.9 percent of the U.S. city average.

Table 3-1. 1977 Revenue, by Source, Illinois Governments (Millions)

Government Unit	*Property Taxes*	*Other Taxes*	*Charges & Misc. Rev.*	*Intergov't Revenue*	*Total*
Counties	$ 321.5	$ 75.1	$ 190.5	$ 364.6	$ 951.8
Municipalities	657.8	705.3	389.8	775.7	2,528.6
Townships	118.2	0.1	6.8	78.8	203.9
Special districts	278.3	—	228.2	356.8	863.3
School districts	2,195.9	2.2	340.3	1,991.7	4,530.1
All local governments	$3,571.7	$782.7	$1,155.6	$3,330.8[a]	$8,840.9[a]

Source: U.S. Bureau of the Census, *Governmental Finances, 1976-77* (Washington, D.C.: U.S. Government Printing Office, 1978), Table 24.

[a]Duplicative intergovernmental transfers are excluded.

Table 3-2. Municipal Revenues by Source, 1976–1977

	Illinois Municipalities		*U.S. Municipalities*	
Revenue Source	*Per Capita*	*Percent*	*Per Capita*	*Percent*
General revenue, total	$269.70	100.0%	$443.10	100.0%
Intergovernmental revenue	82.50	30.6	175.48	39.6
From federal government	40.21	14.9	64.81	14.6
From state government	36.19	13.4	102.92	23.2
From own sources	187.20	69.4	267.62	60.4
Taxes	144.93	53.7	190.48	43.0
Property	69.94	25.9	114.28	25.8
Sales	60.01	22.3	42.39	9.6
Other	14.98	5.6	33.74	7.6
Charges and miscellaneous	42.27	15.7	77.14	17.4

Source: U.S. Bureau of the Census, *Finances of Municipalities and Township Governments, 1977* (Washington, D.C.: Government Printing Office, 1979), Table 17.

LOCAL REVENUE POWERS

One of the most important determinants of the revenue structure used by municipalities is the legal authority to levy taxes. Local governments, as creatures of the state, have only those powers and functions granted by the state. The revenue-raising powers of Illinois cities of 25,000 and over, and those under 25,000 that elect to adopt home rule, were greatly expanded by the passage of the 1970 constitution, which provided for broad home rule powers. The constitution removed tax rate limits and debt limits from home rule units, although the General Assembly retained the power to reinstate these limits with sufficient votes. Home rule authority exists in sharp contrast with the situation prior to 1970, when the powers of the cities were tightly controlled and their use of the property tax circumscribed by statutes limiting the rates that could be imposed for each fund. Since the rates pertained to all cities, population growth or shifts in economic activity caused significant difficulties for cities faced with changing needs for services. The growing complexity of urban problems and the growing divergence among cities in terms of their tax bases created a need for more flexibility in formulating policies to remedy local problems. That flexibility came with home rule.

The home rule powers in Illinois are perhaps the broadest in the nation. Article VII, Section 6(a) states; "Except as limited by this Section, a home rule unit may exercise any power and perform any function pertaining to its government and affairs including, but not limited to, the power to regulate for the protection of the public health, safety, morals and welfare; to license; to tax; and to incur debt." When constitutional delegates established home rule powers, they were cautious not to enumerate the topics covered in them. Either the General Assembly or the courts might have interpreted such a list as inclusive.

The home rule powers are further protected by the inclusion of Section 6(m), which states that "powers and functions of home rule units shall be construed liberally." The apparent intention was to break with earlier restrictive interpretations of municipal authority. If the General Assembly wishes to deny or limit the power to tax and any other power or function of a home rule unit not exercised or performed by the state, a three-fifths majority of both houses is required. To declare an area exclusively a state concern, on the other hand, requires only a simple majority.

The implementation of home rule authority by cities has been very cautious because of the high stakes involved in a restrictive court decision being handed down. Municipal attorneys have carefully watched the court decisions involving home rule powers and have studied the emerging trends in the attitudes of the courts regarding accepted uses of these powers.[2]

The local government article of the constitution did impose several limitations on the financing of services, however. Section 6(d) states that a home rule unit cannot incur debt payable from *ad valorem* property taxes if it matures more than forty years from the date incurred. Sections 6(j) and (k) indicate that the General Assembly may limit the debt payable from sources other than *ad valorem* property tax receipts with a three-fifths vote in both houses. As of this time, debt limits have not been imposed. Section 6(e) states that home rule units have only the powers granted by the General Assembly to "license for revenue or impose taxes measured by income or earnings or upon occupations." This means that cities would have to obtain approval from the General Assembly prior to imposing an income tax, for example.

Although the home rule provisions of the Illinois constitution are among the most liberal in the United States, the adoption of the 1970 constitution did not mean that officials in home rule municipalities would find it easy to raise revenues. The number of new or unused forms of taxation that would yield significant amounts of revenue remained quite limited, and new taxes were apt to encounter strong resistance from taxpayers. The removal of local income taxes from home rule power eliminated one possible "new tax," while an early decision of the Illinois Supreme Court made it clear that property tax adminstration was not a home rule function. Striking down an attempt by Cook County, a home rule county, to provide for the payment of the property tax in four annual installments, the court stated:

> Although obviously there are powers and functions of county government which pertain to its government and affairs within the contemplation of section 6 of article VII... the collection of property taxes is not one of them. In the process of collecting and distributing tax monies the county acts both for itself and the other taxing bodies authorized to levy taxes on property within the county, and the function thus performed does not pertain to its government and affairs to any greater extent than to the government and affairs of the other taxing bodies for whose benefits it acts. We find no provision for the constitution of 1970 or in the proceedings of the [constitutional] convention which leads us to believe that the collection of property taxes is a home-rule power or function within the contemplation of section 6 of article VII.[3]

This decision emphasizes that even home rule governments are in no sense independent fiscal entities free to develop revenue programs independent of other units or independent of the past. Local government fiscal affairs interact in complex ways with those of other local units and with the state. Also, they are greatly affected by tradition and past practices. For these reasons, considerable space is devoted to the property tax in this chapter. No other revenue source involves such complex interrelations with other units of local governments, and no other revenue source has so greatly affected fiscal procedures and decision-making processes.

THE PROPERTY TAX IN PERSPECTIVE

For decades the property tax was the major source of both state and local revenue in the United States. In 1902, the first year for which complete data are available, 82 percent of all state and local tax collections and 87 percent of all local taxes were derived from the property tax. Not only were property taxes lucrative, they were also considered to provide an equitable form of taxation. Many state constitutions written in the second half of the nineteenth century contained provisions attempting to mandate the universal, uniform general property tax as the major source of state and local revenue.

Because of the prominence of the property tax, statutes and

procedures covering budgeting and financial reporting were built around the property tax levy process. They remain so today. Municipal bonds are often secured by property tax levies, and bond rating agencies give much attention to the size and quality of the tax base in their rating process. Legislative attempts to control the size of local governments often involve limiting tax rates (or levies) and debt, usually expressed as a percent of the property tax base.

In the simple agrarian economy of the Civil War period, the property tax had much to commend it. Much wealth was in the form of land, livestock, or simple agricultural tools. Taxation in proportion to wealth was widely considered to be an equitable system. Assessment was relatively easy because the values of the most common kinds of property were well known to the township assessor.

As property became more diverse, though, discontent with property taxation increased. Many kinds of personal property were difficult to tax, and there was a growing belief that not all types of property represented the same ability to pay. States began to classify property so that different kinds of personal and real property were taxed at different rates. By 1939 at least twenty-one states permitted some type of classification.[4] While legal classification was not allowed in Illinois, *de facto* or administrative classification systems arose in many counties, most notably in Cook County. The *de facto* classification systems exempted intangible property, or assessed it at a small fraction of its true value. Household goods and private automobiles were exempted from assessment in Chicago, and a *de facto* system of real estate classification that favored homeowners and small apartment owners at the expense of large office and industrial properties was adopted for all of Cook County. Real estate classifications were not set forth in any official document, but resulted with the use of assessment manuals and other materials developed by the assessor. The results were clearly evident in the assessment-sales ratios published by class of property.

Informal classifications also developed in some downstate counties. Less systematic and less publicized than those in Cook County, classification systems in downstate counties often favored industrial and agricultural property.

The system of classification in Cook County developed in response to depression conditions, but it also served well in an era of rapid suburbanization. Many observers admitted that there was logic in providing a tax break to homeowners or small apartment owners at a time when middle-class residents were fleeing to the suburbs. While the favoring of small property owners placed a heavy tax burden on the owners of large office and commercial buildings, it was argued that the advantages of the central city location and the fact that many daytime occupants were suburban residents justified higher taxes. In fact, many leading real estate operators and businessmen appeared to accept the situation as inevitable and not intolerable.

It is clear that an abrupt elimination of *de facto* classification would have seriously threatened all elected officials in Cook County. Such an event would have meant a massive shift in tax burden, with many small property owners paying higher taxes to the benefit of a much smaller number of corporations and large property owners. The political implications are obvious.

Given the balance of political forces in Illinois, it is unlikely that the administrative or legislative branches of state government would have taken action to enforce the equal assessment provisions of the constitution, but the possibility of court enforcement was less remote. Such action had occurred in several states, and the decision in several Illinois cases involving railroad property concerned the defenders of *de facto* classification in Cook County.

In 1966, Illinois voters were offered a constitutional amendment permitting a limited income tax and giving the General Assembly power to provide for classification or "in lieu" taxation of personal property. The amendment also allowed the classification of real estate in Cook County to continue.[5] It failed. After this failure, backers of changes in the revenue article began to support the call for constitutional convention as the only hope for securing the desired changes. In fact, this support may have been a decisive factor in the referendum that resulted in the Sixth Illinois Constitutional Convention of December 1969.

Shortly before the Sixth Illinois Constitutional Convention met, two events, which were to have a great influence on the deliberations over the revenue article, occurred. In July 1969, the Illinois Supreme Court upheld a newly passed state income tax in a sweeping decision that removed an earlier, very restrictive interpretation of the state's power to impose nonproperty taxes.[6] This decision did not change the status of the property tax, but it did shift the balance of power in the convention in ways sure to affect property tax provisions.

The other important tax event of 1969 was the passage by the General Assembly of a resolution submitting a proposed constitutional amendment to the electorate in November 1970, which would prohibit the taxation of personal property "as to individuals." This amendment complicated the work of the constitutional convention. First of all, it tied the hands of the constitutional convention in the matter of personal property taxation. It clearly would be poor strategy to present to the voters a proposed new constitution restoring a tax that they had eliminated by an amendment to the old constitution. Another problem lay with the ambiguity and possible unconstitutionality of the phrase "as to individuals." It was not clear just what the phrase meant, and a number of well-qualified tax attorneys were of the opinion that classifying property on the basis of ownership by an individual or a corporation would be held unconstitutional in federal courts.

After months of negotiations and numerous compromises, the convention produced a revenue article making a number of important changes in the Illinois system of property taxation.[7] The new revenue article begins with a section involving the state's revenue power and then turns to the matter of nonproperty tax classification. A third section places limits on the income tax. Sections 4 and 5 concern the property tax and read as follows:

> *Section 4. Real Property Taxation.* (a) Except as otherwise provided in this Section, taxes upon real property shall be levied uniformly by valuation ascertained as the General Assembly shall provide by law. (b) Subject to such limitations as the General Assembly may hereafter prescribe by law, counties with a population of more than 200,000 may classify or continue to classify real property for purposes of taxation. Any such classification shall be reasonable and assessments shall be uniform within each class. The level of assessment or rate of tax of the highest class in a county shall not exceed two and one-half times the level of assessment or rate of tax of the lowest class in that county. Real property used in farming in a county shall not be assessed at a higher level of assessment than a single family residential real property in that county. (c) Any depreciation in the value of real estate occasioned by a public easement may be deducted in assessing such property.
>
> *Section 5. Personal Property Taxation.* (a) The General Assembly by law may classify personal property for purposes of taxation by valuation, abolish such taxes on any or all classes and authorize the levy of taxes in lieu of the taxation of personal property by valuation. (b) Any ad valorem personal property tax abolished on or before the effective date of this Constitution shall not be reinstated. (c) On or before January 1, 1979, the General Asembly by law shall abolish all ad valorem personal property taxes and concur-

rently therewith and thereafter shall replace all revenue lost by units of local government and school districts as a result of the abolition of ad valorem personal property taxes subsequent to January 2, 1979. Such revenue shall be replaced by imposing statewide taxes, other than ad valorem taxes on real estate, solely on those classes relieved of the burden of paying ad valorem personal property taxes because of the abolition of such taxes subsequent to January 2, 1979. If any taxes imposed for such replacement purposes are taxes on or measured by income, such replacement taxes shall not be considered for purposes of the limitations of one tax and the ratio of 8 to 5 set forth in Section 3(a) of this Article.

In revising the constitution, delegates clearly understood that classification of real property had to be preserved if the necessary support from the Cook County Democratic organization was to be received. With respect to other counties, however, the final solution was to allow classification in counties containing over 200,000 residents. On or before January 1, 1979, the General Assembly had to abolish all *ad valorem* personal property taxation. This was finally accomplished in August 1979 with the passage of H. B. 2569, which replaced the personal property tax on corporations with an increase in income taxes. In part because of the poor wording in the constitution, which created much confusion and uncertainty, the replacement of the personal property tax was a difficult process.[8] The replacement provision provided no guidance for how to distribute the replacement revenue among local governments, and there was considerable disagreement about the amount of tax to be replaced. In November 1978, the legislature proposed a constitutional amendment making the question of eliminating business personal property taxes optional. The Illinois voters narrowly defeated this proposal. The issue was of great importance to cities since business personal property taxes constituted as much as one-third of the property taxes extended in some cities.

Some of the most important provisions affecting local finance are found in the local government article of the new constitution. For home rule municipalities, the local government article of the constitution removed property tax rate limits that had in previous years played such a restrictive role in local government finance.[9] This is an especially interesting development in view of the national trend toward more restrictive limits on local government taxation, which began about the time the Illinois constitution was adopted and was dramaticized by the passage of Proposition 13 in California.

The local government article also granted home rule units the power to levy or impose additional taxes on areas within their boundaries (special service areas) for provision of special services provided to those areas.[10] This provision modified the "geographic uniformity" rule requiring that the tax rates of a unit of government be uniform throughout its territory.

Since the adoption of the new constitution, there have been several developments in property taxation. Some of these, which involve changes in assessment levels and in equalization practices, will be discussed in later sections of this chapter. One important development was the passage of legislation in 1973 implementing the provision for special tax areas as described above.[11]

Another development relating to property taxation came in the 1972 "circuit breaker" legislation. This act provided for state grants to persons sixty-five years of age or older and to disabled persons paying property taxes. The program, which has a counterpart in many states, is intended to reduce the property tax burden for these people. Because payments are made from the state treasury, the legislation has no direct effect on local government tax collections.

Legislation passed in 1976 provided that agricultural land be assessed on the basis of fair cash value offered voluntarily by a buyer intending to use the land for agricultural purposes. In 1977, the General Assembly passed legislation basing assessments on productivity and established a formula to determine the best or highest grade of agricultural land in each county.[12] The formula involves (1) average value of agricultural products sold per acre from the county, (2) three-year average value per acre per year of four principal crops, and (3) a 10-percent of sale price (for the same three years) of land transferred for agricultural use. Lands of lesser value are to scaled down from the ceiling imposed by the formula. Farm dwellings are to be assessed separately from the land, and other improvements to the land are to be assessed on the basis of their contribution to the productivity of the farm.

These preferential assessment acts presented substantial constitutional questions, but the Illinois Supreme Court has sustained the special service areas and the 1977 farmland assessment legislation.[13] Since its original passage, the farmland assessment legislation has been modified several times.

Local government property tax collections were also affected by homestead exemption legislation allowing an exemption of assessed valuation for persons sixty-five years and older.[14] In 1978 an exemption was provided for disabled veterans and their spouses under certain conditions.[15] An annual exemption of up to $25,000 for new improvements was also provided for residential properties. The exemption, which covers the actual cost of the improvements, can continue for four years following completion and occupancy or until the next quadrennial assessment, whichever comes later. Provision was also made for improvements in cooperatives. These programs, of course, indicate a loss in property tax revenues to local governments.

PROPERTY TAX ADMINISTRATION

The property tax is probably the most poorly administered major tax in America. The inherent difficulty of determining the value of property, combined with the highly fragmented nature of the administrative process, causes inequitable taxation and much taxpayer confusion about how tax liabilities are determined.

Municipal officials have only a minor role in the administration of property taxes even though the property tax is a major element in the municipal finance picture. The problem for municipal officials is compounded by the fact that many urban residents attribute to municipal officials both the administration and the levying of property taxes. Actually, many county and state officials share responsibility for the assessment and equalization of property values and for the extension and collection of the tax. The taxes are levied by the governing boards of the various units of government in accordance with procedures and limitations spelled out by the state.

Assessment and Review

Property tax liabilities are distributed among property owners in a taxing district on the basis of assessed value. The assessor must find, list, and appraise all taxable property within the district. Assessed value is presently defined as 33⅓ percent of fair market value.

Assessors in Illinois, as specified by statute, are county or township officials. Every four years, Cook County elects a county assessor. Township assessors are elected for areas outside Chicago. In the St. Louis area, St. Clair County elects a five-member board of assessors with staggered six-year terms and township assessors with four-year terms. In the seventeen counties with the commission form of government, the presiding officer of the county board, with the advice and consent of the board, appoints an assessor chosen from the three persons earning the highest grade on an examination conducted by the Illinois Department of Revenue.[16] Counties with the township form of organization elect township assessors who work with supervisors of assessment appointed in the same way as assessors in commission counties.[17]

Every county, except Cook, has a board of review responsible for adjusting individual assessments upon complaint.[18] The board may adjust assessments between classes of property and among assessment districts. If dissatisfied with the decision of the county board of review, a downstate taxpayer may appeal to the state Property Tax Appeals Board. The decisions of this board are subject to judicial review pursuant to the Administrative Review Act. Cook County taxpayers may appeal to the Cook County Board of Tax Appeals. The taxpayer's rights to appeal to the courts are limited to cases of fraudulent overvaluation or to cases in which the assessor violated the applicable statutory or constitutional requirements.[19]

In today's complex, rapidly changing economy, the assessor has a difficult job. Property is constructed for or devoted to highly specialized uses. Values change rapidly, especially in an era of inflation, and the assessor must assign a value to properties that rarely sell. This is not to say that it is impossible to do a good job. The appraisal profession is highly developed, with very sophisticated methods for appraising property. These appraisal methods are designed to permit the appraiser to determine the amount that could be obtained for the property if it were sold in a voluntary, arms-length transaction under circumstances in which both buyer and seller were well informed about the property.

Three major approaches are used to determine market value of property. The comparative sales approach is used for types of property that are frequently sold, such as residences, small apartments, or small commercial buildings. As the name implies, the sales prices of similar properties serve as data on which to base the appraisal of the property in question. Because the properties sold are never exactly identical to the property being appraised, adjustments must be made for differences. To make these adjustments, the assessor uses tables showing standard amounts to be added or subracted for various features. When computer facilities are available, the assessor can use multiple-regression analysis to make the adjustments more rapidly and completely.

The income approach to determine market value of property is based on the concept that a buyer is interested in the return (income) that a property will yield. After estimating the income that a property will yield over a period of years, the assessor converts this flow of income into a capital value. The income approach is most suitable for properties such as office buildings or apartments that are commonly rented, but it can be used for properties not commonly rented by "imputing" the rent that the owner would have to pay if he were to rent it from someone else.

The cost, or "brick-and-mortar," approach involves estimating the cost of building a similar building and then making proper allowances for depreciation and obsolescence. This approach to determining market value of property is most useful when the building is relatively new or is of a type economically feasible to construct under present conditions. It is less useful when the property is functionally obsolete and, of course, cannot be used for nonreproducible property, such as land.

A skilled appraiser will choose the method (or methods) most suitable for the property in question. Unfortunately, partially trained personnel in an assessor's office often become so absorbed in the procedural aspects of one of the approaches that they apply it mechanically even to properties for which the procedure is ill suited.

Successful application of these methods to the assessing (mass-appraisal) process requires competent, professionally trained appraisers who have adequate staff and sufficient operating funds. Up-to-date property records containing physical descriptions of each parcel of real estate; information about zoning, sales, costs, and dates of alterations to the property; and similar data must be maintained. The office must also have aerial maps properly cross-indexed to the property records, and files containing all kinds of information that may affect property values in the city.[20] Ideally, appraisal should be an ongoing process with values updated regularly, even though official assessments are made only at specified periods.

The development of the computer has greatly facilitated the assessment process. Not only do computers store and retrieve data needed for conventional assessment methods, they also permit the use of new methods such as multiple-regression appraisal.[21] Multiple-regression analysis is basically a comparative sales approach that permits property values to be updated almost instantaneously.

There are, of course, some circumstances affecting values that cannot be readily handled by multiple regression. In such cases, constant review by a qualified appraiser is necessary. The use of multiple-regression analysis in the assessment of properties most amenable to the approach, such as residences and perhaps small commercial properties, makes it even more important that the appraisal of other types of property be kept current. Otherwise, in an inflationary period, the computer-assisted assessments will be high relative to those assessed in the conventional fashion.

Whereas the assessment process is basically similar throughout Illinois, it is important to note that properties in Cook County are classified. The result is that residents in many of the suburban cities in the present study currently have their property assessed at 16.0 percent (Group II in Table 3–4) rather than at the 33.3 percent rate used in downstate counties.

Equalization of Assessments

Although the terms "equalization" and "review" are often used interchangeably in common speech, they are technically different. Review refers to the process of correcting individual assessments within an assessment district. Interdistrict equalization, sometimes simply called equalization, refers to across-the-board changes of assessments for the purpose of equalizing the level of assessment between two or more districts. Review is necessary to correct inequities among individual property owners within a district. Equalization is necessary to ensure that taxpayers in a district, taken as a group, pay their fair share of the tax levies of taxing districts that lie in more than one assessment district. Equalization is also necessary to ensure the fair distribution of state grants-in-aid when property valuation is one of the factors in the distribution formula.

In counties other than Cook, the county boards of review may equalize property by raising or lowering the valuation of property or a class of property in a township or part thereof.[22] Generally, this power is used sparingly.

At the state level, the Department of Revenue has the power and responsibility to equalize among counties by assigning a "multiplier" to each county. This figure, when multiplied by every assessment in the county, should bring the average level of assessment to the statutorily prescribed percentage of fair cash value. The multiplier is also highly unpopular. An assigned multiplier of more than 1.000 means that every assessment in the county will be increased and that local authorities will be able to blame the increase on "the state" or "the governor." As a result, there have been long periods in Illinois history when state authorities have made little effort to equalize assessment levels among counties. Thus, residents in some counties pay more than their share of the taxes of governmental units that overlap county lines, and receive less than their share of school aid and other grants that use property valuation as a factor in the distribution formula.

In 1975, the Illinois Supreme Court ruled that the Department of Local Government must assign a multiplier that would bring the equalized assessed value in every county to the statutorily prescribed 50 percent.[23] Because many counties were assessing far below the 50-percent level, immediate implementation of this order would have created much confusion. To reduce the severity of the adjustment, the General Assembly passed HB 990, which reduced the statutory rate of assessment to 33⅓ percent and provided for a three-year transition period during which the multipliers were to be calculated to reach the statutory level in three equal annual steps. No counties were to be assigned multipliers reducing the total assessed valuation in the county below the 1974 assessed value. In accordance with the new statute, the Department of Local Government assigned multipliers for tax year 1975 ranging from 5.0983 to .8005.[24]

Quality of Assessment and Equalization

With the presence of many types of highly specialized properties, the assessment of property for tax purposes is difficult at best. Values fluctuate rapidly because of technological change or changes in economic conditions. Property rights are defined by law, and legal complexities affect the values of certain properties.

To assess property accurately requires a commitment of resources and of political will that is rarely present. Appraisal of property would have to be entrusted to specialized, well-trained, professionally oriented appraisers whose only function would be to determine the current market value of the property. Ideally, assessors would have to be insulated, not just from blatant political attempts to secure favorable treatment of particular parcels of property, but also from the consequences of general unrest and dissatisfaction resulting from changes in assessed values.

In practice, there is often a mixture of "administrative" and "political" decision making when it comes to property tax assessments. The large number of participants in the process are well aware that the decisions they must make could potentially cause conflict. Because they hope to be reelected or simply because of the normal human aversion to conflict, they tend to take actions that create the least controversy. This means that procedures once developed are generally accepted and that assessed values once assigned to particular parcels of property tend to remain unchanged. The result of this administrative conservatism is that assessed values often differ greatly from the standards required by property tax theory or by relevant state statutes. In a period of rapidly changing values, such as the current inflationary period, inequities are magnified.

Because market value is the standard underlying the legally specified assessed value, it is appropriate to test the quality of assessment by comparing the prices at which a property sells and the assessed value assigned to it. The Department of Revenue makes such comparisons, known as assessment-sales ratio studies, part of its regular duties. In fact, these studies are the basis for the multipliers assigned in the equalization process.

Table 3-3 provides information about assessment levels and dispersion for cities or parts of cities. The column labeled "Number of Transfers" shows the number of valid, arms-length transactions included in each case. The first step in analyzing the data is to compute the assessment-sales ratio for each sale. If, for example, a parcel of property that is assessed at $3,000 sells for $10,000, the assessment-sales ratio for that parcel is 30 percent. If assessment were perfect, all ratios would be 33⅓ percent, the legally prescribed level.

The final column of the table shows the median ratio for each city. Most of the medians are below 33⅓ percent, indicating that as of 1976 underassessment had not be corrected by the equalization program ordered by HB 990.

It is also possible to measure the extent to which individual assessments deviate from the median. This is accomplished by computing a coefficient of dispersion. This coefficient of dispersion is the average deviation from the mean divided by the median and expressed as a percent. More simply, it is the average percentage by which assessments vary from the median level.

Examination of the data reveals that the coefficients of dispersion range from a low of 8.0 in Park Forest in Will County to a high of 105.2 in East St. Louis in St. Clair County. There is some disagreement over what significance should be attached to these coefficients. However, a recent publication of the International Association of Assessing Officers states:

> Coefficients of dispersion for residential properties should generally range from 5 and 15 percent. In areas of similar single-family resi-

Table 3-3. Coefficients of Dispersion and Median Assessment Ratios, Selected Cities Outside Cook County, 1976

City	*County*	*No. of Transfers*	*Coefficient of Dispersion*	*Median Assessment Ratio*
Addison	DuPage	1,408	13.7	25.03
Alton	Madison	464	36.4	35.72
Aurora	Kane	1,383	17.8	31.19
Belleville	St. Clair	740	36.6	25.01
Bloomington	McLean	762	16.7	27.48
Bolingbrook	Will	807	11.1	33.81
Carpentersville	Kane	597	9.6	29.46
Champaign	Champaign	782	22.4	28.80
Danville	Vermillion	668	35.4	29.10
Decatur	Macon	1,175	31.1	30.88
DeKalb	DeKalb	405	21.6	29.50
Downers Grove	DuPage	747	15.0	25.61
East St. Louis	St. Clair	560	105.2	47.37
Elgin	Kane	962	14.5	28.58
Elmhurst	DuPage	836	16.5	23.42
Freeport	Stephenson	414	24.6	30.82
Galesburg	Knox	932	29.3	25.64
Granite City	Madison	571	32.2	31.22
Highland Park	Lake	332	12.9	26.30
Joliet	Will	960	28.3	25.83
Kankakee	Kankakee	437	26.6	30.42
Moline	Rock Island	710	24.5	23.58
Naperville	DuPage	820	13.4	23.22
Normal	McLean	401	14.4	29.77
North Chicago	Lake	96	37.3	29.10
Park Forest	Will	69	8.0	28.00
Pekin	Tazewell	967	18.5	36.68
Peoria	Peoria	2,738	31.7	28.72
Quincy	Adams	782	21.0	36.88
Rockford	Winnebago	2,081	15.4	37.46
Rock Island	Rock Island	121	30.5	26.10
Springfield	Sangamon	2,326	25.5	27.20
Urbana	Champaign	782	22.4	28.80
Waukegan	Lake	681	21.9	28.21
Wheaton	DuPage	878	12.1	26.73

Source: Assessment/Sales Ratio Study Findings—1976 (Springfield: Illinois Department of Local Government Affairs), Table I.

dential properties, coefficients closer to 5 percent are attainable. In older, dissimilar areas, a coefficient at the upper end of the range might indicate good performance. A similar range in coefficients of dispersion should be attainable for multi-family and other income-

> producing properties. The market for vacant land, however, is much more volatile and therefore difficult to predict. Coefficients of dispersion in the area of 20 percent may therefore indicate good performance.[25]

In any case, it is clear that the coefficient of dispersion measures more than the skill of the assessor. To take the above example, it is easier to assess property in Park Forest, an area of relatively new, above-average-quality homes, than it is to assess property in East St. Louis, a depressed area with falling property values. Properties in Park Forest are apt to be assessed at a relatively constant proportion of the selling price, while properties in East St. Louis tend to be assessed at greatly varying percentages of these figures.

Because classification of property for taxation in counties of 200,000 was legalized by the 1970 Illinois Constitution, separate coefficients of dispersion must be computed for each class of property in Cook County—the only county to use this provision. The Department of Revenue does this, but it does not publish separate ratios for each city in the county. Table 3-4 shows the 1976 ratios for four groups of property in the city of Chicago. Data are broken down for each of the four assessment districts into which the county is divided and are also provided for the county as a whole. Not surprisingly, these data reveal that the most uniform assessment is achieved for residential property of six units or less (Group II). Even within this class of property, however, there are significant inequalities in assessment. The lowest coefficient is 21.7, meaning that the average property in the sales sample was assessed 21.7 percent above or below the median assessment level. This degree of inequity probably would not be tolerated in any other form of taxation.

There are, of course, those who argue that sales-assessment ratios are not fair measures of administrative performance. One claim is that sales—even those that survive the editing process—do not represent "true" value. There is some validity to this criticism of the sales ratio studies, but the market remains the best guide to value. Although relatively few taxpayers know and understand the coefficient of dispersion for their area, they are often aware of the market value of their property and of assessment discrepancies between their property and similar property. This fact is, without doubt, the source of many property tax complaints and the unpopularity of the tax.

Table 3-4. Coefficients of Dispersion and Median Assessment Ratios, Cook County, 1976

Property	*Coefficients of Dispersion*				*Median Assessment Ratios*			
	Property Group I	*Property Group II*	*Property Group III*	*Property Group V*	*Property Group I*	*Property Group II*	*Property Group III*	*Property Group V*
City of Chicago	132.8	35.5	81.9	89.1	18.66	15.79	33.56	43.23
Assessment District 1	87.4	21.7	48.7	77.1	16.86	14.81	31.59	38.96
Assessment District 2	79.4	24.2	65.0	105.3	20.20	13.92	35.28	39.15
Assessment District 3	113.9	36.1	87.8	111.5	18.19	15.96	33.40	42.84
Assessment District 4	141.1	37.9	125.5	89.0	14.88	17.11	35.09	40.45
County total	108.5	31.5	81.6	101.7	17.38	15.28	33.42	40.70
Legal ratio (1976)	—	—	—	—	22.00	17.00[a]	33.00	40.00

Source: Office of Financial Affairs, Department of Local Government Affairs, *Assessment/Sales Ratio Study Findings, 1976* (Springfield, 1978), pp. 6–7.

Note: The classes are: Group I—Unimproved real estate or real estate used as a farm. Group II—Real estate used for residential purposes when improved with a house or apartment building of not more than six living units, as residential condominium, or a residential cooperative. Group III—All improved real estate used for residential purposes not included in Class II. Group IV—Nonresidential real estate owned and used by not-for-profit corporations for purposes set forth in charter. Group V—All real estate not included in above classes.

[a]Changed to 16.0 percent in 1977.

Tax Levies

Tax levies, passed by the governing boards of local units of government, are based on an appropriation or previously adopted budget ordinance. Levies are usually in dollar amounts, but non-home rule units are often subject to limits on the rate that can be levied for particular purposes. To ensure compliance with these statutes, levies are made for particular funds, such as refuse collection or police protection. Expenditures are then made from the designated fund as authorized in the budget or appropriate ordinance. Since home rule units are no longer subject to mill rate tax limits, it is possible for home rule municipalities to consolidate some of the many funds that have complicated municipal budgeting, making it easier for a citizen to understand financial reports.

Nonproperty tax revenues and unexpended fund balances are subtracted from appropriations to arrive at the amount to be raised by property tax levies. Thus the property tax, a residual tax, can be varied in small increments to close the gap between authorized expenditures and expected receipts from fixed-rate taxes and intergovernmental revenues.

Extension of Taxes

The county clerk's duty, after receiving all certified tax levy ordinances, is to extend the taxes on the equalized assessed value of the respective taxing districts. Because tax levies are usually stated in dollar amounts and segmented by funds, the county clerk must divide the dollars levied for each fund (plus estimated loss in collections) by the equalized assessed value of the taxing unit to determine the rate to extend for each fund. In non-home rule cities the clerk must check to see that the rate so determined does not exceed the tax limit set by the legislature. If it does, the maximum legal rate is extended. The levies for bonds and interest are adopted and certified to the clerk at the time the bonds are issued. The clerk extends the maximum legal rate for this purpose regardless of whether the annual tax levy ordinance includes such sums.

The county clerk then aggregates the rates to be extended against the properties in a given tax code area. Because of the irregular way in which local governments overlap, the county clerk establishes tax code areas that include all the area subject to the same tax rates. Any given governmental unit (taxing district) may be carved into several tax code areas, depending on the number of districts and the particular pattern of overlapping. Once the tax code areas have been established, the clerk aggregates the authorized rates of the governmental units pertaining to the particular areas and prepares the tax bill for each parcel of property.

Collection

Real estate taxes are paid in two installments. Except in Cook and Lake counties, the first installment becomes due on June 1 and the second on September 1. Cook and Lake counties use an acclerated billing system. The first installment, payable March 1, is an estimate computed as 50 percent of the preceding year's bill. The second installment, covering the balance of taxes due, is to be paid by August 1.

The author of a recent article on Illinois municipal law points out that although the municipality's role in the property tax administration process is virtually over when the levy is filed, "the municipal attorney should be aware that there are rather awesome complex procedures which come into play between the filing of the levy and the receipt of funds. It is the county which has the responsibility of defending and collecting the property tax against challenges to its validity."[26]

An important feature of the collection process is the method of protest. A taxpayer who believes that all or part of the taxes levied against him are incorrect or illegal may pay his taxes under protest and then file an action to obtain a refund of the illegal portion. The county treasurer holds a portion of the taxes paid under protest and does not make the money available to the governmental unit that levied the tax until the case is settled.

In some counties, railroads and other large taxpayers routinely pay their taxes under protest. Grounds for protest range from the allegation that a unit of government has no statutory authority to levy a particular tax to the claim that a tax rate referendum held fifteen years before was void due to improper wording.[27] These cases seldom come to trial, but rather are negotiated at a conference attended by the attorneys for the plaintiff, the state's attorney of the county, and perhaps officials of the governments involved. Then, the judge of the court to which the protest has been submitted accepts the recommendations of the interested parties since both sides are anxious to avoid the publicity, delay, and expense of a trial.

Individuals who do not protest their taxes are ineligible for refunds. Indeed, most taxpayers are unaware that protesting taxpayers regularly receive tax refunds. In some cases, governmental units continue to make the contested levy, even though it is always conceded to protesting taxpayers.

Taxes on real estate automatically become a prior first lien on the property against which they are levied. Procedures for foreclosing the lien when taxes are delinquent and procedures for redeeming property after the tax lien has been sold are spelled out in the statutes. The statutes also provide procedures whereby taxes may be collected from the rents or profits of income-earning property during the foreclosure process.

Real estate tax delinquencies are usually negligible, but in Chicago the delinquency rate for real estate taxes in 1977 was 4.7 percent of the amount billed.[28] While the percentage may seem small, the uncollected real estate taxes in Chicago amounted to $12.7 million in 1977. There is no doubt that delinquencies are a serious problem in certain depressed areas.[29] Owners of property in such areas often decide to "mine" the property of the last bit of return by discontinuing maintenance and stopping payment of property taxes. Eventually, the property is offered at a tax sale. At this sale, tax buyers bid for property, with the expectation that the owner will redeem the property within the allotted two-year period and will repay with interest all the expenses that the tax buyer has incurred.

The problem is that tax buyers rarely bid for property unless they believe its value to be at least six times the amount of the delinquent taxes. Thus, much property in badly depressed neighborhoods is not purchased and its ownership ends up in legal limbo. There are, of course, methods by which a potential redeveloper can obtain title to such property, but long, expensive legal procedures are often involved.[30]

The percentage of personal property taxes collected during the mid-to late 1970s, at least in Cook County, was even lower then for real estate taxes. Corporations simply decided not to file tax returns because of the lengthy delay in enforcement and the tendency for negotiated settlements without penalties. One estimate is that as many as 40 to 50 percent of the corporations in Cook County subject to the personal property tax did not return schedules listing their assests to the assessor's office. The state's attorney's office was nearly two years behind in suing for delinquent assessments in the latter 1970s. The uncertainty about the elimination of the personal property tax on corporations after January 1, 1979, did nothing to encourage compliance or enforcement.[31] At the close of 1976, for example, out of $95.3 million personal property taxes extended in the city of Chicago, only $41.7 million had been collected, yielding a delinquency rate of 43.8 percent.[32] These data must be viewed with caution, however, due to the administrative practice of making arbitrary assessments when a return is not filed. Although detailed information about delinquency rates in other counties is not available by type of property, none of the counties containing municipalities larger than 25,000 had a total delinquency rate approaching Cook County's.

THE PROPERTY TAX AS A REVENUE SOURCE

Assessed value as determined by the assessor and equalized by the Department of Revenue is the base against which the property tax is levied. It also serves as security for many municipal bonds and plays an important role in the determination of a municipality's credit rating.

Table 3A-1, an appendix to this chapter, shows the 1975 assessed value per capita of each of the study cities and the percentage change over the preceding ten years. It should be remembered that the 1975 assessments provide the base for the 1976 tax year and that much of the revenue obtained is spent during the 1977 fiscal year. An examination of these data reveals large differences in the size of the property tax base available to the municipalities. North Chicago, an independent city in Lake County, has an assessed value of only $1,405 per capita, but this figure is affected by the large number of military personnel in the population. Data for Normal and Champaign-Urbana are likewise affected by the presence of college students. The assessed value in Niles, a suburban municipality in Cook County, was $8,474 in 1975—more than six times as large as North Chicago's.

The mean for the Chicago suburban municipalities in 1975 was $4,899, or 23.0 percent higher than the mean for the independent cities. There is, of course, considerable variation within each group, with the variation among the suburban group slightly higher than that among the independent cities. The 1975 per capita assessed value of $3,946 for Chicago is close to the average for the independent cities, but well below the suburban average. The average of $3,397 for cities in the St. Louis area, however, is well below all other group averages.

The percentage increases from 1966 to 1975 also show marked differences, ranging from 0.4 percent for Freeport to 90.4 percent for Calumet City. The average rate of growth in Chicago suburban municipalities was 32.3 percent, compared with 20.1 percent for the independent municipalities. The growth rate in Chicago was 29.3 percent.

The amount of the assessed value is a function of assessment practices and the value of taxable property within the boundaries of the municipality. Each of these, in turn, is affected by a complex series of political and economic interactions. Very high assessed values per capita often result from a concentration of commercial and industrial property within the limits of a municipality or other taxing jurisdiction with a small population. Such tax enclaves may be created deliberately by property owners seeking the advantages of lower tax rates that result from the combination of much valuable property and few people. Once these enclaves exist, they tend to be self-expanding. New industrial or commercial construction is attracted, and steps are taken through zoning or other methods to discourage new residential development. Some of the study cities may be adversely affected by these enclaves on their borders.

Another reason for variations in assessed value per capita is that the value of residential property differs from city to city and the rates at which the property is assessed may also vary. This is especially likely in suburban areas where the various suburban municipalities tend to attract residents of similar economic circumstances. Zoning and land development practices tend to perpetrate and accelerate these differences. In Cook County, for instance, single-family houses (Group II) are assessed at 17 percent, whereas in other counties they are assessed at 33.3 percent of their market value.

Clearly, the status of the local economy affects both service needs and the property tax base. The existence of large amounts of commercial and industrial property increases the per capita tax base, but may also increase service needs and at the same time discourage the construction of high-value residential property. Unfortunately, Illinois does not collect very much useful information about municipal property tax bases. Prior to the discontinuance of the personal property tax, the extensions against personal property were available separately from extensions against real estate. Data for the 1975 tax year show that extensions on personal property averaged 14.8 percent of the total in independent cities and 9.9 percent in suburban cities. The figures for Chicago and the suburban St. Louis group were 22.4 and 25.3 percent, respectively. Because taxes on the personal property of individuals had been discontinued, these data reflect how much business personal property the assessor was successful in locating and valuing. More recently, the proceeds of state taxes on corporations have replaced the revenues from personal property taxation.

It is possible to use multiple-regression analysis to gain some indirect knowledge of the factors affecting the tax base. The multiple-regression technique was designed to isolate factors associated with variations in a particular variable. In this case, the aim is to determine the extent to which variations in the per capita assessed valuation (1975) are associated with differences in city characteristics.[33] The regression equation is shown in Table 3-5.

We have used multiple regression to analyze five socioeconomic characteristics for cities. Hypothetically, we might expect that a city with more expensive homes, a larger business district, and a larger population would have a greater tax base. We might also hypothesize that in a city experiencing greater population growth there would be new housing construction activity and an expanding tax base. Since real estate property can be single-family, multifamily, commercial, or industrial, it seems reasonable that population density (population per square mile) might also affect the tax base in the municipality. In particular, a city with higher density would be expected to have a lower per capita tax base.

The findings in Table 3-5 generally support these expectations.

Table 3-5. Determinants of 1975 Per Capita Assessed Valuation

Variable	*Regression Coefficient*	*Beta*
Median housing value	.083 (7.37)*	.590
Population density	-.028 (.67)	-.061
1975 population	.009 (2.38)*	.182
Sales tax receipts	49.14 (6.58)*	.586
Population change, 1970-1975	7.391 (.55)	.050

*Significantly different from zero at 5 percent
R^2 adjusted = .701
Standard error of estimate = 681
F = ratio = 26.729
Constant = 178.82
N of cases = 56

On the average, we found that cities with higher median housing values, greater sales tax receipts, and larger populations have significantly above-average per capita assessed valuations (t-statistics greater than 1.95). Population density is negatively associated with the tax base, but the relationship is not significantly different from zero. These variables can predict per capita valuation reasonably well with approximately 70 percent of the variation among cities in assessed valuation being associated with differences in these characteristics ($R^2 = .701$).

The beta coefficients show that the median value of housing is the variable most closely related to per capita assessed value. Without doubt, this reflects the fact that residential property comprises a large portion of the property tax base. Early regressions included income analysis, but because median value of housing is closely related to per capita income ($r = .895$), we excluded per capita income from later equations to avoid the statistical problem of multicollinearity.

The importance of the sales tax collections in explaining per capita assessed value may also be related to the general level of affluence in the community, but it is probably more closely related to the existence of shopping facilities within the municipal boundaries. Unfortunately, data about the composition of the tax base, which would allow us to verify that hypothesis, are not available.

The third most important variable is the size of the city's population. The fact that larger cities have a higher assessed value, after median value of housing and sales tax collections are taken into account, may reflect the presence of more business activity (other than retail stores) or industrial property in larger municipalities. For whatever reason, larger cities appear to have high assessed valuations per capita.

One might also have expected more densely populated cities to have lower assessed valuations because individual dwelling units would be less costly. However, this was not found to be the case. The correlation coefficient between median housing value and density was .071, not significant at the 5-percent level. One possible explanation is that density and assessed valuation are measured at the city rather than the neighborhood level. Cities with more industrial land use may tend to have lower population density, but they also have higher assessed value per capita.

We found no significant relationship between percent change in population between 1970 and 1975 and assessed value per capita. The inclusion of a regional variable showing independent and suburban city also was not significant when other factors were included. Other socioeconomic characteristics, such as percent poor or percent nonwhite, were explored but found to be insignificant.

While the findings shown in Table 3-5 provide insights into factors affecting the tax base in cities, it is important not to misinterpret the nature of the findings. Although the word "explains" is commonly used to describe regression results, correlation does not prove a cause-effect relationship. It may appear reasonable to assume that the differences in the median value of housing contribute to variations in per capita assessed values, but there is no "absolute proof" of that. A third, unidentified variable could also be involved.

An Appraisal of the Property Tax

The history of the property tax is clearly unique. In the mid-nineteenth century, elaborate constitutional attempts were made to ensure that the property tax would be a major revenue source for state and local governments. The tax was fairly easy to collect and provided a stable revenue source. Today, of course, the situation is very different. Following the passage of Proposition 13 in California in 1978, state after state have imposed limits or added more restrictions to existing limits on the use of property taxes. In Illinois, Governor Thompson called a special session in January 1980 to limit the growth in property tax collections. The governor's proposal called for limits on the rate of increase in tax extensions based on Illinois personal income during the three previous years.[34] In addition, provisions were proposed for the boards of local governments to determine whether surplus revenues were available and, if so, to respond by reducing property taxes. The ability of local governments to abate taxes would also have been expanded. The proposal met with strong opposition from local government officials. The result was passage of an increase in the homestead exemption from $1,500 to $3,000 on residential property.[35]

In part, the unpopularity of the property tax stems from the public's perception that the tax is inequitably administered. Whereas the high coefficients of dispersion confirm the accuracy of this perception, it is ironic that the unpopularity of the tax, the complexity of its administrative machinery, and the closeness of local government to the public often combine to defeat efforts at reform.

Attempts to improve assessment, at least in a period of rising prices, inevitably lead to increased assessments for most parcels of property. Property owners fail to understand, or to believe, that increased assessments do not always result in a proportionate increase in taxes. Their outcry often forces the assessor or legislators into some kind of rollback action. The situation is further complicated by the fact that it is often financially or physically impossible to update all assessments at the same time. This problem is well illustrated by a recent controversy in Cook County. In that county, assessments are revised on a four-year cycle, with one quadrant of the county being reassessed annually. The controversy—some might say revolt—arose in the northeast quadrant as a result of efforts to update assessments.

A 1971 study by the Real Estate Research Corporation recommended major changes in the property evaluation process. Since that time, the Cook County Assessor's Office instituted new procedures, hired or trained a professional staff, initiated a computerized system, and produced an updated cost manual.[36] Multiple-regression analysis was used for the assessment of residential property for the first time in 1976, in the northeast quadrant.[37] After that assessment period, a spokesman for the Civic Federation, a highly respected taxpayer watchdog organization, stated, "We feel that the quality of assessment for homes for 1976 is the best we have had in Cook County for many years."[38]

Unfortunately, some property owners in the quadrant did not fully appreciate the corrections to their assessments. Many residential properties were assessed at higher levels even though the classification system had reduced the assessment level for residential property. At the same time, some local governments in the area, especially school and park districts, substantially increased their tax levies.

The impact of these increases on taxpayers in the northeast quadrant was magnified by the fact that Cook County collected taxes in two installments. The first bill was estimated, based on the previous year's taxes. The bills mailed in the summer of 1977 for the second installment contained the entire increase for the year and were often much higher than the first "half" of the taxes paid earlier. The problem was complicated even more by the fact that increased assessed values in a school district, under the school equalization formula, decreased the amount of state aid and thus required higher property taxes.

In spite of the criticism of the property tax, it remains a major source of local government revenue because of tradition, inertia, and difficulties in changing a system so well established in constitutional and statutory law. There are several other reasons why the property tax continues to be a major source of local government revenue. For one thing, the property tax system is closely interwoven with the complex system of local government.[39] For another, real property is visible and immobile, and thus is easy to locate for tax purposes. And since ability to tax depends on physical location, there are few disputes about which governments have jurisdiction to tax. Finally, the method of tax collection is both automatic and inexpensive. Property taxes are levied *in rem* (against the property) and automatically become liens against the property so that clear title to the property cannot be passed until taxes are paid.

These characteristics—visibility, jurisdictional certainty, and ease of collection—make the tax ideally suited to financing a system of small overlapping governmental units. Only gross incompetency on the part of administrators can prevent most taxable real property from being taxed. No other known tax has these advantages. A few broad-based taxes such as sales and income taxes are successfully employed by local governments, but usually they are collected by the state and employed by only one "layer" of local government. To permit all 6,621 local units in Illinois to levy and administer such taxes would create tremendous administrative costs, difficulties, and confusion.

It would be possible, of course, for local government units to employ state-collected taxes. However, if each unit were allowed to levy the tax at a different rate, the difficulties would be great. Strong pressure would arise for a uniform tax to be allocated by formula rather than by origin, thus transforming the tax into a state grant and increasing the local government's dependence on the state. This is not to say that locally levied nonproperty taxes and state aid to local governments are incompatible with independent local governments, but there are good reasons to believe that such units must have some power to raise their own revenue. At present the property tax meets this need. It is the residual or budget balancing item for local units of government. Deciding how much property tax to levy is the hard task that must be faced after the state or federal grants and the proceeds of state-collected taxes, such as the sales tax, have been estimated.

PROPERTY TAXES IN ILLINOIS CITIES

The property taxes collected by the city government and the relative importance they have in the financing of services depend on many factors. Although a citizen pays one tax bill in two installments, as many as a dozen separate governments might obtain revenues from this source. The city government usually receives a relatively minor portion of the property tax—however, it frequently receives much of the blame for tax increases. Even though city officials make a conscious effort to stabilize or decrease the tax rate, it is very possible for the aggregate rate (the rate of all governments) to increase.

The relative importance of property taxes in financing municipal services partially depends on alternative revenue sources. A prosperous central business district or shopping center will raise significant revenues from the sales tax so that the city can rely less on property taxes. An aggressive policy by city officials to obtain intergovernmental revenues can also reduce property taxes. An attractive strategy for local officials is to shift at least a part of the tax burden to nonresidents so that high-quality services can be provided at acceptable tax rates.

The multitude of governments taxing and providing services to urban residents in Illinois makes it difficult to make a meaningful comparison between the total taxes paid by residents of one city and those paid by residents in another. Services provided by city government in one place may be provided by special districts or by county government in another. Table 3-6 illustrates some of the patterns and variations in the role of the property tax in financing Illinois cities for the year 1975. The first two columns show *city* property taxes per capita and the percentage of total city revenue derived from property taxes. There are wide variations in both columns. Some of the extremes, such as the very low values for North Chicago, are statistical abnormalities. In that particular case, the low values resulted from the large number of military personnel in the population. Even when allowance is made for such instances, however, it is clear that wide variations exist within each group. Interestingly, though, the average city property taxes per capita for the independent and suburban Chicago groups were almost identical, and the degree of variation within the groups was very similar. In the suburban St. Louis group, average property taxes per capita were considerably lower. By contrast, Chicago's per capita property tax was 56.2 percent higher than the suburban Chicago group's.

Column 2 shows that property taxes made up a higher percentage of the total revenue for the suburban Chicago group than they did for the independent cities. However, the difference is not significant at the 5-percent level. Putting it another way, it is clear that the independent cities and the suburban Chicago cities levied about the same property taxes per capita in 1975, but total revenue per capita was higher in independent cities. Chicago and the suburban St. Louis cities received about the same percentage of their city revenues from property taxes as the independent cities.

Column 3 lists estimates of the amount of revenues per capita that taxpayers in the cities paid to overlapping sanitary districts and park districts. These are services that are provided sometimes by cities and sometimes by special districts. By adding the estimates, it is possible to obtain a figure that is approximately adjusted for differences in governmental organization. To determine these estimated figures, we multiplied the tax rate appropriate for each special district by the assessed valuation in the city. We checked detailed tax maps to be certain that the city was contained within the district or that the city was not served by more than one district of the same type.

When the total of "city-plus-special-district" figures are examined, they reveal results quite different from those revealed by the city property tax data alone. The average total property taxes for the suburban cities in the Chicago area was $105.78 per capita. This is significantly higher (at the 5-percent level) than the $87.51 for the independent cities. Obviously, suburban taxpayers paid a higher percentage of their property taxes to these special districts in 1975.

Since Chicago taxpayers paid higher property taxes to special districts than residents in the average suburban city, the addition of special district taxes to city taxes reduces the relative difference between Chicago and its suburbs. The total levy per capita in Chicago was 45.0 percent higher than in the average suburb. This compares with a "city-only" figure, which was 56.2 percent higher.

It is also worthy of note that the total per capita figure for some cities—namely, Chicago Heights, Northbrook, Oak Park, Skokie, and Wilmette—approached the Chicago figure, and that the figure for Highland Park substantially exceeded the Chicago figure. In each of these cases, the percentage of city revenue obtained from the property tax exceeded the average for the group. Evidently these suburbs depended less on nonproperty taxes than did other cities in 1975.

In addition to property taxes used to provide common municipal services, taxpayers also receive services from the county, township, school district, and other special districts. Decisions regarding the taxes to be raised for these districts are made independently by the governing board of each unit, usually without much coordination. Table 3-7 provides a detailed profile of the tax rate used

Table 3-6. City and Overlapping Special District Property Taxes, 1975 Assessment Year

	City Taxes		Estimated Special District Taxes Per Capita	Total Property Taxes Per Capita
	Per Capita	Percent of Revenue		
Independent Cities				
Aurora	$120.54	48.3%	$29.08	$149.62
Bloomington	84.37	24.2	12.64	97.01
Carpentersville	28.77	13.7	13.45	42.22
Champaign	36.85	9.1	27.07	63.92
Danville	67.01	24.9	19.56	86.57
Decatur	44.47	22.5	31.36	75.83
DeKalb	34.76	16.4	20.34	55.10
Elgin	72.41	30.3	42.43	114.84
Freeport	38.84	21.4	13.15	51.97
Galesburg	69.87	32.9	25.51	95.38
Joliet	111.44	43.2	13.70	125.14
Kankakee	55.15	21.7	12.40	67.55
Moline	89.66	16.1	1.55	91.22
Normal	33.48	20.8	6.21	39.69
North Chicago	11.33	13.6	17.52	28.85
Pekin	98.16	43.9	12.75	110.91
Peoria	94.20	37.8	38.05	132.25
Quincy	68.82	15.3	13.59	82.41
Rockford	72.48	34.6	32.09	104.57
Rock Island	93.37	33.0	1.35	94.72
Springfield	77.51	24.1	23.91	101.42
Urbana	49.48	26.6	24.63	74.11
Waukegan	66.62	25.6	60.72	127.34
Average	$ 66.07	26.1	21.44	$ 87.51
(S.D.)	(28.29)	(10.5)	(13.71)	(31.80)
Suburban Chicago				
Addison	$ 44.15	21.3%	$35.63	$ 79.78
Arlington Heights	56.00	24.6	36.84	92.84
Berwyn	36.78	30.9	16.30	53.08
Bolingbrook	51.35	33.1	N/A	N/A
Calumet City	27.81	17.2	32.45	60.26
Chicago Heights	108.36	45.7	35.92	144.28
Cicero	36.90	36.9	56.13	95.03
Des Plaines	71.24	33.1	56.51	127.75
Dolton	32.38	28.6	28.13	60.51
Downers Grove	85.45	40.5	47.72	133.17
Elmhurst	91.03	33.2	34.86	125.89
Elmwood Park	63.97	43.1	16.40	80.37
Evanston	111.65	37.3	20.57	132.22
Glenview	65.83	35.2	43.81	109.64

Table 3-6. *(continued)*

	City Taxes		*Estimated Special District Taxes*	*Total Property Taxes*
	Per Capita	*Percent of Revenue*	*Per Capita*	*Per Capita*
Harvey	53.05	25.1	27.24	80.29
Highland Park	113.45	39.2	91.23	204.68
Lansing	43.82	33.7	29.36	73.18
Lombard	37.56	18.2	33.23	70.79
Maywood	82.59	38.0	20.97	103.56
Morton Grove	65.72	37.3	50.40	116.12
Mt. Prospect	70.15	38.0	40.08	110.23
Naperville	74.05	26.5	39.49	113.54
Niles	33.60	14.9	74.15	107.75
Northbrook	88.58	33.7	59.88	148.46
Oak Lawn	56.04	24.9	35.71	91.75
Oak Park	117.75	41.7	28.87	146.62
Palatine	38.09	21.3	40.76	78.85
Park Forest	37.91	25.0	13.47	51.38
Park Ridge	60.25	30.2	40.68	101.93
Schaumburg	1.25[a]	0.7[a]	59.57	60.82
Skokie	101.01	44.3	51.09	152.10
Wheaton	52.78	30.7	42.45	95.23
Wilmette	82.85	40.9	63.85	146.06
Average	$ 66.00	31.3	40.74	$105.78
(S.D.)	(29.22)	(9.7)	(17.27)	(35.24)
Suburban St. Louis				
Alton	53.90	24.8	N/A	$ 53.90
Belleville	41.98	23.0	5.28	47.26
East St. Louis	51.41	13.9	13.03	64.44
Granite City	56.83	35.1	28.60	85.43
Average	$ 51.03	24.2%	$15.64	$ 62.76
(S.D.)	(6.43)	(8.7)	(11.88)	(16.66)
Chicago	$103.12	25.0	51.29	$153.41
Z = value (independents vs. Chicago suburbs)	.009	1.88	4.65*	2.02*

Source: Compiled from U.S. Bureau of the Census, *Finances of Municipalities and Township Governments, 1977* (Washington, D.C.: Government Printing Office, 1979), Table 22; and *Illinois Property Tax Statistics, 1975* (Springfield: Illinois Department of Local Government Affairs, 1978), Table 2.

*Significant at 5-percent

[a]Excluded from total, Schaumberg did not levy a general property tax in 1977.

Table 3-7. Tax Rate Comparisons

	Nominal Tax Rates				Tax Effort	
	Municipal	Aggregate	Municipal as Percent of Aggregate	Effective Agg. Tax Rate	Mun.	Agg.
Independent						
Aurora	$2.666	$ 9.989	26.7%	3.23%	2.2%	8.1%
Bloomington	1.505	5.958	25.3	1.53	1.5	6.1%
Carpenterville	0.911	6.569	13.9	2.13	0.6	4.6
Champaign	1.547	6.175	25.1	1.55	1.1	4.3
Danville	1.848	6.908	26.8	1.65	1.3	4.8
Decatur	1.008	5.693	17.7	1.44	0.8	4.4
DeKalb	1.070	7.079	15.2	1.82	0.8	5.3
Elgin	1.444	6.233	23.2	2.02	1.2	5.7
Freeport	1.195	6.109	19.6	2.04	0.8	4.2
Galesburg	2.083	6.115	34.1	1.52	1.5	4.4
Joliet	2.527	8.032	31.5	2.06	1.7	5.5
Kankakee	1.228	5.829	21.1	1.53	1.0	4.6
Moline	1.844	5.983	30.8	1.61	1.4	4.6
Normal	1.401	5.900	23.7	1.52	0.9	3.7
North Chicago	0.851	6.673	12.8	1.65	0.3	2.6
Pekin	1.924	6.067	31.7	1.69	1.7	5.4
Peoria	1.620	6.803	23.8	2.05	1.5	6.1
Quincy	1.633	5.203	31.4	1.46	1.5	4.9
Rockford	1.245	5.777	21.6	2.06	1.3	6.1
Rock Island	2.291	5.809	39.4	1.56	1.7	4.2
Springfield	1.581	6.180	25.6	1.55	1.8	5.3
Urbana	1.368	7.073	19.3	1.77	0.8	4.1
Waukegan	1.857	7.699	24.1	1.91	1.5	6.2
Mean	$1.593	$ 6.515	24.5%	1.80%	1.3%	5.0%
(S.D.)	(.487)	(1.009)	(6.6)	(.39)	(.5)	(1.1)
Suburban Chicago						
Addison	$0.715	$ 7.782	9.2%	2.46%	0.7%	7.6%
Arlington Heights	2.623	7.825	33.5	2.54	1.7	5.0
Berwyn	1.182	6.740	17.5	2.19	0.6	3.6
Bolingbrook	N/A	N/A	N/A	N/A	N/A	N/A
Calumet City	0.595	6.119	9.7	1.98	0.4	4.6
Chicago Heights	2.790	9.397	29.7	3.05	2.4	8.2
Cicero	1.216	6.947	17.5	2.25	1.1	6.3
Des Plaines	1.042	7.650	13.6	2.48	1.2	8.6
Dolton	0.911	7.456	12.2	2.42	0.6	4.9
Downers Grove	1.568	7.492	20.9	2.07	1.2	5.7
Elmhurst	1.704	7.649	22.3	2.12	1.3	5.7
Elmwood Park	2.132	7.226	29.5	2.34	1.1	3.7
Evanston	2.572	10.307	25.0	3.34	1.5	6.0
Glenview	0.998	8.094	12.3	2.63	0.6	4.9
Harvey	1.639	8.075	20.3	2.18	1.3	6.6
Highland Park	1.562	8.827	17.7	2.19	0.9	5.3
Lansing	1.119	7.413	15.1	3.67	0.7	4.7

Table 3-7. *(continued)*

	Nominal Tax Rates				*Tax Effort*	
	Municipal	*Aggregate*	*Municipal as Percent of Aggregate*	*Effective Agg. Tax Rate*	*Mun.*	*Agg.*
Lombard	$0.653	$ 7.250	9.0%	2.01%	0.5%	5.8%
Maywood	2.986	9.344	32.0	3.03	1.8	5.6
Morton Grove	1.152	7.089	16.3	2.30	0.9	5.8
Mt. Prospect	1.138	7.939	14.3	2.57	0.8	5.4
Naperville	1.176	7.659	15.4	2.12	1.0	6.2
Niles	0.361	6.313	5.7	2.05	0.5	8.4
Northbrook	1.230	8.452	14.6	2.74	0.9	3.7
Oak Lawn	1.362	7.480	18.2	2.43	0.9	6.5
Oak Park	3.503	10.652	32.9	3.45	1.8	5.5
Palatine	0.753	8.204	9.2	2.66	0.5	6.0
Park Forest	1.492	9.113	16.4	2.96	0.6	3.7
Park Ridge	2.793	8.105	34.5	2.63	1.7	4.8
Schaumburg	N/A	7.270	N/A	2.36	N/A	8.8
Skokie	1.514	8.146	18.6	2.64	1.2	5.8
Wheaton	1.083	7.499	14.4	2.08	0.8	5.2
Wilmette	1.735	9.679	17.9	3.14	0.9	4.8
Mean	$1.526	$ 7.975	18.6%	2.53%	1.0%	5.7%
(S.D.)	(.780)	(1.056)	(7.9)	(.44)	(.5)	(1.4)
Suburban St. Louis						
Alton	$1.396	$ 5.918	23.6%	1.83%	1.2%	4.9%
Belleville	1.093	6.187	17.7	1.68	0.7	4.0
East St. Louis	2.044	8.321	24.6	2.26	1.4	5.9
Granite City	1.361	6.708	20.3	2.07	1.2	5.9
Mean	$1.474	$ 6.784	21.6	1.96	1.1	5.2
(S.D.)	(.404)	(1.076)	(3.2)	(.26)	(.3)	(.9)
Chicago	$3.009	$ 8.690	34.6%	2.82%	2.4%	6.9%
Z = Values (Chicago suburbs vs. independents)	40	5.19*	3.01*	6.44*	2.18*	2.06*

Source: Illinois Property Tax Statistics, 1975 (Springfield: Illinois Department of Local Government Affairs, 1976).

*The difference in means between the Chicago suburbs and the independent cities is significantly different from zero at 5-percent.

by the city, comparing it with the aggregate tax rate, which represents the sum of the rates of all governments. These rates are expressed in terms of dollars per $100 assessed valuation; for example, the $2.666 charged in Aurora represents a tax bill of $266 for a house assessed at $10,000 with a market value of $30,000.

In 1975, the average rate per $100 assessed valuation in independent cities was $1.593, compared with $1.526 in the suburbs. However, this represents only the tax rate pertaining to the city government and does not consider other governments. The aggregate tax rate averaged $6.515 per $100 in the independent cities, but $7.975 in the suburbs. Even considering the variation within each group of cities, this difference is statistically significant.

The relative importance of the city government in the total property taxes collected is shown in column 3 of Table 3-7, which lists the city tax rate as a proportion of the aggregate rate. In the average independent city, the municipal tax rate was 24.5 percent of the aggregate rate, compared with an average of 18.6 percent in the average Chicago suburb. This difference is statistically significant at the 1-percent level.

Up to this point, our discussions have been based on nominal tax rates, the rate per $100 of equalized assessed valuation. Another statistic, the effective tax rate, can be computed to show what percentage of the property's market value is paid as property taxes. This measure adjusts for differences in assessment practices among counties. In the average independent city, residents paid 1.80 percent of the property value in property taxes, compared with an average of 2.53 percent in the Chicago suburbs. Again, the difference is statistically significant at the 1-percent level. In Chicago, 2.82 percent of the property value was paid in property taxes.

Tax Effort

The last two columns of Table 3-7 show property taxes as a percent of personal income. When taxes are measured this way, Chicago has the highest "tax effort": city taxes represented 2.4 percent of income, and taxes paid to all units of local government (aggregate taxes) constituted 6.9 percent of income.

In the Chicago suburbs, 1.0 percent of income went to city property taxes and 5.7 percent for aggregate taxes. In the independent cities 1.3 percent of personal income in 1975 went for city taxes, with 5.0 percent for aggregate taxes. Each of these differences is significant at the 5-percent level. These data again emphasize the greater role played by taxing districts other than city governments in the Chicago suburban area. Alternatively stated, the data point up the larger role that independent city governments play in the financing of government in their areas.

In an attempt to explain these results, we estimated a number of multiple-regression equations, using socioeconomic variables such as population, city government, ratio of manufacturing employment to resident manufacturing employees residing in the city, and income, as well as variables intended to measure the distribution of services among levels of government. Although we encountered the usual data problems associated with these attempts, which make the results somewhat difficult to interpret, we discovered a consistent variable. A binary variable indicating whether the city was an independent or suburban city consistently turned up among the most significant variables when we used property tax collection as a percentage of income as a dependent variable.

Property Tax Trends

Two considerations are important in examining trends in property tax collections. First is the amount of property taxes collected. Second is the relative importance of property taxes in view of the total revenues collected by the city government. Table 3-8 provides data for an analysis. The Chicago suburban cities collected an average of $19 per capita in 1962, but this amount had grown to $66 in 1977, an increase of 245.5 percent. The independent cities, on the other hand, collected an average of $21.71 per capita in

Table 3-8. Trends in Per Capita Property Taxes

		1962	*1977*	*Percent Change*
City Property Taxes				
Suburban Chicago	Current dollars	$19.10	$66.00	245.5%
	Constant dollars	19.10	27.16	42.2
Independent	Current dollars	21.71	66.07	204.3
	Constant dollars	21.71	27.19	25.2
Property Taxes as Percent of Total City Revenues				
Suburban Chicago		37.6%	32.0%	-13.5%
Independent		40.6	26.1	-35.7
Price Increases				
Consumer Price Index		100.0	212.8	
Illinois Municipal Price Index		100.0	243.0	

Source: U.S. Bureau of the Census, *Finances of Municipalities and Township Governments, 1977* (Washington, D.C.: Government Printing Office, 1979), and U.S. Bureau of the Census, *Government in Illinois* (Washington, D.C.: Government Printing Office, 1964).

1962, compared with $66.07 fifteen years later, for an increase of 204.3 percent.

During the period from 1962 to 1977, the prices of government-purchased goods and services increased substantially. According to the Consumer Price Index, for instance, consumer goods and services that would have cost $100 in 1962 would have cost $212.80 in 1977. A price index constructed for the types of purchases made by Illinois municipalities shows even greater price changes.[40] For example, it would have cost a city $243 to purchase the same goods and services that cost $100 fifteen years earlier.

When increases in property taxes collected by the city government are deflated to adjust for price increases, the suburban increase is reduced from 245.5 percent to 42.2 percent and the increase for the independent cities is decreased from 204.3 percent to 25.2 percent. In the case of the independent cities, this increase represents less than 2 percent annual real growth per year from this revenue source. The greater increase in the suburbs is most likely a result of these cities changing from bedroom communities with caretaker services to full-fledged cities with a more complete range of services. The additional services require larger revenues, and the property tax is a logical revenue source.

Whereas the actual property tax collected from 1962 to 1977 increased, its relative importance in the financing of municipal services declined. In 1962, property taxes represented 37.6 percent of the total city revenues in the Chicago suburbs, compared with 40.6 percent in the independent cities. By 1977, however, the property tax as a percentage of total city revenues had decreased to 32.0 percent in the Chicago suburbs and to 26.1 percent in the independent cities.

The growing divergence between the two city types in reliance on property taxes is a function of two main factors. The first is the changing structure of the suburbs, with greater services provided as the cities become more independent from Chicago. The second factor may depend on the way intergovernmental revenues are distributed, particularly at the federal level. In the past decade, more attention has been given to providing larger revenues to cities showing signs of fiscal stress or having disadvantaged populations. Based on the comparison of socioeconomic characteristics in the previous chapter, the independent cities would be expected to benefit from greater attention to formulas using "need" as a basis. We will examine this possibility in more detail in the following chapter.

SUMMARY

The property tax was once the major source of state and local government revenue. While administrative procedures were established by the state, much of the responsibility for the property tax was delegated to township and county officials. As urbanization proceeded, the tax became less satisfactory in many ways. As applied to real property, however, the tax proved itself well suited to financing the multitude of overlapping governments that grew up in many states. The fixed location of real property has made it relatively easy to allocate the revenue among small overlapping units of government.

The 1970 Illinois Constitution provided for the elimination of the personal property tax, effective in 1979, and legalized the *de facto* system of real estate classification that existed in Cook County.

Property is poorly assessed for taxation in most states, including Illinois. Some types of property are especially difficult to assess and reassessment is so unpopular—and so poorly understood—that assessors are unlikely to be given the compensation, resources, and legal authority to do the best possible job. Improvements are being made, however. The adoption of multiple-regression assessment techniques in Cook County and the use of multipliers to bring the level of assessment in downstate counties to the legally required $33\frac{1}{3}$ percent should improve the quality of assessment.

Municipal officials have very limited control over the property tax base. They play little part in the administration of the tax, and only to the extent that municipal policies affect the economic development of the city can they affect the value of property located in their city.

Available data show that there are major variations in the property tax base per capita in the study cities. In 1975 assessed values per capita in Chicago and the independent cities were quite similar. Average assessed values were considerably lower in the St. Louis suburban area and subtantially higher in the Chicago suburban cities. There was considerable variation within the groups. Elimination of the personal property tax in 1979, of course, changed these numbers.

It seems obvious that the composition of the tax base reflects the economic character of the cities, but unfortunately no useful information about the composition of the real estate tax base is available for cities outside Cook County. It is possible to use multiple-regression to infer some relationships between the composition of the tax base and its size. The most important variable turns out to be median value of housing in the city. Because per capita income and median value of housing are closely related, it is not possible to separate the influence of the two, but it is clear that cities whose residents have high incomes and live in high quality houses have higher assessed values per capita. Almost as important are sales tax receipts per capita. This variable could also be related to the general level of affluence, but it is probably closely related to the amount of commercial property in the tax base as well. Population is significant, too; the larger cities have a larger per capita assessed value after the other variables have been considered.

It is known that some smaller cities are industrial tax enclaves, with large amounts of industrial property. However, our data do not permit us to determine the influence of industrial property on assessed values in the study cities.

The average municipal tax rate in independent cities is somewhat higher than in the Chicago suburban cities, but the aggregate rate is considerably higher in the suburban cities. Chicago, of course, has much higher municipal and aggregate rates. Although the difference is narrowed when allowance is made for differences in the assessment levels, it does remain. When differences in assessment levels are adjusted via the effective tax rate, the difference between the aggregate rates in suburban and independent cities is widened. When property taxes as a percent of income are compared, the aggregate tax effort is still higher in the suburbs than in the independent cities, but the municipal tax effort is higher in the independent cities.

It is not easy to disentangle these numbers into a simple conclusion, but Illinois data suggest that aggregate property taxes are higher in the suburbs than in independent cities, although municipal taxes are slightly lower. Taxes in Chicago are the highest among the cities, however measured. These data are consistent with the well-known fact that government expenditures are higher in larger metropolitan areas. Whether or not these higher expenditures represent higher social costs or a higher quality of government services is difficult to determine.

NOTES

1. The percentage of revenues obtained from the state government increased when the personal property tax was replaced by an increase in the state income tax. In FY 1979, for instance, cities in Illinois received 11.3 percent of their revenues from the state, while the national average was 22.0 percent.
2. See report of the *Illinois Municipal League Committee of Home Rule Attorneys,* ed. by Frank M. Pfeifer and Thomas V. Kelty (Springfield: Illinois Municipal League, 1977).
3. Bridgman v. Korzen, 54 Ill.2nd 74, 295 N.E.2d9 (1973).
4. William H. Avery, Jr., "The Property Tax and Its Administration," *Illinois Tax Problems: Proceedings of an Open Forum,* Special Report No. 5 (Springfield: Illinois Tax Commission, 1939), p. 10.
5. For a history of that attempt, see Ann H. Elder and Glenn W. Fisher, *An Attempt to Ammend the Illinois Constitution: A Study in Politics and Taxation* (Urbana: Institute of Government and Public Affairs, University of Illinois, 1969).
6. Thorpe v. Mahin, 43 Ill.2d 36 (1969).
7. For a detailed account of the writing and passage of the revenue article, see Joyce Fishbane and Glenn Fisher, *Politics of the Purse: Revenue and Finance in the Sixth Illinois Constitutional Convention* (Urbana: University of Illinois Press, 1974).
8. The personal property tax replacement issue was resolved in 1979 with an increase in the corporate income tax rate.
9. For a detailed history of property tax limitation in Illinois, see Glenn W. Fisher and Robert P. Fairbanks, *Illinois Municipal Finance* (Urbana: University of Illinois Press, 1968), pp. 86–119.
10. The constitutionality of this practice was recently upheld in a court case involving the city of Moline. *Coryn v. City of Moline,* Ill. Sup. Ct., (March 1977).
11. Ill. Rev. Stat., ch. 120, par. 1301 *et seq.*
12. 1977 Farmland Assessment Act (P.A. 80-247, eff. August 16, 1977). Since its passage, this law has been amended. Because the amendments do not affect property assessment in cities directly, they are not discussed in detail here.
13. Paul W. Hoffman, et al. v. James M. Clark, County Treasurer, 69 Ill.2d 402 (1977).
14. *Ill. Rev. Stat.,* Ch. 120, sec. 500.23.
15. Ibid.
16. This function was formerly carried out by the Illinois Department of Local Government Affairs.
17. *Ill. Rev. Stat.,* ch. 120, secs. 482-487.
18. For makeup and duties of the boards, see *Ill. Rev. Stat.,* ch. 120, secs. 489-491.
19. For a discussion of the different treatment of taxpayer appeals in Cook County and downstate, see Alan S. Ganz and Dixie L. Laswell, "Review of Real Estate Assessments—Cook County (Chicago) v. Remainder of Illinois," *The John Marshall Journal of Practice and Procedure,* Vol. 11, No. 17, pp. 19–90.
20. For a discussion of the use of aerial photography in Cook County, see "Aerial Photography Used in Cook County Assessment," *Assessment Digest* (January/February 1979), pp. 16–17.
21. There is considerable literature regarding computer-assisted assessment. Almost any recent issue of the *Assessors Journal* contains one or more articles on the subject. Two useful introductions are: George W. Gipe, "Understanding Multiple Regression Analysis," *Assessors Journal,* Vol. 12, No. 2 (June 1977),

pp. 81-94, and Albert M. Church and Robert H. Gustafson, *Statistics and Computers in the Appraisal Process* (Chicago: International Association of Assessing Officers, 1976).
22. *Ill. Rev. Stat.*, ch. 120, 589.
23. Hamer v. Lehnhausen, 60 Ill.2d. 400 (1975).
24. *Illinois Property Tax Statistics, 1975* (Springfield: Illinois Department of Local Government Affairs, 1978).
25. International Association of Assessing Officers, *Understanding Real Property Assessment: An Executive Summary for Local Government Officials* (Washington, D.C., 1978).
26. Lee Schwartz, "Finance and Tax," in *Illinois Municipal Law,* ed. by Stewart H. Diamond (Springfield: Illinois Institute for Continuing Legal Education, 1978) p. 13-38.
27. Glenn W. Fisher and Robert P. Fairbanks, "The Politics of Property Taxation," *Administrative Science Quarterly,* Vol. 12, No. 1 (June 1967), p. 60.
28. Civic Federation, *Bulletin 897* (Fall 1978), p. 14.
29. For a more detailed discussion of the delinquency problem in Chicago and other large cities, see J. Lawlor, *Real Property Tax Delinquency and Urban Policy* (Cambridge, Mass: Lincoln Institute of Land Policy, 1977); George Sternlieb and R. W. Lake, "The Dynamics of Real Estate Tax Delinquency," *National Tax Journal,* Vol. 29 (1976), pp. 261-71; and S. Olson and M. Lackham, *Tax Delinquency in the Inner City: The Problem and Its Possible Solutions,* Lexington, Mass.: Lexington Books, D. C. Heath, 1976).
30. An excellent discussion of experience with tax sales and recommendations for improvements can be found in *Final Report Submitted to the Assessor of Cook County by the Commission to Study the Property Tax,* Justin A. Stanley, Chairman, January 18, 1978.
31. Testimony delivered by Pierce and Cahill before Real Estate Tax Study Commission, November 1, 1977.
32. Civic Federation, *Bulletin No. 882* (Fall 1977), Table 11, p. 15.
33. For a better understanding of this statistical technique, refer to the appendix.
34. For a more complete discussion of the tax relief proposal, see *Background Paper: The Proposed "Property Tax Limitation Act of 1980"* (Springfield: Illinois Department of Revenue, 1980).
35. H.B. 2563, 1980.
36. Dona P. Gerson, "Tax Revolt in Cook County," *Illinois Issues,* Vol. 4, No. 1 (January 1978), pp. 4-7.
37. Commission to Study the Property Tax, *Final Report Submitted to the Assessor of Cook County* (Chicago, January 18, 1978).
38. Gerson, "Tax Revolt in Cook County," p. 5.
39. For a more detailed discussion of this argument, see Arthur D. Lynn, Jr., ed., *Property Taxation Land Use & Public Policy,* Chap. I, "Property Taxation and the Political System" by Glenn W. Fisher (Madison: The University of Wisconsin Press, 1976), pp. 5-22.
40. The purchases made by municipalities are much more labor intensive, which means that wage and salary increases are much more prominent than in the private sector. For a more complete discussion of the municipal index, see Norman Walzer and Peter J. Stratton, *Inflation and Municipal Expenditure Increases in Illinois* (Springfield: Illinois Municipal Problems Commission, 1977).

Appendix: Table 3A-1. Per Capita Equalized Assessed Valuation (Illinois Municipalities over 25,000 Population)

	Assessed Value	
	1975	*Percent Increase, 1966–1975*
Independent		
Aurora	$4,315	14.0%
Bloomington	5,569	38.4
Carpentersville	3,051	15.9
Champaign	3,624	4.7
Danville	3,557	13.2
Decatur	4,132	13.5
DeKalb	3,106	32.1
Elgin	4,597	44.9
Freeport	3,233	0.4
Galesburg	3,624	27.4
Joliet	3,558	23.5
Kankakee	4,013	26.4
Moline	4,579	13.8
Normal	2,737	7.7
North Chicago	1,405	—
Pekin	5,039	41.1
Peoria	5,263	26.8
Quincy	4,155	4.8
Rockford	5,590	14.8
Rock Island	3,979	22.3
Springfield	4,961	44.9
Urbana	2,867	1.0
Waukegan	4,635	10.4
Average	$3,982	20.1%
(S.D.)	(1009)	
Chicago Suburban		
Addison	$5,310	47.4%
Arlington Heights	4,571	34.2
Berwyn	3,368	21.5
Bolingbrook	4,433	—
Calumet City	4,403	90.4
Chicago Heights	4,211	21.8
Cicero	4,933	25.0
Des Plaines	7,099	79.4
Dolton	3,658	34.3
Downers Grove	5,338	29.5
Elmhurst	5,219	23.2
Elmwood Park	3,388	23.1
Evanston	4,250	11.5
Glenview	5,203	1.1
Harvey	3,547	20.3

Appendix: Table 3A-1. *(continued)*

	Assessed Value	
	1975	*Percent Increase, 1966–1975*
Highland Park	$6,380	15.8%
Lansing	3,874	55.8
Lombard	4,967	44.3
Maywood	2,699	2.6
Morton Grove	5,827	30.7
Mt. Prospect	4,644	20.6
Naperville	5,732	57.8
Niles	8,474	70.5
Northbrook	7,003	47.9
Oak Lawn	4,241	51.6
Oak Park	3,631	5.0
Palatine	4,430	44.3
Park Forest	2,467	(0.5)
Park Ridge	4,785	22.8
Schaumburg	7,269	—
Skokie	6,714	—
Wheaton	4,639	27.7
Wilmette	4,950	10.8
Average	$4,899	32.3%
(S.D.)	(1317)	
St. Louis Suburban		
Alton	$3,750	37.8%
Belleville	3,450	7.1
E. St. Louis	2,176	(0.3)
Granite City	4,212	14.6
Average	$3,397	14.8%
(S.D.)	(872)	
Chicago	$3,946	29.3%

Source: Illinois Property Tax Statistics 1975 (Springfield: Illinois Department of Local Government Affairs, 1976), Table VI.

Note: The 1975 assessments are the base for taxes levied in the 1976 calendar year. Much of this revenue is spent in the 1977 fiscal year.

Chapter 4

Nonproperty Tax Revenues

Property taxes remain an important revenue source for cities, although their relative importance has declined considerably during the past several decades as they have been supplemented by a host of other local revenue sources such as taxes on sales, incomes, and utilities. In addition, cities have made much greater use of charges for services. However, one of the most prominent changes in revenue sources has been the increase in intergovernmental revenues received from state and federal governments. The wider range of revenue sources available has provided municipal officials with an opportunity to tailor the revenue structure in their cities to the types of economic activities that can be taxed most effectively.

This chapter provides a detailed description of the nonproperty tax revenue sources in Illinois cities and illustrates the extent to which they have been used to finance services. Particular attention is focused on the role of intergovernmental revenue because of its recent growth in importance. The discussion concludes with an examination of the extent to which cities are borrowing to finance services.

LOCAL REVENUES

Illinois municipalities receive 26 percent of their general revenue from property taxes, 28 percent from other local taxes, 15 percent from charges and miscellaneous sources, and 31 percent from state and federal grants. Table 4-1 shows the average revenue from taxes, charges, and miscellaneous revenue received by the study cities, excluding Chicago and East St. Louis. The averages shown represent only cities actually receiving revenues from a particular source.

The Illinois constitution, adopted in 1970, significantly altered the powers of some municipalities to levy nonproperty taxes. Prior to that time, municipalities could levy taxes only as specifically authorized by the General Assembly. The 1970 constitution gives home rule municipalities much greater authority to levy local taxes. The only exception is that they cannot "license for revenue or impose taxes upon or measured by income or earnings upon occupations" without authorization from the General Assembly.[1] Although the courts have interpreted the home rule provisions liberally, as they were instructed to do in the last subsection of the local government article, practices in matters as sensitive as taxation change slowly. For this reason, most of the nonproperty tax revenues received by Illinois municipalities are derived from taxes that were statutorily authorized prior to the adoption of the new constitution.

Municipal Sales Tax

Table 4-1 clearly shows the general sales tax to be a major revenue source for Illinois municipal governments. Since 1955, municipalities have had statutory authority to impose the tax through legislative action by the city council.[2] The tax is collected in conjunction with the state sales tax and returned to the municipality in which the sale occurred. The maximum tax rate is 1 percent, with counties imposing the tax in unincorporated areas of the county. On the average in 1977, the study cities collected $46.32 per person in sales taxes. Considerable variation was found among the cities, with receipts ranging from a low of $7.08 per capita in North Chicago to a high of $106.65 in Schaumburg. These extremes reflect the large military population in North Chicago and a large shopping center in Schaumburg.

A more detailed profile of sales tax collections by city is provided in Appendix Table 4A-1.

Table 4-1. 1977 Per Capita Revenue Sources

Revenue Source	*Amount Per Capita*	*Number Reporting*
Local Sources		
Property taxes	$65.65	59
Sales taxes	46.32	59
Foreign fire insurance tax	.34	52
Gross receipts on utilities	21.87	22
Vehicle tax	5.59	47
Intergovernmental Revenue		
Motor fuel tax	$12.20	59
Illinois income tax	13.47	59
State grants	2.48	48
Federal grants	14.06	45
General Revenue Sharing	11.11	59
Other intergovernmental revenue	13.71	36
Fees and Licenses		
Liquor	1.40	55
Other licenses	1.39	55
Franchise fees	.76	23
Building and inspection fees	2.56	58
Fines	2.91	59
Charges for Services		
Sanitation	$3.69	25
Parking	1.87	20
Libraries	.89	38
Recreation	3.02	21
Other services	4.10	43
Interest Income	8.29	59
Other Receipts	41.11	59
Total Revenues	$235.73	59

Source: Statewide Summary of Municipal Finances, 1977 (Springfield: Office of the Comptroller, 1978).

Note: Chicago and East St. Louis are not included due to lack of comparable data. Because the averages are based on cities reporting each revenue source, the sum of averages will not equal the total.

The local sales tax, levied as a supplement to the state tax, offers several distinct advantages for municipalities. First, it responds to inflation because price increases mean revenue growth. Second, the sales tax—at least the local share—is not highly visible and many taxpayers view it as a state-imposed tax. Third, there are no local administrative problems since municipal authorities need only pass an ordinance imposing the tax and the state assumes collection for a small fee.

One potential problem with the local sales tax is that shifts in population and economic activity can contribute to a growing disparity between local needs and revenue-raising potential. This situation is illustrated by Schaumburg, where a regional shopping center located in a relatively small city generates enough revenue so a general property tax in not needed. Surrounding cities, on the other hand, may experience relative declines in sales tax receipts and be forced into relying more heavily on property taxes. This not only results in chance inequalities in the distribution of the tax burden, but also encourages competition among municipalities, thus contributing further to distorted economic development in urban areas.

In response to growing pressure from officials in cities surrounding major shopping complexes, legislation was introduced in the Illinois General Assembly in 1975 (H. B. 1667) whereby the local sales tax for counties and municipalities would be replaced by an increased state sales tax. The bill proposed distributing sales taxes to county areas based on point of sale and to municipal governments within a county on a population basis. This proposed legislation met with considerable opposition and did not pass, but it does suggest concern about the disparity in sales tax revenues.

The continued growth and concentration of sales activity will, without question, create renewed pressures to revise the sales tax distribution system. In the meantime, cities needing additional revenue will continue to compete for commercial developments to increase sales tax revenue. Unfortunately, the market for retail sales is not unlimited, and continued efforts by cities to expand sales tax revenues will at some point be at the expense of neighboring municipalities.

Utilities Tax

By statute, Illinois municipalities impose a tax on the gross receipts of people engaged in the businesses of transmitting messages and of selling gas, electricity, or water for use or consumption in the city limits and not for resale. This tax is over and above a franchise fee charged for the utility's use of city streets, alleys, and other services. While interviews with municipal officials did not reveal definite patterns with respect to franchise fees, it is common for a city government to receive services in exchange for extending permission for a utility to use public facilities.

Taxes on receipts from utilities offer several attractions. First, this revenue source has been a hedge against inflation since utility rates have increased with energy prices during the 1970s. Second, the tax cannot be easily avoided and is relatively easy to collect.

On the average, the utility tax on electricity, gas, telephone, and water raised $21.87 per person in 22 cities where it was in effect in 1977. Most cities impose a 5-percent rate. The utility tax ranks as the third largest revenue source in these cities, following property and sales taxes. During the study year, Evanston reported the highest collection, $50.76, closely followed by Oak Park, with collections of $37.18 per capita.

With current high utility costs, this tax is not particularly popular among residents. In fact, in recent years several cities have repealed the utility tax as a concession to taxpayers. According to a survey conducted by the Illinois Municipal League in 1978, at least four municipalities with populations over 25,000 had removed the tax since 1973. Three of the communities (Arlington Heights, Berwyn, and Chicago Heights) are in the Chicago SMSA, while the fourth, Kankakee, is downstate. The situation surrounding the repeal of the tax was unique in each city, so it is difficult to generalize about possible trends.

Motor Vehicle Taxes

The imposition of a wheel tax on vehicles operated within city limits is popular among municipalities. Statutes dictate how high a tax non-home rule cities can levy and exactly how they can use the funds.[3] Whereas the cities in this study are not governed by these requirements, one might reasonably expect that practices in a city are affected by similar actions in neighboring communities since citizens are quick to compare the charges they pay with those paid by others.

An advantage of a wheel tax is that it can be promoted as a charge for operating a vehicle in the city rather than a tax, especially if the revenues are earmarked for street purposes. A wheel tax is usually difficult to enforce, especially in cities with transient populations. In many instances, routine patrols are established soon after the deadline for obtaining a sticker; violators are fined and required to purchase a sticker.

As of 1977, 47 of the 59 municipalities had a motor vehicle tax. On the average, it brought in $5.59 per resident.[4] Wheel tax revenues commonly provide supplemental funds for street maintenance and can represent a significant amount of revenue.

Foreign Fire Insurance Tax

The foreign fire insurance company tax is a 2-percent tax on the gross premiums of policies issued on property within the municipality by insurance companies not incorporated in Illinois.[5] This revenue source is relatively small: in 1977, it amounted to an average of 34 cents per capita.

Licenses

Illinois municipalities, by statute, have wide latitude in determining the occupations and businesses that can be licensed for regulation. The 1970 constitution states that cities may "license for revenue or impose taxes upon or measured by income or earning or upon occupations" only as specifically permitted by the legislature. Thus, cities do not license for revenue, but rather license for regulation and attempt to collect enough revenue to offset the administrative costs. One source has estimated that municipalities, both home rule and non-home rule, have the power to license at least 101 activities.[6] Whereas municipalities can tax or regulate, the fee must resemble the cost of carrying out the enforcement if they are licensing for regulation.

Municipalities license a wide variety of activities. Among 42 Illinois cities with populations over 25,000 responding to a survey in 1978, nearly every city reported licensing taxicabs, followed closely by the licensing of coin-operated machines.[7] Bowling alleys and billiard halls are also commonly licensed. While only broad estimates of the revenues collected from each licensed activity are available, data in Table 4-1 indicate that revenues collected from licenses other than on motor vehicles are quite small.

Franchise Fees

Detailed information about the franchise fees collected from utilities is not available, but data concerning total receipts (including cable television) show that 23 municipalities collected 76 cents per person in franchise fees. Personal interviews revealed that free services provided to municipalities in lieu of franchise fees are common. These in-kind payments are not reported as revenue.

Service Charges

Table 4-1 reveals that Illinois municipalities obtain revenue from several types of service charges, such as those for parking, libraries, recreational facilities, sewage disposal, and sanitation. In most instances, these receipts are collected as part of an enterprise operation, and wide variations among municipalities are found.

Refuse collection, for example, may be conducted entirely by a municipality, entirely by private collectors, or by a combination of both.

There is a strong economic rationale for using service charges to offset the costs of operating services when those benefitting can be identified and when the charges are easily collected. This method of financing places costs directly on consumers and provides an automatic and relatively simple way of determining the amount of service to be provided.

Table 4-1 also provides information about four specific services for which charges are imposed in the study cities. In 1977, the most revenue was obtained from refuse collection, which provided an average of $3.69 per capita in 25 cities. Charges for recreation ranked second, having generated an average of $3.02 per capita in 21 cities. Although 38 cities reported charging for library services, the average amount collected was only 89 cents per capita.

While the revenues generated from charges were relatively small in 1977, it is likely that they will increase in importance as cities face tighter budgets. Cutbacks in federal aid and more pressure to keep property taxes down will cause local officials to look for ways to charge residents directly for services. However, given the nature of the services provided, the opportunities for imposing fees are limited and such charges will probably never be a major revenue source.

Special Assessments

There are many times when public projects benefit a particular group of residents in a specific neighborhood more than residents in other areas. A common case is street improvements. To finance these improvements, the city government can assess a special tax against property owners benefiting from the project and, in this manner, can offset at least a portion of the cost to the city. This is known as special assessment financing.

Like property taxes, special assessments are levied against property rather than against persons or organizations. Special assessments are included in the property tax statements, and collection and foreclosure procedures are similar to other property taxes. There are, however, important differences between property taxes and special assessments. Property taxes are levied for general public purposes with no requirement that owners of the taxed property receive services or benefits in proportion to the tax levy. Property taxes are levied on the assessed value of property, but special assessments are levied to finance specific projects—usually capital improvements. The levy is distributed on the basis of a formula or procedure, relating the charge against a parcel of property to the services or benefits received.

Special assessments and service charges are somewhat similar. Both are related to the use of or benefit from a specific government program or project. In each case an attempt is made to distribute the assessment or charge in proportion to the use or benefit. They differ in that the service charge is levied against people rather than against property. Service charges are also more apt to be levied for repetitive or continuous services, whereas special assessments are usually used to finance capital improvements.

Normally, the cost of the project is prorated among properties in the area in proportion to benefits received. Part of the cost may be assessed against the city as a public benefit. Bonds payable from the proceeds are issued, and property owners are permitted to pay their assessments in annual installments.

Special assessments have not been levied as widely in Illinois as in some other states, partially because of the lingering memory of the widespread defaults of the 1930s and the restrictive procedures surrounding the use of special assessments and the issue of special assessment bonds. These procedures, which are statutory in part, are a result of practices followed by the legal and financial communities involved in issuing bonds. The prevailing conservatism is illustrated by the fact that a special assessment law passed in 1947 to simplify procedures has not been used because bond houses are reluctant to handle bonds issued according to those procedures. The law has never been tested in court, and no case law interpreting the act is available.

The constitution of 1970 specifically provides both home rule and non-home rule units with the power to levy special assessments and stipulates that the power of home rule units cannot be denied or limited.[8] This raises the question of whether Article 9 of the Illinois Municipal Code, which spells out special assessment procedures in detail, must be followed. The importance of the investor and his representatives is again primary. The authors of the special assessment chapter in a recent and authoritative work on Illinois Municipal law state:

> Prior to making changes in the Article 9 procedures, however, the municipal attorney should be aware that there is a wealth of cases interpreting present Article 9 upon which the investors in special assessment bonds have come to rely. These investors may initially

> refuse to invest in special assessment bonds based on radical innovations. For example, Division 3 of Article 9 is a simplified legislative method for financing through special assessments. Although it has been on the books for over 25 years, it has, to the authors' knowledge, never been used because of the lack of supporting case law.[9]

In spite of the complexity and cost of following established procedures for levying special assessments and issuing special assessment bonds, there are definite advantages to using this method of raising revenue. The principal attraction is that, like a service charge, a special assessment makes it possible to assess the cost of certain services against those who benefit. The installation of public improvements such as streets, sewers, sidewalks, and water mains usually increases the value of property, but it may be of limited benefit to the public at large. Considerations of equity and economic efficiency suggest that it is proper to charge the cost of such improvements to the owner of the benefited property rather than to all taxpayers in the municipality.

Another advantage is that, while part of the project cost is covered by special assessment, general revenue sources can be used to finance the estimated public benefit of the project. This method can also finance improvements desired by a majority of property owners in a particular area but opposed by a majority of voters within the municipality.

Special Service Areas

The 1970 constitution provides another option for financing public improvements: the levy of additional property taxes within a defined district for the purposes of providing special services to those areas and for the payment of debt subsequently incurred. In *Oak Park Federal Savings and Loan Association* vs. *Village Of Oak Park,* the Illinois Supreme Court held that the General Assembly must enact legislation to expressly implement section 6(l) of the local government article.[10] The General Assembly passed the implementing legislation, and several municipalities have since used the provisions.

Because the property tax is *ad valorem*, the cost of improvements financed this way are distributed according to the value of the property. On the other hand, when the special assessment procedure is used, the assessor has considerable discretion in spreading the costs among properties in the special assessment district. While it is common to use front footage as the basis of distribution, factors such as area, zoning, and best use are also considered. The statutes stipulate only that the amount assessed cannot exceed the benefit received.

INTERGOVERNMENTAL REVENUES

One of the most significant changes in the financing of local public services during the past two decades has been the growth in intergovernmental revenues. The Advisory Commission on Intergovernmental Relations, for instance, estimates that in 1959 combined state and federal aid to local governments represented 42.2 percent of general revenue from own sources. In 1977, the ACIR estimated that state and federal aid, nationwide, had increased to 75.4 percent.[11] The growth in federal and state support has been of major assistance to municipal governments in meeting increasing demands for services. Of course, some intergovernmental aid is in response to mandated programs, and the revenues provided are less than the costs involved. This section examines the changing nature of the intergovernmental revenue programs and describes their effects on the financing of municipal services.

Table 4-2 provides a profile of the major intergovernmental revenue sources for Illinois cities, by type. The data indicate that intergovernmental receipts differ widely according to type of city. In particular, independent cities in 1977 collected an average of $70.32 per capita in total intergovernmental revenue, compared with the Chicago suburbs' average of $43.10. It is also apparent in Table 4-2 that independent cities received nearly three times the amount of federal government assistance as did the Chicago suburbs. As expected, relatively little difference is found in state grants, since the motor fuel tax and income tax rebates are based on population. Each of the revenue sources will be discussed in greater detail below.

In making comparisons of intergovernmental revenues, one must recognize that variations in governmental arrangements throughout the state can affect the findings. For example, if a city government has responsibility for providing a sewage system and receives a federal grant to construct one, the city rates high in intergovernmental receipts. However, in a special district such a receipt will not appear as intergovernmental revenue to the city. This difference accounts for some of the variation between the Chicago suburbs and the independent cities. In addition, since special district boundaries and city boundaries usually do not coincide, it

Table 4-2. 1977 Per Capita Intergovernmental Revenues

Revenue Source	*Independent Cities*	*Chicago Suburbs*	*St. Louis Suburbs*
Total intergovernmental revenue	$70.32	$43.10	$42.61
(S.D.)	(29.78)	(11.14)	(5.05)
From federal government	34.57	11.28	18.08
(S.D.)	(25.30)	(5.63)	(7.65)
General Revenue Sharing	14.50	8.61	12.95
(S.D.)	(3.02)	(3.17)	(4.64)
Grants	25.37	4.91	1.07
(S.D.)	(26.25)	(6.14)	(0.0)
From state government	28.62	27.49	26.57
(S.D.)	(3.20)	(4.79)	(1.11)
Income tax	13.56	13.41	13.60
(S.D.)	(0.63)	(0.59)	(0.80)
Motor fuel tax	12.44	11.99	12.58
(S.D.)	(0.82)	(0.50)	(0.71)
Grants	2.32	2.76	0.59
(S.D.)	(2.29)	(5.06)	(0.81)
Other intergovernmental revenue	4.41	3.57	1.64
(S.D.)	(4.52)	(4.69)	(1.15)

Source: Statewide Summary of Municipal Finance in Illinois, 1977 (Springfield: Office of the Comptroller, 1978).

is difficult, if not impossible, to correct for these variations. However, they should be kept in mind.

Types of Intergovernmental Grants

Intergovernmental grants are commonly classified by the degree of control that the granting government exercises over the use of the funds. *Unrestricted grants* impose no limits on the use of funds except for very general procedural restrictions. These may require that the funds be deposited in the treasury and that standard budgeting and accounting procedures be followed, for instance. Some states provide unrestricted grants to local governments. And the federal government imposes almost no restrictions on the uses of General Revenue Sharing funds. There are, however, certain conditions to be met, such as the payment of prevailing wages and nondiscrimination in hiring practices.

Categorical grants, in contrast, have specific purposes. Although methods for determining eligibility and the exact restrictions vary greatly, categorical grants can generally be subdivided into four classes:[12]

1. *Project grants.* Potential recipients must compete for such grants by submitting applications for each proposed project.
2. *Formula-project grants.* A specified formula is used to determine the amount available for each project area.
3. *Formula-apportioned grants.* The grants are allocated among recipients according to factors specified by in the legislation or regulations.
4. *Open-ended reimbursement grants.* The granting government commits itself to reimbursing a specified proportion of program costs.

Block grants, the third type of intergovernmental grant, lie midway between unrestricted grants and categorical grants. They must be used in a broad area such as health or public safety, and are far less restricted in purpose than are categorical grants.

Each type of grant produces different economic and political effects. Unrestricted grants provide maximum financial relief for the recipient government and maximize the power of individuals or political factions that influence the decisions of that government. Categorical grants, on the other hand, permit the granting government to decide how the funds will be used and to establish a uniform program in all areas. Administrative costs are often higher, and the opportunities for friction between grantee and grantor are multiplied. Block grants usually allow the recipient government considerable freedom in designing programs, but they do require that the funds be spent in the specified functional program area.

The extent to which a municipality relies on intergovernmental assistance is related to many factors, but of primary importance are local officials' attitudes and an adequate number of staff members who will apply for grants. In some instances, grant applications are not needed; the city receives funds automatically. The vast majority of programs, however, require active solicitation by the city government. A limited staff or conservative attitude about outside interference in local programs may cause a city not to apply for federal funds even though they are available.

THE DEVELOPMENT OF FEDERAL GRANT PROGRAMS

Although earlier precedents can be cited, it is common to date the beginning of the existing federal grant-in-aid structure from the enactment of the Morrill Act of 1862. This act provided assistance to states to establish state colleges for the promotion of education in agriculture and the mechanical arts. Three programs established during the first 20 years of this century are still significant elements in the categorical aid structure: the Federal Aid Highway Program (1916) and two programs for vocational education and rehabilitation (1917 and 1920).

The 1930s saw a dramatic growth in federal aid as a number of emergency relief and income maintenance programs were enacted. Some of these programs have been terminated, but a number of them, such as the public assistance programs, have grown dramatically in scope and cost. In the 15 years following World War II, about 30 new grant programs were inaugurated. Included were programs providing funds for school lunches, federal impact area school aid, urban renewal, and pollution control.

The 1960s saw the introduction of a multitude of categorical grants consisting of funding for specific projects usually based on application and with a requirement of matching local funds. The categorical grants were a logical continuation of the construction projects financed during the 1950s. Cities with skilled grantsmen were able to attract considerable federal support for building new facilities and expanding services. During the 1960s, the Great Society programs were introduced with the purpose of improving the living environment and employment opportunities of disadvantaged citizens. A vast array of social programs aimed at bettering the plight of central city residents was created. In 1961, for example, the Advisory Commission on Intergovernmental Relations was able to identify 40 grant programs estabished prior to 1958 still in effect. By 1969, according to Wright, "there were an estimated 150 major programs, 400 specific legislative authorizations, and 1300 different federal assistance activities for which monetary amounts, application deadlines, agency contracts, and use restrictions could be identified."[13] Wright estimates that from 1964 to 1966, more than 100 additional project grants were established.

The new grant programs were accompanied by requirements for planning the impact of the project on the community, as well as a greater role for public participation in the decision-making process. Emphasis was placed on greater accountability. Techniques such as planning-programming-budgeting systems and other management techniques from the private sector were introduced into public decision making. These requirements, plus the need for a more sophisticated record-keeping system, caused an explosion in the number of demands placed on the administrative capabilities of municipalities.

Not only did categorical grants increase substantially during the 1960s, but their orientation also changed. In the early 1960s, for example, transportation and social security were the main focus, comprising about 80 percent of the funding. During the late 1960s and early 1970s, many new grants relating to health, employment, training, social services, natural resources, and environmental concerns were established. This period saw a decided shift in the relative proportion of grants from the nonurban areas to metropolitan areas.[14]

The 1960s brought growing displeasure over the complexity of the grants process, the federal regulations involved in administering the programs, and the financing of agencies independent of municipal governments. Sufficient pressures were mounted in the late 1960s to usher in a movement away from categorical grants toward block grants and General Revenue Sharing. Supporters believed this shift would result in a reduction of administrative costs, wider latitude for local officials to meet local needs, and an allocation of funds according to need rather than the abilities of a grantee's consultants or resident grantsmen.

Politically, the struggle over the form of grants has often pitted elected officials (generalists) against functional specialists. Included among the latter are planners, professionals in fields such as health and education, social workers, and public works engineers. The professionals tend to favor rather restricted categorical programs because they believe these programs are more apt to result in uniformly high-quality services. Elected officials, on the other hand, often resent the influence of such professionals and think that categorical programs lessen their control. They feel forced to accept programs so they do not "lose" federal aid, even when a greater need for other programs exists. The battle between the lobbyists for the elected officials, represented by a group of organizations called the public interest groups (PIGs), and the lobbyists for the functional groups is well described by Haider in his book about the enactment of General Revenue Sharing.[15]

The waging of this battle in Washington has not resulted in a clear victory for either side, but the 1970s saw the enactment of revenue sharing and the consolidation of many categorical programs into broader block grant programs. However, a typical mid-sized municipality still needs specialists to prepare federal grant applications, and a considerable amount of time and money is spent complying with federal requirements.

It is difficult to provide even a brief summary of all the federal programs from which Illinois municipalities might obtain funds.

We will attempt, however, to provide some understanding of the situation by describing revenue sharing and three of the more important block grant programs, and then catalogue, by type, other federal programs available to municipalities in this study.

General Revenue Sharing

In 1972, the State and Local Fiscal Assistance Act was passed and signed into law. It provided $30.2 billion to more than 39,000 state and local governments nationwide between its enactment and December 31, 1976. The program was subsequently extended for an additional three and three-quarters years at an annual funding level of $6.85 billion, with some changes in requirements concerning public participation and antidiscrimination safeguards, and with fewer restrictions on the uses of the funds.[16] General Revenue Sharing meets the objectives of decision making decentralization with a minimization of reporting, planning, and administrative requirements.

1. Allocation Formula. The allocation of revenue sharing funds to state areas is based on either a three-factor or a five-factor formula, depending on which provides the greater revenue. The three factors are population, per capita income, and tax effort (taxes collected compared with income). The five-factor formula also includes the percentage of state revenue obtained from the income tax and the percentage of population residing in urban areas.[17] Of the total General Revenue Sharing funds to which governments within a state are entitled, one-third are for use by the state government itself. In Illinois, virtually all the state's share is used to support local school districts.[18]

The funds are provided only to general-purpose governments, which in Illinois include counties, townships, and municipalities. The moneys are allocated to county areas based on relative income (per capita income in the county compared with that of the state), population, and tax effort (adjusted taxes collected in the county divided by total personal income in the county). After the funds have been divided between types of governments based on shares of taxes collected, the moneys are further allocated to individual government units based on relative income, population, and tax effort.

The revenue sharing allocation formula has both advantages and limitations. One strong point is that it does allow for a regularity of funding that permits local officials to improve their revenue-planning processes. In addition, the formula benefits cities in greater need (based on relative income) and those already taxing themselves at higher levels (as measured by tax effort). Questions have been raised, however, about whether the formula goes far enough in assisting the central cities with major fiscal and social problems.[19]

Disadvantages of the formula are that no recognition is given to cities providing services to residents outside the corporate limits (benefit spillovers), and that no attempt is made to correct for the condition of housing stock or the blighted areas within a city. To some extent, these problems are addressed by community development grants (to be discussed later).

Table 4-2(page 109) shows that independent cities in 1977 received an average of $14.50 per capita in General Revenue Sharing funds. The Chicago suburbs received $8.61. This difference, which is statistically significant at the 1-percent level, is related to the poorer condition of independent cities and their greater reliance on property tax collections.

2. Expenditures. A major attraction of the General Revenue Sharing program is the flexibility local officials have in allocating funds. The initial legislation mandated the use of priority categories, including public safety, transportation, environmental protection, social services for the poor and aged, health, recreation, and libraries. Virtually the only restrictions were that moneys could not be spent on education and welfare, which are funded under separate programs. Likewise, cities could not use revenue sharing funds as matching funds for other federal grants. If revenue sharing funds constituted a significant portion of a construction project, Davis-Bacon Act provisions, requiring the payment of prevailing wages, had to be followed. Also, cities were prohibited from engaging in discriminatory practices in hiring and project development.

With the renewal of the State and Local Fiscal Assistance Act in 1976, both the priority categories and the prohibition against the use of revenue sharing for purposes of matching were dropped. Citizen participation requirements were increased, with cities required to hold hearings on how the General Revenue Sharing funds would interact with other programs in the city budget. At least in the early years of revenue sharing, cities tended to focus their expenditures on one-time capital projects to prevent unpopular cutbacks in case the program was not renewed in 1976. Interviews in recent years have disclosed a greater tendency to include the revenue sharing funds in the regular budgeting process, as well as a reduced emphasis on one-time projects. However, city officials vary considerably in their approach to the use of the funds. In Champaign, for instance, a competition is held among civic groups for revenue sharing allotments. The awards are based on proposals presented at the first of two required public hearings. In 1978, the city council reserved between $150,000 and $175,000 of an estimated $800,000 for social service agencies within the city.[20]

In other instances, city officials indicated that, as much as possible, revenue sharing is used for capital projects rather than for personal services and related purposes. It is unclear whether this attitude reflects a cautious approach to financing services or whether, within the budgeting process, it simply is easier for cities to spend revenue sharing funds for capital purposes.[21]

When revenue sharing was introduced, one of its stated aims was to reduce pressures on the property tax. Among Illinois municipalities over 25,000 surveyed in 1975, only 6.5 percent responded that the rate of a major tax had been reduced, but 58.9 percent indicated that revenue sharing had prevented an increase in the rate of a major tax. In all probability these responses are attributable to the persistence of inflation in the early 1970s. A comparable survey in 1979 revealed that 56 percent of the cities would either raise taxes or cut back services, or some combination of both, if General Revenue Sharing funds were eliminated.[22]

Overall, General Revenue Sharing has provided an infusion of intergovernmental revenue at a time when inflation has been challenging the cities' abilities to provide services. It has provided considerable certainty in the funding process with a minimum of red tape and regulations. Municipalities have not had to spend time locating appropriate funding agencies and negotiating projects. Local governments generally have the authority to decide what types of projects to undertake with revenue sharing funds, with the "generalists" gaining considerably more say in the resource allocation process.

Block Grants

Block grants, like revenue sharing, represent a shift in the philosophy of intergovernmental relations underlying categorical programs. The new approach enhances the flexibility and freedom of state and local generalists as compared with the categorical programs that strengthened the influence of program specialists.

There is some question regarding the classification of grants as either block grants or categoricals. Most observers now associate the term block grant with the five programs established under the

Partnership for Health Act, the Omnibus Crime Control and Safe Streets Act, the Comprehensive Employment and Training Act of 1973, the 1974 amendments to the Social Security Act, and the Housing and Community Development Act of 1974. At least three of these programs have had a major impact on municipal government finance.

1. Omnibus Crime Control and Safe Streets Act. This act, passed two years after the Partnership for Health Act of 1966, provided the second major block grant. The aim of this legislation was to help state and local governments improve their criminal justice systems. Whereas the Partnership for Health Act resulted from a consolidation of categorical grants, the Omnibus Crime Control legislation began as a block grant aimed at providing wide discretionary power to recipient governments within the broad area of criminal justice. The act established the Law Enforcement Assistance Administration of the Department of Justice as the main funding agency; as of 1976, nearly three-fourths of the federal funds in this area were disbursed through LEAA.[23]

Because of the need for political compromise and because traditionally state and local governments are responsible for criminal justice, the funding in this block grant involves state government coordination. States were required to establish a state planning agency (the Illinois Law Enforcement Commission) responsible for administering the program within the state. To promote even greater cooperation, a network of regional planning commissions within the state was established, with membership from the various segments of the criminal justice system. In sum, the funding procedure goes like this: grant applications begin with the individual government obtaining the approval of the regional commission. That commission then carries the request to the state planning agency. The state planning agency is responsible for preparing a comprehensive statewide plan for improving the criminal justice system, and this plan provides the basis for much of the funding in the subsequent period.

In 1974, the Juvenile Justice and Delinquency Prevention Act was passed to provide additional support for juvenile delinquency programs, The states were required to maintain their funding at the fiscal year 1972 level. The legislation was very specific, with 19.15 percent of all LEAA funds being earmarked for juvenile justice and an additional $15 million set aside annually for neighborhood crime prevention.[24] In addition, other requirements including funding judicial planning committees were imposed.

Although the recipient governments had considerable latitude in determining what types of projects would receive funding, matching requirements encouraged the spending of funds according to specific priorities. For instance, initially the federal government paid 75 percent of riot and civil disorder control program costs, 50 percent of construction costs, and 60 percent of other action program costs. This federal aid could not be used to pay for more than a third of the personnel costs within a project so that, at least in the beginning, a definite incentive was provided for local governments to purchase hardware. One of the basic criticisms of the program was that municipalities and other law enforcement agencies were tempted to purchase unnecessary equipment.

This brief overview of the program suggests that considerable energy might be devoted to completing plans and compiling data to meet program requirements. Because the local government had to apply to the state planning agency for funds, future funding was not always certain. This, of course, affected the development of local programs. A popular local program that could be discontinued at a future date or that might someday require funding from local resources could create serious problems for local officials.

Recently, the LEAA approach to criminal justice system improvement has been sharply criticized; in fact, attempts have been made to do away with the entire program. Proponents claim that the funding is a vital part of the criminal justice system and that its removal would be devastating. However, based on ACIR estimates, the LEAA appropriations in 1976 amounted to "less than 5 percent of annual state and local own-source outlays for crime reduction purposes."[25]

Appropriately, the Omnibus Crime Control and Safe Streets Act has been labeled "creeping categorization." The considerable red tape and maintenance efforts required to qualify for new funding programs, combined with the differential matching requirements, have significantly reduced local decision making. Thus, one of the major attractive features of the block grant approach has been eroded.

2. Community Development Block Grants. In 1974, the Community Development Block Grant (CDBG) program was instituted. Unlike the Omnibus Crime Control and Safe Streets Act, this block grant program provided funding directly to local governments, bypassing states. The CDBG program consolidated several community development programs, including urban renewal, Model Cities, open space, urban beautification and historic site preservation, neighborhood facilities, water and sewer, and public facilities loans.[26] Two programs, Section 312 (involving rehabilitation loans) and Section 701 (providing planning and management funds) were not included in the new block grant.

The main objective of the CDBG program, "the development of viable urban communities," was to be accomplished through the provision of decent housing and a suitable living environment. In addition, economic opportunities for people with low and moderate incomes were to be increased. Seven specific objectives for the program were enumerated: elimination and prevention of slums and blight; elimination of unhealthy and unsafe conditions; conservation and expansion of the nation's housing stock; expansion and improvement of community services; more rational use of land; reduction of the isolation of income groups; and historic preservation.[27]

Cities qualify for assistance under the CDBG program in one of three ways. Cities of 50,000 and larger are "entitlement cities" eligible to apply for a grant directly. The amount to which each city is entitled is based on three measures—population, poverty status (weighted twice using regional income data), and housing overcrowding. A hold-harmless provision assures that for three years these cities do not receive less than they would have been awarded under the replaced programs. The hold-harmless level is the sum of:

1. The average of all grants, loans, or advances received during FY 68–FY 72 under each of the consolidated programs except Neighborhood Development programs and Model Cities, and
2. The average annual grant made under Model Cities during FY 68–FY 72, and
3. The average annual grant made under the Neighborhood Development Program during FY 68–FY 72, or during FY 73 for the first time NDPs.[28]

Nonentitlement cities in metropolitan areas obtain funds from moneys set aside for discretionary grants. The remaining cities, nonentitlement municipalities in nonmetropolitan areas, are funded from a small discretionary grant category. The entitlement cities, and those funded under the discretionary grant program, account for about 80 percent of the CDBG funding level. The remaining 20 percent is used by cities in nonmetropolitan areas or by those obtaining funds from the small discretionary grant program. The allocation formula has been criticized as discriminating against cities with large abandonment problems because they score low on the housing overcrowding index. The use of population estimates, which often are dated, can also discriminate against cities undergoing large population growth. In addition, the lack of a definite relationship between population size and fiscal need has been emphasized.

A significant disadvantage of the CDBG approach as compared with General Revenue Sharing is the four-part grant application required. The first part contains a three-year development plan summary showing short-and long-term objectives, an assessment of the city's development needs, and a comprehensive strategy for meeting those needs. Second, an annual plan showing activities to be performed, cost, and location within the city must be provided, with importance attached to outside sources for revenue to supplement the federally funded work projects. Third, cities must design their work plans around the national objectives of eliminating and preventing slums, blight, and deterioration within the city. The final component, and perhaps the most important, is a housing assistance plan containing a survey of housing conditions as well as an assessment of the present and future needs of lower-income residents. The housing assistance plan must present reasonable annual goals for the number of dwelling units improved or the number of individuals to be assisted, and it must specify exactly where the proposed housing for low-income residents will be constructed.

When the funds have been received, local officials face several restrictions on their use. A maintenance-of-effort clause requires that cities maintain support for housing at the level of the previous period. An inclusive list of the types of activities on which funds can be spent is also provided. This list includes acquisition and disposition of real property and public facilities or improvements, rehabilitation of housing, economic development activities, planning and environmental design costs, and other aspects of the block grant activities.[29]

Table 4-3 compares the Community Development Block Grants received by Illinois cities from 1975 to 1977. The annual average for the independent cities was $18.02 per capita, and for the Chicago suburbs, $6.01. East St. Louis received an average of $53.28—the largest amount shown. As noted, several cities did not apply for funds. Apparently the municipal officials were not interested in completing the detailed application process or did not wish to comply with some of the requirements imposed on the funds.

3. Comprehensive Employment and Training Act. In the

Table 4-3. Community Development Block Grants, 1975-1977 (Dollars Per Capita)

	FY75	FY76	FY77	Average
Independent				
Aurora	$3.16	$7.03	11.73	$7.31
Bloomington	52.25	52.25	52.25	52.25
Champaign	6.42	8.53	14.31	9.75
Danville	28.75	28.75	28.75	28.75
Decatur	5.75	8.68	14.23	9.55
DeKalb	28.42	28.42	28.42	28.42
Elgin	2.63	5.82	9.71	6.05
Galesburg	9.69	9.69	9.69	9.69
Joliet	3.97	8.82	14.37	9.05
Kankakee	—	4.97	10.73	7.85
Moline	3.89	7.52	12.25	7.89
Normal	2.43	5.37	9.51	5.77
North Chicago	11.87	11.87	11.87	11.87
Peoria	16.79	16.79	16.79	16.79
Rockford	17.92	17.92	17.92	17.92
Rock Island	50.62	45.13	39.65	45.13
Springfield	51.63	51.63	51.63	51.63
Urbana	3.86	8.57	14.15	8.86
Waukegan	7.77	7.77	7.77	7.77
Average				$18.02
Suburban Chicago				
Arlington Heights	$1.73	$1.91	$4.56	$3.24
Berwyn	2.66	2.96	3.20	—
Calumet City	—	7.24	0.84	4.04
Chicago Heights	1.26	18.72	39.77	19.91
Cicero	2.17	3.51	3.81	—
Des Plaines	2.42	2.69	2.87	—
Evanston	2.90	6.43	10.40	6.58
Harvey	9.11	7.29	23.86	13.42
Maywood	1.76	1.76	1.76	1.76
Morton Grove	—	3.83	11.99	7.91
Mt. Prospect	—	1.81	—	1.81
Naperville	—	—	3.99	3.99
Niles	—	3.47	—	3.47
Northbrook	—	—	1.21	1.21
Oak Lawn	2.63	2.92	3.24	—
Oak Park	2.61	5.81	9.40	5.94
Palatine	—	3.28	—	3.28
Park Forest	—	—	14.72	14.27
Skokie	1.93	4.24	7.03	4.40

Table 4-3. *(continued)*

	FY75	*FY76*	*FY77*	*Average*
Wilmette	$ 0.31	$ —	$ 1.54	$ 0.92
Average				$6.01
Suburban St. Louis				
East St. Louis	$60.28	$53.27	$46.28	$53.28

Source: Community Development Block Grant Program: Directory of Allocations for Fiscal Year 1977 (Washington, D.C.: U.S. Department of Housing and Urban Development, 1977).

Funded at hold-harmless level.

Did not apply.

early 1970s high inflation coincided with an economic recession that forced state and local governments to cut back on spending while the federal government was following expansionary policies. The recession created pressures for programs aimed at providing assistance to local governments to stimulate employment. One of the programs directed especially at the chronically unemployed was the Comprehensive Employment and Training Act (CETA), passed in 1973. This act replaced all or a portion of three earlier programs—The Manpower Development and Training Act (MDTA) of 1962, the Emergency Employment Act of 1971, and the Ecomic Opportunity Act of 1964.

Funding under CETA is provided directly to governments of at least 100,000, including three Illinois municipalities—Chicago, Rockford and Peoria. Among these cities, only Chicago is a prime sponsor; Rockford and Peoria are part of countywide agencies. East St. Louis is the only prime sponsor that has a population under 100,000. This treatment reflects the special needs in East St. Louis that result from its high unemployment, minority population, and concentration of residents below the poverty level.

Grants are allocated to prime sponsors according to the following formula: 50 percent based on the previous year's allocation; 37.5 percent based on relative numbers of unemployed; and 12.5 percent based on relative numbers of adults in families below the Bureau of Labor Statistics (BLS) lower-level standard of living.

Three titles in the act are of prime interest for present purposes: Title I (Community Job Training programs); Title II (Public Service Employment); and Title IV (Emergency Jobs Program). The funds under Titles II and VI are aimed at providing public service jobs in areas with high unemployment, defined as 6.5 percent or more for three consecutive months. Under Title VI, individuals hired must be from families at or below 70 percent of the BLS lower-level standard of living and must meet one of the following conditions: (1) be a recipient of Aid to Families with Dependent Children (AFDC); (2) be receiving unemployment compensation and be unemployed for at least 15 weeks; (3) be an individual whose unemployment compensation benefits have expired and who is unemployed.

The intent of the CETA program was to create employment and improve skills of individuals rather than only providing financial assistance to local governments. Depending on the actions followed by cities, however, the funds can be of considerable help to local governments. Indirectly, a municipality benefits as incomes are increased and residents improve their living environments, thus increasing the tax base and revenues to the city. More directly, cities obtain subsidized employment for services that, without the CETA program, might not have been provided.

Concern was expressed, however, that cities may use CETA employees to replace municipal employees who would have been funded from tax revenues. Thus a basic purpose of the program—creating employment—would be frustrated. Although we found no detailed study of the impact of CETA programs in Illinois, one estimate is that approximately 80 percent of CETA funds at the national level have been used to create additional jobs, while 8 to 21 percent have involved displacement of existing employees.[30]

Discussions with municipal officials indicated that Illinois cities have followed various approaches to the CETA program. In some instances, cities have had limited involvement because officials were wary of the program's duration and feared that employees would have to be dismissed later. Other cities reported that CETA employees, many with limited backgrounds, were less motivated than regular workers and that such situations created dissention among city employees. Still others reported difficulties with unions or civil service organizations within the city. Pressure was sometimes applied to make the positions permanent. CETA workers may not have met the regular age or height requirements for a particular position. When a permanent position became available, city officials were pressured to waive the requirements.

City officials differed widely in their opinions of the CETA program's effectiveness. The funds provided relief to cities using the moneys and provided assistance to unemployed residents within the city. In this respect, the program accomplished its goals. However, the overall effect on municipal finance is hard to assess because of the variations among cities in their degree of participation in the program. In one city, for instance, nearly 25 percent of the city work force were paid from CETA funds, whereas several other cities hired few, if any, CETA employees.

Categorical Grants

Space limitations do not permit even a brief description of all the categorical grants for which municipal governments may be eligible. However, it is possible to provide an overview of the number, functions, and type of grants from which a municipal official might seek financial assistance. Table 4-4 classifies, by type and subfunction, categorical grants available to state and local governments and to local governments only during fiscal year 1978.

Although federal grant programs have been reported to number more than 1,000, the counting method used by the Advisory Commission on Intergovernmental Relations yields 492 categorical grants. Excluding grants for which Illinois governments are obviously ineligible, such as those for Appalachian development, reduces the number to 405. Of these, 191 are available to state governments only. Sixty-six are available to state and local governments, and 24 are available only to local governments. The remainder pertain to governmental and nongovernmental recipients including, at least in some cases, local governments. Of the 24 "local government only" grant programs, 16 are for educational purposes and therefore probably are not available to Illinois municipalities.

Classification of the grant programs by type clearly reveals the importance of project grants. Of the 66 state and local grants, only 8 are pure formula grants. Eleven others are project grants but are subject to a formula for distributing funds. Eight of the 24 local grants are formula grants, but 7 of these are for educational purposes.

As the importance of block grants increased in the federal intergovernmental revenue system during the 1970s, the importance of categorical grants diminished. In 1966 categorical grants represented 98 percent of the total intergovernmental revenues, but in 1976 they represented 79 percent.[31] However, in spite of the drop in categorical grants awarded, there remains a concerted effort by state and local governments for consolidation of the categorical

Table 4-4. Categorical Grant Programs, by Budget Subfunction and Grant Type, Available to State and Local Governments Only, FY1978

	State and Local Governments				Only Local Governments				
Budget Subfunction	*F/P*	*F*	*P*	*T*	*F/P*	*F*	*P*	*T*	*Total No. of Grants Available*[a]
Department of Defense—Military	1	—	2	3	—	—	—	—	5
Water resources	—	—	3	3	—	—	—	—	7
Recreational resources	—	—	2	2	—	—	—	—	10
Pollution control and abatement	5	—	2	7	1	—	—	1	35
Other advancement and regulation of commerce	—	—	1	1	—	—	—	—	2
Ground transportation	—	1	2	3	—	—	—	—	36
Mass transportation	—	—	6	6	—	1	—	1	8
Air transportation	2	—	1	3	—	—	—	—	3
Community development	—	—	1	1	—	—	1	1	5
Area and regional development[b]	—	—	5	5	—	—	—	—	19
Disaster relief and insurance	—	—	4	4	—	—	—	—	9
Elementary, secondary, and vocational education	1	3	2	6	—	7	7	15	70
Research and general education aids	—	—	3	3	—	—	1	1	21
Training and employment	1	3	1	5	2	—	1	3	23
Social services	—	—	1	1	1	—	—	1	47
Health care services	—	—	4	4	—	—	1	1	56
Consumer and occupational health and safety	—	—	1	1	—	—	—	—	7
Public assistance and other income supplements	—	—	4	4	—	—	—	—	27
Criminal justice assistance	—	1	1	2	—	—	—	—	13
Other general government	1	—	1	2	—	—	—	—	2
Total	11	8	47	66	4	8	11	24	405

Source: Advisory Commission on Intergovernmental Relations, *A Catalog of Federal Grant-In-Aid Programs to State and Local Governments: Grants Funded FY1978* (Washington, D.C., February 1979), pp. 9–44.

Key: F/P Project grant subject to formula for distribution.
F Formula grant.
P Project grant.

[a]Total number of grants available to state governments only, state and Local governments, local governments only, and governmental and otherwise.

[b]Excludes grants not applicable to Illinois.

grant programs into a more manageable number.[32] Although several proposals for consolidating and reorganizing the categorical grants process have been made, it is too early to determine the likelihood of their success.

The importance of federal intergovernmental revenues in the

financing of cities was shown in Table 4-2. A wide divergence between the independent and suburban city groups was apparent in regard to per capita federal revenues received. Although not shown in Table 4-2, revenues obtained from the federal government differed significantly when considered as a percentage of total city revenues. The independent cities received an average $34.57 per resident from federal intergovernmental revenues, compared with an average of $11.28 per capita for the suburban cities. Federal revenues represented 13.7 percent of the total in the independent cities, compared with an average of 5.2 percent in the suburbs. Both differences are statistically significant at the 1-percent level.

At least two factors contribute to the differences between the cities in federal revenues received. First is the fact that the suburbs receive a greater share of their services from special districts such as sanitary and park districts. Thus, the intergovernmental revenues received by these governments are not included in the city totals. Second, the federal grants such as CDBG and General Revenue Sharing include funding elements to direct funds toward cities with lower average incomes, poorer housing, and similar characteristics. The independent cities are more likely to conform to those characteristics.

STATE AID TO MUNICIPALITIES

Although much attention has been focused on federal aid programs in recent years, state aid to local governments has a long history in the U.S. and actually provides local governments with more dollars than does federal aid. Comparisons of the amount of aid from federal and state governments is complicated by the fact that some of the funds coming from the state are actually federal funds which have been passed along to the states under mandatory or discretionary authority. Nevertheless, it is clear that states raise a large amount of the revenue expended by local governments. A large amount of this revenue is earmarked for the traditionally large state aid programs in the fields of education and highway construction. Since schools in Illinois are financed by school districts, cities do not receive aid to education.

Illinois provides financial aid to municipalities in three main ways: income tax rebates, motor fuel tax rebates, and a number of relatively small grants.

1. State Income Tax Rebates. Effective August 1, 1969, Illinois began levying a state income tax of 2.5 percent on the adjusted gross income of individuals and 4 percent on the net incomes of corporations.[33] As part of this legislation, one-twelfth of the net proceeds is transferred to the "Local Government Distributive Fund," from which rebates to municipalities, based on population, are provided.[34] The income tax payments are unrestricted and are distributed automatically. The funds need not be separated for auditing. Because municipalities are prohibited from imposing a tax on income without statutory authority, the shared income tax provides an opportunity to benefit from revenue growth as incomes increase.

2. State Motor Fuel Tax (MFT) Rebates. The State of Illinois collects a tax of 7.5 cents per gallon on motor fuel sold in the state. By statute, municipalities receive 32 percent of the funds to be allocated to local governments.[35] Of the net collections, (gross collections minus refunds) cities received 29.1 percent. In fiscal year 1977, allotments to municipalities were $118.5 million, as shown in Table 4-5. The apportionment among municipalities, based on population, was $12.11 per resident in 1977.[36]

Table 4-5. Motor Fuel Tax Allotments, December 1, 1976–November 30, 1977

Gross Collections		$424,120,345
Transferred to Road Fund	$28,274,690	
Highway Administration	3,310,021	
Revenue Administration	3,384,452	
Refunds	16,673,323	
State Boating Act Fund	2,016,000	
		-53,658,486
		$370,461,859
Allocations		
Dept. of Transportation		$128,994,819
Municipalities	$118,547,795	
Counties over 1,000,000 pop.	40,417,389	
All other counties	44,122,007	
Road districts	38,379,848	
Total to local governments		241,467,039
		$370,461,859
1977 per capita distribution		$12.11
1976 per capita distribution		11.61

Source: Unpublished data, Illinois Department of Transportation.

Cities can sometimes take action to increase their motor fuel and income tax allotments. For example, North Chicago has been able to annex an adjoining military base, thereby including military personnel in the population count for purposes of income tax and motor fuel tax rebates. Cities with universities include students in their population counts. It is also common for growing cities to undertake a special census to increase the population count used in distributing revenue.

The permitted uses of the MFT funds are specified in the statutes. Although the accepted uses are broad (Figure 4-1), fairly strict controls are imposed on the projects qualifying for reimbursement. Street designs, for instance, are stated in width, surface, and base. Beginning in 1971, municipalities over 5,000 were required to develop and keep updated a twenty-year, long-range highway transportation plan with an estimate of available revenues and a statement of work to be undertaken. A detailed plan showing location of existing streets, projecting traffic per street, and listing major expected improvements within the next five years was to be included.

While the preparation of this plan may serve a worthwhile planning function, there exists no penalty in the statutes for noncompliance. As a result, a significant number of cities have apparently chosen to ignore the mandate. Of those providing plans, a substantial number are not detailed enough to be of much use in planning.

Regulations involving standards for the transportation facilities within a city have caused administrative problems in some municipalities. Cities often have engineering staffs (or hire a consulting engineer) to determine construction standards based on soil conditions, traffic flow, and related measures. If these standards differ from those prescribed by the state, funds can be withheld until an agreement is reached. This can lead to long delays, which, during inflationary periods, mean substantial increases in the costs of a project. In the final analysis, the design originally proposed by the local officials may be the one used, but it has probably become a more expensive project.

The close supervision of the Illinois Department of Transportation serves positive purposes, however. The fact that engineering services from the state are available can reduce the need for specialists to evaluate projects. The state department supervises the project, making sure that the appropriate standards are in use. This can be a valuable service, particularly in smaller cities.

State regulations also provide an opportunity for municipal

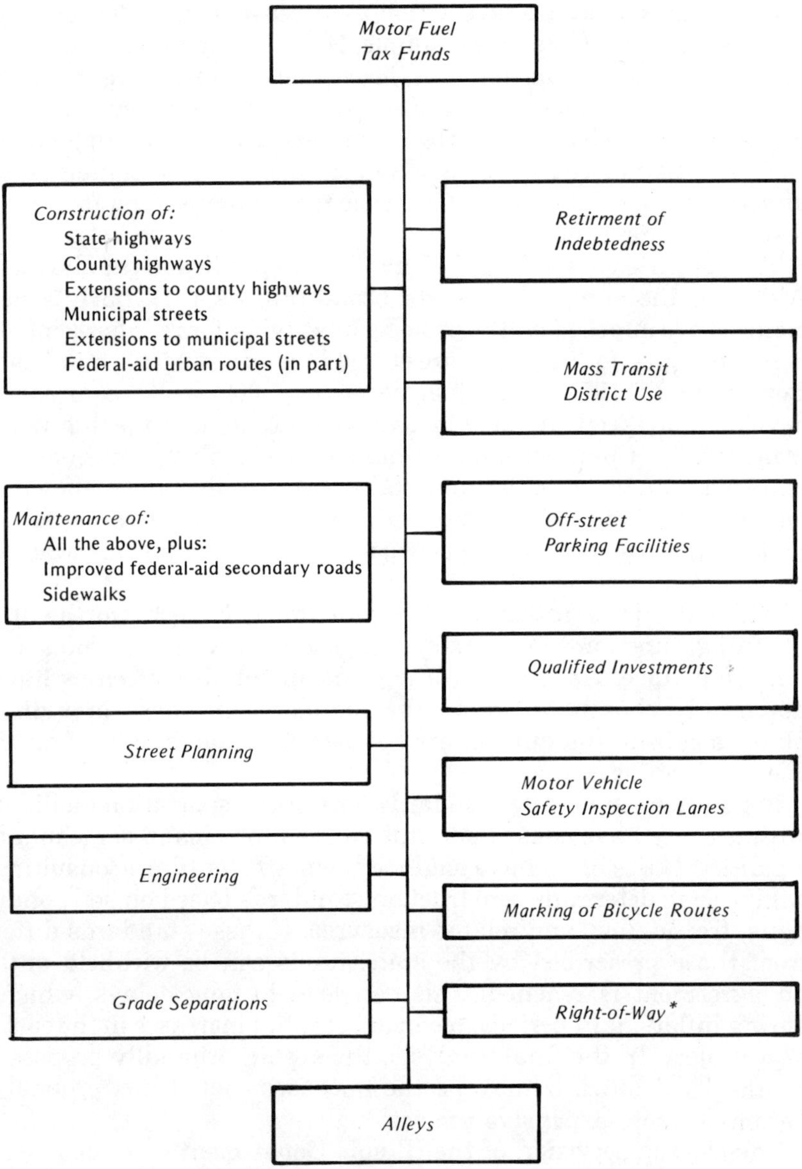

*Although the statutes do not spell out that motor fuel tax funds can be used to purchase right-of-way for MFT improvements, the department has interpreted that these costs are a part of construction costs and are eligible for MFT expenditures.

Source: Illinois Department of Transportation

Figure 4–1. Permissible uses of motor fuel tax funds by municipalities.

officials to separate the motor fuel tax funds from the regular budgeting process. In particular, keeping the funds separate may reduce pressures for projects that are popular with a particular group but are not justified on the basis of professional planning and engineering criteria.

At present, MFT funds represent approximately 5 percent of total municipal revenue in Illinois. Unless rates are changed, however, this percentage will decline. Because the tax is based on gallons sold rather than on dollar sales, conservation attempts reducing the consumption of gasoline will result in the inability of this revenue source to keep pace with price increases for street construction materials.

Until 1979, a tax on motor fuels was also used to finance transportation facilities in the six-county Chicago metropolitan area. A 5-percent tax was imposed on sales in this region, with the Regional Transit Authority (RTA) having responsiblity for financing mass transit. In 1979, this additional 5-percent tax was replaced by an increase in the general sales tax in the area. Financing the RTA has been a persistent problem facing policy makers and, as of this writing, another financing arrangement is being negotiated.

3. State Grants to Municipalities. Several relatively small state grant programs reimburse cities for expenses incurred in providing services. Since programs are located in many different state agencies, considerable difficulty is encountered in obtaining a comprehensive picture of funds available. The Bureau of the Census does provide a tabulation, by purpose; these data for FY 1977 are given in Table 4-6. These data are for all cities in Illinois, not only the study group. The two largest entries, income tax rebates and motor fuel sales tax rebates, have already been discussed. Several other programs provide funds to local governments, but the proportion paid to cities could not be identified, so these programs are not included in this list. It should also be remembered that the state payments shown may represent federal funds passing through the state, such as funds for highways or sewage treatment facilities.

THE COMPLEXITY OF INTERGOVERNMENTAL RELATIONS

Intergovernmental fiscal relations are very complex. Part of the complexity is an inevitable result of growth in the size of government and the nature of the tasks undertaken by government. The rapid suburbanization of metropolitan areas after World War II, for example, was unintentionally encouraged and facilitated by federal housing and transportation policies. This, in turn, had a major impact on local government organization and finance and was partly responsible for some of the problems that later federal grant programs have attempted to correct. In an effort to foresee and prevent undesirable consequences, all these programs have imposed a variety of restrictions on local governments. Some have been subjected to criticisms from local officials who are sometimes caught between the demands of two or more federal or state requirements.

One of the requirements increasing local costs resulted from the Davis–Bacon Act, which stipulated that prevailing wages must be paid if federal funds are used on a project. Often this has meant that the union scale has been accepted rather uncritically as the

Table 4–6. Selected State Payments to Illinois Municipalities, 1977 (in Thousands of Dollars)

Purpose	*Amount*
Education	
Transportation	$ 130
Public welfare	
Hospitals & medical services	2,247
General local government support	
Income tax	126,945
Highways	
Motor fuel sales tax	120,319
Federal aid for highways	559
Health and hospitals	
Hospital construction	27
Local health services	838
Mental health services	2,035
Sewage	
Treatment facilities	29,800
Miscellaneous	
Transportation of elderly	64
Public transportation facilities	34
Rural public transportation	272
Port facilities	112
Snowmobile trails	1,430
Libraries	10,431
Outdoor recreation	2,268
Airport construction	188

Source: U.S. Bureau of the Census, *State Payments to Local Governments in 1977* (Washington, D.C.: Government Printing Office, 1979), Table 7.

prevailing wage, with dramatic increases in cost. Because federal funds were involved, there was little incentive for local officials to brave the controversy and strife that might be necessary to hold down costs.

Even more complex are the requirements of the Occupational Safety and Health Act of 1970, designed to improve working conditions. Not only does the act require the implementation of many protection devices involving time and exposure, but it also insists on the maintenance of a detailed record-keeping system.[37] While we could review "horror stories" of problems created by the administration of OSHA, the point here is simply to note that federal funding often brings federal requirements. These can both greatly increase the cost of providing local services and complicate decision making.

Although the standards and mandates in federal legislation are often accompanied by federal grants to help offset the costs, other mandates, sometimes issued by the state government, are not accompanied by financial aid. The increases in pension costs arising from benefits set at the state level have contributed to increases in the property tax at the local level.[38]

Benefit levels for worker's compensation were increased substantially in 1975, triggering major increases in insurance rates paid by cities. In some instances, policies were cancelled and local officials had difficulty obtaining coverage. The insurance rates for certain municipal employee classifications more than doubled over several years. In neither the pension benefit nor worker's compensation program was there state reimbursement.[39]

After spending so much time discussing intergovernmental assistance programs available to cities, one might inquire about their likely impact on municipal finance. Local officials faced with the prospect of additional aid from other governments have two basic choices. They can use the federal or state assistance in lieu of local revenues to finance existing services or perhaps to grant property tax relief. Alternatively, they can use the outside aid to implement new programs that otherwise would not have been possible. Given the earlier finding that suburban residents face higher aggregate property tax burdens while the cities receive less intergovernmental aid, one is tempted to conclude that one effect of intergovernmental aid has been to help independent cities keep property taxes down. This scenario makes sense in light of our discussions with municipal officials. However, differences in responsibility for services and corresponding differences in intergovernmental receipts by type of government prevent a conclusive test of this hypothesis.

In Chapter 5, we will consider the possibility that additional intergovernmental revenues lead to higher expenditures for services. Given that local officials are constrained by available revenues, it seems likely that the prospect of additional funds obtained without raising taxes would result in the provision of additional services.

FINANCING THROUGH BORROWING

While the preceding discussion focused on nonproperty tax revenues available to Illinois cities, this section will cover the financing of services through borrowing. With the adoption of home rule in 1970, restrictions on debt were removed and cities with home rule authority became free to finance projects subject only to market conditions. In addition to their usual construction projects, cities in recent years have become involved in helping private industry locate in cities. These ventures make use of industrial revenue bonds, which permit businesses to borrow at lower interest rates. The city lends its name to the bonds, qualifying them for special tax treatment, and the bonds are retired from the proceeds of the project for which they were issued.

Types of Debt Instruments

Municipal debt can be classified by method of financing or by length of issue. A common classification is by tax-supported (general obligation) issues and revenue bonds (bonds retired from revenues generated by the project). An alternative classification system is to group debt with an expiration date in excess of one year as long-term debt and instruments with a shorter maturity date as short-term debt.[40] Short-term debt frequently includes tax anticipation warrants and bonds issued for the purpose of permitting the city to pay its bills until property taxes or other revenues are received. Long-term debt, on the other hand, includes revenue for the financing of capital projects benefiting future generations.

Table 4–7 provides a profile of outstanding debt by major type during 1977. The average outstanding debt for the independent cities was $344.93 per capita, compared with an average of $230.97 per capita for the Chicago suburbs. The difference between the two city groups was not statistically significant at the usual levels. Major differences are found within the two groups, however. While

Springfield reported the highest debt, the figure includes the debt for a utility plant operated by the city. Much of the high outstanding debt reported is related to special circumstances in the cities, making comparisons difficult without more detailed information.

The fact that in each case the vast majority of debt is long-term indicates that funds are being used to construct facilities and provide services extending into the future. Relatively little use was found of tax anticipation warrants or other short-term debt, with the exception of cities such as Peoria, Rock Island, Oak Park, and Danville. Whereas the reason for the short-term borrowing in these cities is not known, it most likely is related to a mismatch between tax receipts and current expenditure requirements. In most instances, the amounts are relatively small. The disadvantage of short-term borrowing, of course, is the additional interest expense involved.

A more interesting breakdown is between full faith and credit debt and nonguaranteed debt. Cities varied considerably in the distribution between these two types of debt as can be seen from an examination of the full faith and credit debt in Table 4-7. In the majority of instances, the full faith and credit debt was small compared with the total. Cities may have been helping private industrial concerns locate in the city or perhaps financing public improvements such as parking facilities with revenue bonds. In some cities, however, there was considerable full faith and credit debt outstanding. One possibility is that cities have been borrowing for capital improvements using guaranteed issues, but with the intention of paying them off with revenues generated from the projects. This approach offers the advantage of lower interest costs with no drain on municipal resources. Of course, if the venture were to fail, the issues would have to be retired from property taxes or other municipal revenues.

One measure of a city's debt management is the rating that it receives from bond rating companies. For comparison purposes, Moody's bond rating for 1977 is shown in Table 4-7. Bond rating firms are contacted to estimate the creditworthiness of an offering and, after reviewing the available material on the city's finances, the firm assigns a rating. The rating assigned to the city is partly subjective, and city officials can sometimes develop strategies to emphasize fiscal stability and revenue-raising potential to obtain a better rating. Obtaining the highest rating possible is very important because a higher rating means lower interest costs. It is not uncommon for city officials to make trips to the rating agencies,

Table 4-7. 1977 Per Capita Municipal Debt

	Total Debt Outstanding	Long-Term	Full Faith and Credit	Moody's Bond Rating
Independent Cities				
Aurora	$ 327.27	$ 327.27	$250.86	Aa
Bloomington	536.99	523.74	523.74	Aa
Carpentersville	103.75	103.75	55.61	A
Champaign	223.57	217.54	185.19	Aa
Danville	289.62	233.49	233.28	Aa
DeKalb	75.88	75.88	20.84	A
Decatur	306.45	290.60	142.79	A
Elgin	188.66	188.66	158.48	—
Freeport	141.19	141.19	—	—
Galesburg	138.57	129.83	47.15	A1
Joliet	406.28	392.84	40.32	Baa1
Kankakee	194.02	192.23	4.83	—
Moline	292.79	292.79	225.83	Aa
Normal	457.40	457.40	411.99	Aa
North Chicago	86.82	86.82	86.82	—
Pekin	1,028.24	1,028.24	13.02	—
Peoria	173.93	147.93	15.95	Aa
Quincy	315.62	315.64	256.94	Aa
Rock Island	724.43	699.97	567.78	Aa
Rockford	164.55	137.96	45.15	Aa
Springfield	1,553.94	1,553.94	8.47	Aa
Urbana	95.73	95.73	26.58	Aa
Waukegan	107.78	107.78	7.68	A1
Average	$ 344.93	$ 336.57	$151.33	
(S.D.)	(347.57)	(348.25)	(168.32)	
Suburban Chicago				
Addison	$ 442.80	$ 442.80	$442.80	A1
Arlington Heights	1,020.75	1,020.75	5.71	Aa
Berwyn	46.96	46.96	36.57	A
Bolingbrook	308.84	308.84	308.84	A
Calumet City	188.68	188.68	—	—
Chicago Heights	305.11	305.11	141.80	A
Cicero	51.07	51.07	5.67	A
Des Plaines	282.28	282.28	153.88	Aa
Dolton	37.73	37.73	26.38	A
Downers Grove	145.40	145.40	82.91	A1
Elmhurst	200.62	200.62	117.06	A1
Elmwood Park	37.69	37.69	27.16	Baa1
Evanston	216.66	216.66	93.02	Aaa
Glenview	85.92	85.92	64.81	A1
Harvey	126.07	126.07	97.23	Baa
Highland Park	179.22	179.22	96.76	Aa
Lansing	127.25	127.25	35.51	A
Lombard	340.57	340.57	217.04	A1

Table 4-7. *(continued)*

	Total Debt Outstanding	Long-Term	Full Faith and Credit	Moody's Bond Rating
Maywood	$ 93.36	$ 93.36	$ 23.55	—
Morton Grove	87.76	87.76	47.90	A1
Mt. Prospect	163.37	161.84	124.56	Aa
Naperville	701.59	701.59	218.78	A1
Niles	55.10	55.10	4.93	—
Northbrook	265.22	265.22	113.67	Aa
Oak Lawn	382.21	382.21	28.32	A
Oak Park	421.22	387.77	247.77	Aa
Palatine	158.78	158.78	5.04	A1
Park Forest	107.61	107.61	17.69	A
Park Ridge	493.63	485.56	469.12	Aa
Schaumburg	93.17	93.17	6.30	—
Skokie	41.05	41.05	32.76	A1
Wheaton	207.37	207.37	99.12	A1
Wilmette	207.11	207.11	53.73	Aa
Average	$ 230.97	$ 229.67	$107.69	
(S.D.)	(208.70)	(207.52)	(119.56)	
Suburban St. Louis				
Alton	$1,170.16	$1,170.16	$ 14.93	Aa
Belleville	193.48	193.48	9.51	—
East St. Louis	228.56	205.09	23.56	—
Granite City	155.89	154.03	30.03	A1
Average	$ 437.02	$ 430.69	$ 19.51	
(S.D.)	(489.66)	(493.46)	(9.09)	
Chicago	$ 436.07	$ 365.89	$ 99.20	Aa

Z = value: Total debt outstanding (Chicago suburban vs. independent) = 1.40

Source: U.S. Bureau of the Census, *Finances of Municipalities and Township Governments, 1977* (Washington, D.C.: Government Printing Office, 1979), Table 22; *1978 Municipal Yearbook* (Washington, D.C.: International City Management Association, 1978), Table 1/1.

bearing financial documents and other materials to convince them that the city is a good risk. An investment in this strategy can pay handsome dividends if the rating is improved.

Borrowing Trends

Changes in the type of borrowing and the extent to which borrowing takes place are shown in Table 4-8. The Chicago suburbs' total outstanding debt increased from an average of $96.67 per capita in 1962 to $230.97 in 1977. In the independent cities, on the

Table 4-8. Trends in Debt, Illinois Municipalities

	Chicago Suburbs			Independent Cities		
Debt Type	*1962*	*1977*	*% Change*	*1962*	*1977*	*% Change*
Total debt outstanding						
Current dollars	$96.67	$230.97	138.9%	$106.06	$344.93	225.2%
Constant dollars[a]	96.67	95.05	-1.7	106.06	141.95	33.8
Long-term						
Current dollars	94.66	229.67	142.6	102.65	336.57	227.9
Constant dollars[a]	94.66	94.51	-0.2	102.65	138.51	34.9
Full faith and credit						
Current dollars	38.92	107.69	179.7	28.85	151.33	424.5
Constant dollars[a]	38.92	44.32	13.9	28.85	62.28	115.9

Source: U.S. Bureau of the Census, *Finances of Municipalities and Township Governments, 1977* (Washington, D.C.: Government Printing Office, 1979); U.S. Bureau of the Census, *Governments in Illinois* (Washington, D.C.: Government Printing Office, 1964).

[a]Deflated by Illinois Municipal Price Index.

other hand, an average of $106.06 per capita was outstanding in 1962 compared with $344.93 per resident 15 years later. In real terms, however, the outstanding debt in the average suburb decreased by 1.7 percent, while the real increase for the independent cities was 33.8 percent.

The debt shown in Table 4-8 represents only that incurred by the city. One explanation of the differences between the city types is the differences in responsibilites for services. Independent cities, for instance, may have to borrow to improve a sewage treatment facility while special districts incur this debt in the suburbs. In either case, urban residents must pay a portion of the taxes to retire the debt. The vast majority of the outstanding debt for both city types was long-term in both 1962 and 1977. In 1962, the average suburb had $38.92 per capita in general obligation debt, approximately 40.3 percent of the total. By 1977, the general obligation debt of $107.69 per capita represented 46.6 percent of the outstanding debt. In the independent cities, full faith and credit borrowing was $28.85 per capita in 1962, or 27.2 percent, but by 1977 the $151.33 outstanding represented 43.9 percent of the total.

Although the debt in the study cities has increased during the past 15 years, the level of debt is not likely to be troublesome. For instance, estimated at the average, the 1977 general obligation debt of $151.33 per capita in the independent cities averaged only 3.8 percent of the assessed valuation during the 1975 assessment year. Likewise, the $107.69 per capita in general obligation debt of the suburbs averaged 2.2 percent of the assessed valuation in the average city. These levels are well within an easily manageable range of debt finance.

SUMMARY

Tables showing sources of municipal revenue by broad categories such as property taxation or intergovernmental revenues are likely to conceal much complexity. This chapter and the previous one have shown that the simple uniform property tax that was the source of much state and local revenue in the early days of statehood has become a complicated system of taxation governed by statutory and case law. Administration and levy responsibility are shared by state, county, and other local governments in a way that often confuses both taxpayers and municipal officials.

The wide variety of revenue sources available for financing municipal services in Illinois allows an enterprising municipal official to tailor the revenue structure to meet the city's economic base. Some cities have relied heavily on sales tax receipts and have spent considerable time and energy attracting a shopping center or rebuilding the central business district. Other cities have made effective use of business taxes such as those on hotels, motels, and eating establishments. Still others have obtained significant amounts of intergovernmental revenues as they worked to upgrade streets, sewers, and other neighborhood facilities.

This chapter's discussions of revenues emphasize two points. First is that a wide variety of methods are used to obtain revenues for city services. This range of revenue sources attests to the flexibility for generating revenues that Illinois municipal officials have.

Second is that the independent cities and the suburbs differ in the types of revenues obtained. Underlying some of these differences is that fact that independent cities provide a greater share of services than the suburbs do. Special districts are more important in providing services in the Chicago area.

A major finding of this chapter is the relatively greater importance of intergovernmental assistance in the total revenue picture of the independent cities. Part of this difference can be assigned to variations in governmental arrangements, but it is equally clear that federal programs such as the Community Development Block Grants and General Revenue Sharing are providing more funds per capita to independent cities than to suburbs. This, of course, is consistent with the earlier finding that independent cities manifest more of the signs of distress than do their suburban counterparts.

The collection of revenues, of course, is only a means to an end, namely, the provision of public services. The decision-making process of matching expenditures with revenues is long and involved, and the outcomes in terms of services provided may differ widely by type of city and region within the state. The next chapter examines these outcomes and attempts to provide insight as to why independent cities and suburbs differ in spending patterns.

NOTES

1. Illinois Constitution of 1970, Article VII, Sec. (6e).
2. A detailed history of the municipal sales tax is available in Jack F. Isakoff, Gilbert Y. Steiner, and June G. Cabe, *Illinois Municipal Review,* 2nd ed. (Urbana, Ill.: Institute of Government and Public Affairs, 1958), and Glenn W. Fisher and Robert F. Fairbanks, *Illinois Municipal Finance* (Urbana: University of Illinois Press, 1968), pp. 141–144.
3. *Ill. Rev. Stat.,* chap. 24, sec. 8-11-5.
4. Part of this revenue may be from truck license fees also.
5. *Ill. Rev. Stat.,* chap. 24, sec. 11-10-1.
6. Frank M. Pfeifer, "Local Sources of Municipal Revenue" (Springfield: Illinois Municipal League, 1978).
7. Norman Walzer and Vickie S. Winters, "License Fees and User Charges in Illinois Cities," *Illinois Municipal Review,* Vol. 58, No. 6 (June 1979), pp. 12–15.
8. Illinois Constitution of 1970, Article VII, Sec. 6(1) and 7.
9. Arthur C. Thorpe, Jr., and Patrick A. Lucansky, "Special Assessment and Special Service Areas" in *Illinois Municipal Law,* ed. by Steward H. Diamond (Springfield: Illinois Institute for Continuing Legal Education, 1978), chap. 20, p. 20–11.
10. 54 Ill.2d. 200 (1973).
11. *Significant Features of Fiscal Federalism,* 1978–79 ed. (Washington, D.C.: Advisory Commission on Intergovernmental Relations, 1979), M-115, Table 54.
12. David B. Walker, "Categorical Grants: Some Clarifications and Continuing Concerns," *Intergovernmental Perspective,* Vol. 3, No. 2 (Spring 1977), pp. 14–15. Also see *Restructuring Federal Assistance: The Consolidation Approach* (Washington, D.C.: Advisory Commission on Intergovernmental Relations, 1979) 79-6, p. 3.
13. Deil S. Wright, *Understanding Intergovernmental Relations* (Belmont, Calif.: Wadsworth Publishing Co., 1978), p. 54.
14. Ibid., pp. 15–16.
15. Donald H. Haider, *When Governments Come to Washington* (New York: The Free Press, 1974).
16. A clear discussion of the controversies that developed during the passage of the renewal legislation is available in Richard P. Nathan and Charles F. Adams, Jr., *Revenue Sharing: The Second Round* (Washington, D.C.: Brookings Institution, 1977), esp. chapter 1.
17. The three-factor formula was the Senate version; the five factors were inserted

by the House. Because of the importance of the income tax and the high percentage of residents in urban areas, the allocation to governments in Illinois is based on the five factors.
18. With the revenue-sharing renewal, the state government share was eliminated in 1981 and made subject to the annual appropriations process for 1982 and 1983.
19. Nathan and Adams, *Revenue Sharing,* chap. 3.
20. Jim Dey, "Agencies Make Revenue Sharing Bids," *Champaign News-Gazette,* March 1, 1978.
21. In 1974, the ratio of capital expenditures to operating-maintenance expenditures was 1.92 to 1.0, whereas in 1976 this ratio had been reduced, on the average, to 1.66 to 1.0.
22. Norman Walzer and Randy Nyberg, *Revenue Sharing in Illinois Municipalities* (Springfield: Illinois Municipal Problems Commission, 1977).
23. An excellent discussion of how the various block grants compare to a set of common criteria regarding functional scope, discretion to recipient governments, program conditions and requirements, certainty of funds, and generalist involvement is provided in *Block Grants: A Comparative Analysis* (Washington, D.C.: Advisory Commission on Intergovernmental Relations, 1977). The following section relies heavily on this analysis.
24. Ibid., p. 19.
25. Ibid.
26. Ibid., pp. 31-36.
27. Several excellent publications describe the block grant programs. See *Community Development: The Workings of a Federal-Local Block Grant* (Washington, D.C.: Advisory Commission on Intergovernmental Relations, 1977), A-57; "Community Development Block Grants: The First Year," *Nation's Cities* (July 1975), pp. 22-36; David Garrison, "Community Development Block Grants: A Whole New Ball Game for City Hall," *Nation's Cities* (November 1974), pp. 49-58; and Paul R. Dommel et al., *Decentralizing Community Development* (Washington, D.C.: Department of Housing and Urban Development, 1978).
28. Garrison, "Community Development Block Grants," pp. 55-56.
29. A more complete treatment of the regulations and requirements can be found in the *Federal Register,* Vol. 43, No. 41 (March 11, 1978), pp. 8434-8490.
30. Richard P. Nathan et al., "Executive Summary, Preliminary Report on the Brookings Institution Monitoring Study of the Public Service Employment Program" (mimeo, 1978), Table 1. For additional discussion see *An Interim Report to the Congress of the National Commission for Manpower Policy: Job Creation Through Public Service Employment,* (Washington, D.C.: National Commission for Manpower Policy, 1978).
31. Carl W. Sternberg, "Block Grants: The Middlemen of the Federal Aid System," *Intergovernmental Perspective,* Vol. 3, No. 2 (Spring 1977), pp. 8-13.
32. See *Restructuring Federal Assistance: The Consolidation Approach* (Washington, D.C.: Advisory Commission on Intergovernmental Relations, 1979), 79-6.
33. As noted earlier, the income tax rates on corporations were increased in 1979 as part of the personal property tax replacement.
34. *Ill. Rev. Stat.,* chap 120, sec. 9-901(b).
35. *Ill. Rev. Stat.,* chap. 120, sec. 424.
36. Municipalities use different fiscal years. Thus in later analyses data will show that not all cities received the same amount per capita, since the amounts received during a particular year depend on the timing of the distribution.
37. U.S. Department of Labor, Occupational Safety and Health Administration,

Record-keeping Requirements Under the Occupational Safety and Health Act of 1970, (Washington, D.C.: Government Printing Office, 1975).

38. One estimate is that for Illinois cities larger than 25,000 the percent of property taxes levied for pension contributions was 27 percent, with four cities reporting that pensions represented more than 40 percent of the tax levy in 1976. See Norman Walzer, *Fiscal Note and Reimbursement Programs for State Mandates* (Springfield: Illinois Municipal Problems Commission, 1978), p. 55.
39. Legislation was passed in 1979 that provides for reimbursement of certain state mandates.
40. A more complete discussion of municipal borrowing procedures is available in Steward H. Diamond, ed., *Illinois Municipal Law* (Springfield: Illinois Institute for Continuing Legal Education, 1978), chap. 13.

Appendix: Table 4A–1. 1977 Per Capita Municipal Revenues

	Property Taxes	Gen. Sales Tax	Foreign Fire Ins.	Gross Receipts (Utilities)	Other Taxes	Total Local Taxes	Motor Vehicle License	Liquor License	Fran-chise Fee	Permit Inspection Fee	Fine Forfeit Fees	Other Licenses	Total Licenses
Independent													
Aurora	$120.54	$54.94	$0.37	—	—	$175.85	$2.10	$1.34	$0.32	$2.30	$2.97	$0.24	$ 9.27
Bloomington	84.37	69.44	0.43	—	$ 1.88	156.12	—	2.10	3.98	4.13	3.64	1.32	15.17
Carpentersville	28.77	19.23	—	$11.24	—	59.24	5.34	0.64	0.35	0.58	1.49	0.57	8.97
Champaign	36.85	51.44	0.36	14.56	—	102.88	—	2.03	—	1.90	3.12	0.50	7.55
Danville	67.01	54.58	0.61	—	11.86	134.06	—	1.47	0.82	1.09	1.55	0.61	5.54
Decatur	44.47	55.20	0.40	7.82	—	107.89	—	1.16	0.93	1.24	2.89	0.93	7.15
DeKalb	34.76	36.47	0.29	32.33	—	103.85	—	1.54	0.40	0.81	2.68	0.84	6.27
Elgin	72.41	54.44	0.40	—	0.91	128.16	5.68	1.13	0.08	3.10	3.83	0.59	14.41
Freeport	38.84	43.66	0.31	—	—	82.81	0.01	1.70	0.80	0.29	3.70	0.06	6.56
Galesburg	69.87	55.70	0.35	—	—	125.92	2.88	2.75	0.66	0.12	2.35	0.03	8.79
Joliet	111.44	56.21	0.50	—	—	168.15	4.56	2.11	—	2.81	3.84	0.22	13.54
Kankakee	55.15	71.47	0.49	—	—	127.11	0.20	2.16	0.62	1.16	2.77	—	6.91
Moline	89.66	65.09	0.62	—	12.52	167.89	2.48	1.93	0.49	2.36	3.55	0.72	11.53
Normal	33.48	16.42	0.13	21.02	1.31	72.36	—	1.11	1.18	1.80	3.39	—	7.48
North Chicago	11.33	7.08	0.11	15.49	—	34.01	0.97	0.86	—	0.73	1.51	1.28	5.35
Pekin	98.16	52.47	0.39	—	11.50	162.52	—	0.73	0.25	—	4.05	0.98	6.01
Peoria	94.20	66.07	0.43	—	—	160.70	—	1.22	1.14	2.40	5.57	0.80	8.97
Quincy	68.82	43.81	—	—	—	112.63	—	1.57	0.11	0.54	3.40	0.28	5.90
Rockford	72.48	52.97	0.43	—	—	125.88	5.57	1.66	0.59	2.16	4.32	0.52	14.82
Rock Island	93.37	28.20	0.31	—	—	121.88	2.98	2.26	0.63	1.93	2.71	0.98	11.49
Springfield	77.51	67.04	0.64	0.43	2.89	148.51	—	1.30	—	1.27	2.71	0.77	6.05
Urbana	49.48	29.92	0.28	28.66	—	108.34	—	1.43	—	1.69	5.40	0.49	9.01
Waukegan	66.62	51.52	0.32	—	—	118.46	4.40	1.57	—	2.36	4.77	0.74	13.84
Average	$ 66.07	$47.97	$0.39	$16.44	$ 6.12	$121.97	$3.10	$1.56	$0.80	$1.67	$3.31	$0.64	$ 9.29
(S.D.)	(28.29)	(17.53)	(0.14)	(10.59)	(5.50)	(36.46)	(2.04)	(0.53)	(0.86)	(1.00)	(1.09)	(0.36)	(3.26)

Appendix: Table 4A–1. *(continued)*

	Revenue from Services							State			Federal			
	Parking	Garbage Col- lection	Library	Rec./ Parks	Total	Invest- ments	All Other Rev.	Inc. Tax	Motor Fuel	Grants	Rev. Sharing	Grants	Other IGR	Total IGR	Total Revenue
Independent															
Aurora	$2.34	$—	$0.27	$2.76	$ 5.37	$13.16	$ 0.71	$13.16	$12.41	$1.02	$19.44	$12.98	$ 0.92	$ 59.93	$264.29
Bloomington	—	—	0.32	6.28	6.70	10.16	38.11	13.01	12.34	1.02	17.10	57.79	4.50	143.87	370.13
Carpentersville	—	—	—	—	—	5.33	3.24	12.83	11.29	0.56	9.15	88.91	0.58	123.32	200.10
Champaign	—	0.80	—	—	0.80	6.34	2.51	14.50	15.37	7.44	12.34	—	3.97	53.62	173.70
Danville	—	0.21	—	2.81	3.02	1.68	5.09	12.02	11.86	0.73	13.00	71.15	1.25	110.01	259.40
Decatur	9.81	—	0.25	—	10.06	11.73	61.02	13.24	11.76	0.62	11.83	9.81	18.12	65.38	269.40
DeKalb	—	—	—	0.35	0.35	8.99	32.77	14.19	13.05	—	15.02	21.71	4.63	68.60	220.83
Elgin	—	0.44	—	2.49	2.93	13.26	15.05	14.25	12.54	4.54	8.63	11.83	0.63	67.47	241.28
Freeport	—	2.05	0.53	0.20	2.78	12.00	5.59	13.71	12.62	—	13.00	1.09	1.28	41.70	151.44
Galesburg	—	2.80	0.95	3.92	7.67	6.34	0.33	13.57	12.90	3.69	16.21	5.06	7.45	58.88	207.93
Joliet	—	—	0.30	0.06	0.36	12.26	97.15	13.56	11.98	6.52	17.78	23.58	2.48	75.90	367.36
Kankakee	—	0.78	0.50	—	1.28	9.75	5.95	14.53	12.78	1.65	12.78	1.83	5.83	49.40	200.40
Moline	—	—	0.62	1.75	2.37	11.03	31.59	13.53	12.52	1.87	17.23	6.21	3.06	54.42	278.83
Normal	—	5.36	—	2.55	7.91	4.98	88.86	12.78	11.36	2.47	9.63	—	3.48	39.72	221.31
North Chicago	0.08	—	0.11	—	0.19	0.94	3.87	14.46	13.32	0.93	8.99	1.52	0.77	39.99	84.35
Pekin	1.37	8.05	—	—	9.42	5.01	28.52	13.47	13.73	3.73	14.97	—	0.53	46.43	257.91
Peoria	1.67	—	0.89	—	2.56	18.30	219.10[a]	13.72	12.73	7.55	17.01	42.75	5.28	99.04	508.67
Quincy	—	—	2.04	—	2.04	10.24	7.01	13.49	13.73	2.54	17.27	13.73	263.77[a]	311.04[a]	448.86
Rockford	—	0.65	0.28	—	0.93	12.73	68.96	13.98	12.42	0.90	17.27	0.85	5.68	51.10	274.42
Rock Island	—	6.21	—	8.08	14.29	8.33	35.84	13.34	12.29	1.23	15.25	46.63	7.94	96.68	288.51
Springfield	—	—	0.44	3.27	3.71	11.29	13.92	13.28	12.57	3.07	14.74	58.77	14.41	116.84	300.32
Urbana	7.45	0.88	0.29	—	8.62	6.76	5.85	14.34	12.23	0.16	11.68	9.06	0.15	47.62	180.35
Waukegan	2.40	—	0.48	—	2.88	4.59	54.45	13.13	11.55	0.67	14.49	16.35	4.08	60.27	254.49
Average	3.59	2.50	0.55	2.88	4.37	8.92	27.56	13.56	12.58	2.32	14.50	25.37	4.41	70.32	261.93
(S.D.)	(3.60)	(2.78)	(0.47)	(2.39)	(3.84)	(4.15)	(29.53)	(0.63)	(0.82)	(2.29)	(3.02)	(26.25)	(4.52)	(29.78)	(93.88)

	Property Taxes	Gen. Sales Tax	Foreign Fire Ins.	Gross Receipts (Utilities)	Other Taxes	Total Local Taxes	Motor Vehicle License	Liquor License	Fran-chise Fees	Permit Inspection Fees	Fines Forfeits Etc.	License Other	Total License
Chicago Suburban													
Addison	$ 44.15	$ 44.85	—	—	—	$ 89.01	$ 5.82	$0.59	—	$ 5.43	$2.92	$ 2.38	$17.12
Arlington Heights	56.00	39.08	$0.31	$18.62	$2.71	116.73	7.63	1.22	—	1.45	3.07	2.33	15.70
Berwyn	36.78	32.70	o.28	—	—	69.76	5.08	4.02	—	0.78	1.17	1.67	12.71
Bolingbrook	51.35	21.50	0.01	—	6.07	78.93	5.09	0.81	$0.13	7.26	2.22	0.59	16.01
Calumet City	27.81	67.41	0.16	—	0.12	95.51	7.33	3.12	—	1.99	1.37	1.65	15.45
Chicago Heights	108.36	46.22	0.43	—	—	155.01	5.54	1.66	—	1.46	1.48	2.41	12.55
Cicero	36.90	31.26	—	—	—	68.16	5.97	2.76	—	1.56	3.70	10.00	23.99
Des Plaines	71.24	69.64	0.50	—	1.31	142.69	8.72	1.73	—	6.13	2.11	4.04	23.56
Dolton	32.36	31.77	—	—	0.08	64.23	5.72	0.70	—	0.70	1.38	1.41	9.90
Downers Grove	85.45	59.85	0.31	—	—	145.61	—	0.46	—	2.66	2.37	0.23	5.72
Elmhurst	91.03	60.22	0.25	—	—	151.50	4.05	1.49	—	1.52	0.93	0.26	8.24
Elmwood Park	63.97	21.00	0.23	—	—	85.20	7.24	—	—	1.05	3.13	1.65	13.07
Evanston	118.65	34.04	0.41	50.76	0.72	204.58	12.12	0.58	—	2.65	7.74	2.21	25.29
Glenview	65.83	30.39	0.39	26.62	1.74	124.61	8.22	1.21	—	2.78	4.26	1.57	18.04
Harvey	53.05	39.27	0.26	22.75	—	115.33	5.63	0.81	—	0.61	2.74	2.14	11.93
Highland Park	113.45	44.48	0.38	32.80	—	191.11	8.43	1.32	—	3.79	1.57	0.63	15.75
Lansing	48.82	28.15	0.19	—	—	77.16	5.84	0.22	—	2.12	1.16	0.58	9.91
Lombard	37.56	76.64	0.27	—	0.74	115.21	4.80	1.38	—	2.13	2.08	0.72	11.11
Maywood	82.59	18.63	0.16	21.19	—	122.57	6.04	0.63	—	0.52	2.18	1.16	10.53
Morton Grove	65.72	48.42	0.34	—	0.94	115.43	8.60	1.52	—	2.26	3.18	1.85	17.40
Mt. Prospect	70.15	47.55	0.22	—	—	117.92	8.81	0.89	0.21	3.20	3.04	1.55	17.70
Naperville	74.05	48.51	0.27	35.97	—	158.79	4.66	1.16	—	5.56	2.32	0.14	13.83
Niles	33.60	95.40	0.33	26.72	0.60	156.66	6.78	1.68	—	2.98	2.78	3.42	17.64
Northbrook	88.58	63.02	0.53	—	—	152.13	7.77	1.04	—	12.00	1.67	1.82	23.29
Oak Lawn	56.04	52.47	0.24	—	1.01	110.66	8.01	1.06	—	2.61	1.55	2.83	16.06
Oak Park	117.75	31.83	0.25	37.18	—	187.01	10.34	—	—	3.23	7.57	—	21.14

Appendix: Table 4A–1. *(continued)*

	Property Taxes	*Gen. Sales Tax*	*Foreign Fire Ins.*	*Gross Receipts (Utilities)*	*Other Taxes*	*Total Local Taxes*	*Motor Vehicle License*	*Liquor License*	*Fran-chise Fees*	*Permit Inspection Fees*	*Fines Forfeits Etc.*	*License Other*	*Total License*
Palatine	38.09	43.49	0.32	—	1.58	83.48	3.48	1.52	—	3.30	3.88	1.17	14.16
Park Forest	37.91	21.39	0.27	9.55	—	69.12	6.43	0.75	—	0.42	2.64	1.10	11.34
Park Ridge	60.25	37.67	0.22	15.62	—	113.76	9.31	—	1.85	2.03	2.38	3.13	18.70
Schaumburg	1.25	106.65	—	—	—	107.90	5.08	2.19	—	17.12	3.27	2.54	30.20
Skokie	101.01	59.14	0.39	—	1.70	162.24	6.57	0.95	—	1.37	2.37	1.83	13.09
Wheaton	52.78	23.77	0.29	14.97	—	91.81	4.60	—	—	4.59	1.79	0.45	11.45
Wilmette	82.85	31.55	0.24	24.80	—	139.44	8.61	1.03	—	1.17	3.00	0.69	14.49
Average	66.00	15.64	0.29	25.97	1.49	122.68	6.82	1.33	0.76	3.29	2.70	1.90	15.70
(S.D.)	(29.22)	(20.78)	(0.11)	(11.08)	(1.55)	(38.12)	(1.95)	(0.83)	(0.79)	(3.42)	(1.52)	(1.77)	(5.38)
St. Louis Suburban													
Alton	$ 54.03	$ 43.29	$0.33	$12.11	—	$109.76	$2.40	$1.09	—	$ 2.39	$3.63	$ 1.50	$11.01
Belleville	41.98	47.99	0.48	—	—	90.45	2.47	1.15	0.11	0.73	1.75	0.74	6.95
Granite City	56.83	32.42	—	—	—	89.25	2.32	0.44	—	0.40	1.26	—	4.42
Average	50.95	41.23	0.41	12.11	—	96.49	2.40	0.89	0.11	1.17	2.21	1.12	7.46
(S.D.)	(1.73)	(7.99)	(0.11)	—	—	(11.51)	(0.08)	(0.39)	—	(1.07)	(1.25)	(0.54)	(3.32)

	Revenue from Services							State			Federal				
	Parking	Garbage Col-lection	Library	Rec./Parks	Total	Invest-ments	All Other Rev.	Income Tax	Motor Fuel	Grants	Rev. Sharing	Grants	Other IGR	Total IGR	Total Revenue
Chicago Suburban															
Addison	$ —	$ 0.61	$0.65	$—	$ 1.26	$ 9.51	$ 2.71	$12.92	$11.49	$—	$14.59	$—	$ 0.81	$39.81	$159.42
Arlington Heights	—	—	—	—	—	9.16	91.29	12.97	12.00	4.15	6.56	1.16	1.89	38.73	271.67
Berwyn	1.38	—	0.15	1.06	1.21	2.37	3.00	14.40	12.91	0.23	9.33	0.64	0.23	37.74	126.79
Bolingbrook	—	—	—	—	1.38	1.52	224.50[a]	14.24	12.35	1.02	7.97	5.78	3.79	45.15	367.49
Calumet City	—	1.53	0.06	—	1.59	7.33	20.09	13.18	11.47	0.88	9.46	1.31	7.25	43.55	183.52
Chicago Heights	—	1.37	0.74	—	2.11	6.40	11.18	13.50	11.95	0.24	17.39	1.14	9.94	54.16	241.41
Cicero	1.87	—	0.06	—	1.93	1.90	1.30	14.49	12.80	—	9.33	6.61	0.97	44.20	141.48
Des Plaines	—	10.21	0.76	—	10.97	10.49	19.34	14.30	12.82	—	10.17	—	—	37.29	244.34
Dolton	—	—	—	—	—	5.40	8.79	12.98	11.42	0.12	7.19	0.43	0.83	32.97	121.19
Downers Grove	—	7.46	0.98	—	8.44	13.74	8.84	13.19	11.61	0.80	8.86	—	0.19	34.65	217.00
Elmhurst	—	8.92	0.51	—	9.43	14.94	12.99	14.25	12.54	4.55	8.63	11.83	—	51.80	248.90
Elmwood Park	0.35	7.44	—	1.06	8.85	3.84	8.65	13.05	11.56	0.15	6.72	—	—	31.48	151.09
Evanston	—	—	2.45	4.94	7.39	10.76	53.64	14.22	12.75	4.21	9.79	26.92	12.16	80.05	381.71
Glenview	—	1.65	—	—	1.65	4.92	12.87	13.04	11.73	—	4.12	0.26	2.04	31.19	193.28
Harvey	0.12	—	0.20	—	0.32	5.77	6.06	13.80	12.15	25.70	13.54	0.84	8.26	74.29	213.70
Highland Park	—	2.19	1.74	9.76	13.69	9.68	3.63	13.31	11.74	2.73	4.85	6.45	—	39.08	272.96
Lansing	—	6.10	0.41	—	6.51	1.94	2.31	12.88	11.91	—	4.64	0.72	—	30.15	127.98
Lombard	1.18	—	0.78	—	1.96	17.62	6.71	13.86	12.21	—	11.01	0.26	—	37.34	189.95
Maywood	0.22	4.48	0.09	0.32	5.11	7.77	13.29	13.67	12.03	0.11	12.52	—	18.76	57.09	216.09
Morton Grove	—	—	3.11	—	3.11	9.23	4.83	13.26	11.67	5.37	6.95	—	—	37.25	187.25
Mt. Prospect	1.29	—	0.62	—	1.91	6.44	12.65	13.00	12.68	4.55	6.91	—	0.26	37.40	194.02
Naperville	1.22	—	0.94	—	2.16	9.35	105.35	13.50	12.23	1.51	9.14	3.93	8.11	48.42	337.91
Niles	—	—	—	—	—	10.46	7.71	14.08	12.39	0.48	12.01	—	5.60	44.56	237.03
Northbrook	—	—	2.76	—	2.76	5.81	12.09	12.59	11.53	0.60	5.11	0.28	7.74	37.85	235.93
Oak Lawn	—	5.78	—	—	5.78	13.77	87.46	12.55	12.10	0.65	8.29	6.21	4.88	44.68	278.41
Oak Park	—	—	2.69	3.52	6.21	10.59	12.72	14.23	12.76	3.22	11.36	11.83	0.37	53.77	291.44

Appendix: Table 4A–1. *(continued)*

	Revenue from Services							State			Federal				
	Parking	Garbage Col-lection	Library	Rec./ Parks	Total	Invest-ments	All Other Rev.	Income Tax	Motor Fuel	Grants	Rev. Sharing	Grants	Other IGR	Total IGR	Total Revenue
Palatine	—	—	—	—	—	5.89	21.61	12.62	11.13	3.02	5.22	2.95	13.16	48.10	173.24
Park Forest	1.21	—	1.29	4.82	7.32	4.61	4.96	13.12	11.75	1.18	6.45	10.77	0.15	43.42	140.77
Park Ridge	—	—	0.94	—	—	10.67	34.84	13.23	11.64	1.22	4.94	—	2.81	33.84	211.81
Schaumburg	—	—	—	—	—	10.63	11.17	13.18	12.10	—	11.64	0.46	1.73	39.11	199.01
Skokie	0.91	—	—	—	0.91	9.60	20.90	13.34	11.76	0.62	7.08	6.82	0.61	40.23	246.97
Wheaton	—	—	3.19	—	3.19	5.33	7.20	12.51	11.20	—	7.91	—	2.43	34.05	153.03
Wilmette	0.76	4.04	—	—	4.80	9.55	7.11	13.02	11.46	1.68	4.37	5.29	2.97	38.79	214.18
Average	0.96	4.75	1.14	3.64	4.52	8.09	19.92	13.41	11.99	2.76	8.61	4.91	3.57	43.10	217.31
(S.D.)	(0.55)	(3.17)	(1.04)	(3.29)	(3.54)	(3.88)	(26.61)	(0.59)	(0.50)	(5.06)	(3.17)	(6.14)	(4.69)	(11.14)	(65.78)
St. Louis Suburban															
Alton	$0.88	$—	$—	$3.04	$ 3.92	$ 7.94	$ 12.66	$14.49	$13.34	$ 0.02	$17.79	$—	$ 2.68	$48.32	$194.54
Belleville	—	3.04	0.35	0.30	3.69	7.52	3.27	12.96	11.94	1.16	8.53	1.07	1.84	40.77	150.89
Granite City	0.86	—	—	—	0.86	1.33	9.73	13.34	12.47	—	12.53	—	0.40	38.74	156.06
Average	0.87	3.04	0.35	1.67	2.82	5.60	8.55	13.60	12.58	0.59	12.95	1.07	1.64	42.61	167.16
(S.D.)	(0.01)	—	—	(1.94)	(1.70)	(3.70)	(4.80)	(0.80)	(0.71)	(0.81)	(4.64)	—	(1.15)	· (5.05)	(23.85)

Source: Statewide Summary of Municipal Finance in Illinois, 1977 (Springfield, Ill.: Office of the Comptroller, 1978).
Excluded from average.

Chapter 5

City Expenditures for Services

If asked about public services, most urban residents could list police protection, fire protection, and street maintenance, but relatively few could provide a detailed list of the many diverse activities in which city governments are involved. Running airports, hospitals, and mass transit systems, treating sewage, and disposing of refuse are just a few of the activities on which city governments spend tax dollars. In addition, cities have taken on a whole new array of basically private-sector development activities in recent years, including downtown rehabilitation, industrial development, and the issuance of mortgage revenue bonds.

Many factors determine the variety of services provided directly to residents and the other programs in which the city government is connected in some way. Historical trends and community leaders' philosophical attitudes are very important. Cities will have fewer services and generally lower expenditures, for instance, if council members do not trust or want to become involved with federal programs. The vitality of the economic base and fiscal resources available for financing services can also play an important role. Wealthy cities may provide a very different set of services than relatively poor cities. A city's location may also affect spending patterns because of institutional arrangements with other governments. In a closely settled area, a city may be able to enjoy cost reductions by making a cooperative arrangement with another city or cities to provide a particular service.

Although measuring public services is difficult without a large amount of data on types of services provided and estimates of their quality, it is possible to provide insight into spending patterns in the study cities and to relate the major variations to differences in city characteristics in some way. These comparisons will be imprecise. A multitude of sophisticated statistical analyses have produced diverse and sometimes inconsistent findings regarding which variables "explain" city government expenditures. It is particularly useful to compare the expenditures of suburban cities with the independent cities in an attempt to determine whether, as a result of the suburbanization process, any notable differences in expenditure patterns exist. While we would like to compare services, by necessity we must settle for per capita expenditures. However, to provide better insight into the expenditure components, information on employment and wages is also included.

This chapter examines city government expenditures and levels of employment for each major city service. Per capita expenditures and employment are used to permit a comparison between cities of different size. Comparisons are made mainly between independent cities and Chicago suburbs. At times, however, we compare Chicago with its suburbs. In a few instances, cities showed abnormally large or small expenditures because of a large federal grant or a large population component not common to other cities. As noted in the discussion, we dropped these cities from the analysis.

TOTAL EXPENDITURES BY CITY GOVERNMENTS

A brief picture of city government expenditures is provided in Table 5-1. Since city residents sometimes obtain a specific service from other governments, there are instances in which cities did not report an expenditure in a particular category. Later in the analysis, expenditures by special districts will be added to compute the total expenditures for services received by urban residents. The figures in Table 5-1 are unweighted averages, meaning that each city received equal weight regardless of population size. Data for Chicago are not included.

The Census Bureau shows four broad types of expenditures. The largest category, general expenditures, encompasses the common municipal functions and is used as the basis for comparisons in this chapter. General expenditures include all city expenditures except for utility, liquor store, and employee retirement or insurance trust expenditures. The term "general expenditures" used by the Census Bureau should not be confused with the "general fund" concept used in municipal budgeting. Payments for city services may be made from many different funds within a city budget. The largest of these funds is the general or corporate fund. General expenditure, as used in subsequent analyses, refers to all city expenditures—excluding the three types listed above—regardless of the fund from which payments are made.

According to Table 5-1, the average 1977 city government expenditure of the 60 cities was $161.85 per capita for functions provided by most cities. (The Census Bureau reports expenditures for other services, but these are provided by select cities and will be covered later in this chapter.) Police protection, fire protection, and streets clearly represented the largest city government expenditures, accounting for more than 50 percent of the total. Cities in the study spent an average of $97.64 per capita for these three services.

Table 5-1. 1977 Per Capita City Government Expenditures

Function	*Average Expenditure*	*Standard Deviation*	*No. of Cities Reporting*
Total city expenditures for common functions[a]	$161.85	$52.54	60
Public safety			
Police protection	38.14	10.74	60
Fire protection	25.87	7.71	58
Transportation			
streets	33.63	17.13	60
Environment and housing			
Sewage	11.64	14.88	50
Other sanitation	9.13	5.41	56
Parks and recreation	9.35	10.45	38
Government administration			
General government	12.36	5.90	60
General public buildings	4.77	6.97	58
Libraries	11.68	9.10	50
Interest on general debt	7.53	6.48	58
Other	30.14	27.17	58

Source: U.S. Bureau of the Census, *Finances of Municipalities and Township Governments, 1977* (Washington, D.C.: Government Printing Office, 1979), Table 22.

Note: *Because of size, Chicago was not included.

[a]Since the number of cities reporting differs, the individual entries will not sum to the total.

The cities vary in their arrangements with other governments for providing services. For example, only 38 cities reported expenditures for parks and recreation, and 50 reported library expenditures. Sewerage expenditures were not reported by some cities because sanitary districts treat and dispose of sewage. A city can report a low expenditure when it is responsible only for maintaining sewer lines within its boundaries, the major processing and disposal costs being covered by the sanitary district through a separate tax levy on urban residents. Differences in service arrangements can therefore explain the relatively large standard deviation for sewage expenditures. Likewise, health and hospital expenditures differ because only a few cities maintain hospitals. Certainly part of the wide variation in spending levels can be explained by differences in the quality of services.

City government expenditures are affected by many factors, including available revenues. In most instances, the final budget is a compromise among many participants in the decision-making process, each of whom has favorite projects to support. The resulting level of expenditures is almost impossible to predict with any certainty. Because budget decision making starts with existing spending levels, historical patterns play a large role in determining the levels of service. In other words, budgeting is incremental.

However, it seems reasonable to expect that city government expenditures are related to broad city characteristics such as the wealth of residents, population size or composition, form of government, and the possibility of financing additional services without increasing property taxes. A climate of taxpayer resistance to property tax increases is certain to have a major effect on expenditure levels.

Before launching into a detailed comparison of city expenditures on each service, we might attempt to identify some of the city characteristics associated with variations in expenditure levels.[1] Insight into some of the more important relationships will help explain the differences. We used multiple-regression analysis to unravel the relationships between per capita city expenditures and five city characteristics (Table 5-2).[2]

A major difficulty in comparing city government expenditures is that cost of living varies among cities. Higher expenditures in one city may result from wage differences, which only reflect variations in living costs. Ideally, one would like to have a cost-of-living index to use in a statistical analysis. However, detailed information about living costs, or even earnings, is not regularly collected for this group of cities. The most recent detailed comparisons of earnings are from the 1970 Census of Population.

Table 5-2. Correlates of Per Capita City Expenditures (*t*-Values in Parentheses)

Variables	*Regression Coefficients*	*Beta Coefficients*
Intergovernmental revenue per capita	1.08* (3.35)	0.43
Average monthly police earnings	.019* (2.89)	0.33
Assessed valuation per capita	14.42* (2.77)	0.31
Form of government (manager = 1; mayor = 0)	23.93* (1.96)	0.21
Population change	–0.62 (0.85)	–0.09
Type of city (independent vs. suburb)	7.12 (0.51)	0.06

Constant = 58.25   *F*-ratio = 9.57
R^2 adj. = 0.52   *N* = 51
Standard Error of Estimate = 39.57

*Significant at 5-percent.

Lacking a cost-of-living index, one possible way to adjust for differences in living costs is to include a wage or earnings variable for an occupation that is comparable among cities. Since we could not obtain information about private-sector wages for all cities, we included the average monthly earnings for police officers as a proxy for living costs. Due to training requirements, police officers provide a fairly comparable employment category across the sample. This variable appears to be the best available proxy for wage and living cost variations.

Hypothetically, one might expect that cities with greater wealth spend more on public services. Greater wealth certainly means that more police protection and fire protection is desirable. If greater wealth is associated with lower population density, greater per capita expenditures on streets are necessary. For these hypotheses to be supported, we must establish a positive relationship between per capita assessed valuation and expenditures. Later findings generally support this hypothesis.

In the previous chapter, we discussed the importance of intergovernmental aid in the financing of local services. City officials frequently find it possible to augment local revenues through a state or federal grant, provided that they spend local moneys on certain projects. In other cases, such as General Revenue Sharing, the funds are provided virtually without restrictions. When cities obtain additional intergovernmental aid, their expenditures are expected to increase.

One might also expect that form of government would be an important factor in expenditure determination. However, it is difficult to state in precisely which direction this variable will operate. City managers are usually hired on the grounds that a more professionally run city will be more efficient. But without detailed information about services provided, it is impossible to differentiate waste in expenditures from a preference for higher-quality services. Thus, we can determine only whether the presence of a city manager makes a difference in expenditure level.

Population change might also be expected to affect expenditure levels. It is reasonable to assume that growing cities need more capital construction such as sewage facilities and streets. These improvements will require higher expenditures, although not necessarily more per capita. Declining cities, on the other hand, might have less need for employees and might be able to cut back on services as their populations shrink. Certainly, these expenditure changes operate with a lag. Because of rigidities caused by unions or other institutions, it may be difficult for a city to eliminate positions even though the population is decreasing. In extreme cases, it may take several years for new property to be put on the tax rolls and for tax revenues to flow into the city treasury. During this adjustment process, one might find growing cities spending less per capita and declining cities spending more. In fact, this was Muller's conclusion in a study of large urban areas in 1975. Ladd, on the other hand, found a U-shaped relationship between per capita spending and population change.[3]

To determine whether population growth or decline during the first half of the 1970s is associated with per capita city expenditures, we included the percentage change in population between 1970 and 1975 in the regression equation. Given the above reasoning and Muller's earlier findings, a negative coefficient is expected. This is especially true because population change for only five years is considered.

Finally, type of city—independent or suburb—was included in the regression equation. A priori, we have no expectation of which sign will be found. The cities clearly differ in age, population composition, and economic base. Exactly how these characteristics translate into expenditure differences is difficult to conceptualize. We included a binary variable indicating type of city in the equation to determine whether any variation not associated with the other variables could be assigned to the city type. The regression results are provided in Table 5-2.

Data reported in Table 5-2 permit us to generalize about the sample cities and their expenditures before undertaking a more detailed examination of each expenditure type. First, cities in which living costs are higher had higher expenditures for municipal services. This is as expected since the cost of providing public services should be related to the level of wages in a city, and wages, in turn will vary with living costs. Cities in which wages are higher will have to spend more to provide the same number of inputs.

Second, cities receiving above average per capita intergovernmental assistance tend to have higher total expenditures. This in itself is not surprising.

The findings in Table 5-2 indicate that cities receiving $1 dollar per capita more in intergovernmental assistance spent, on the average, $1.08 more when the other factors had been considered.[4]

Third, cities with greater wealth (as measured by per capita assessed valuation) spent more for public services. On the average, an additional $100 per capita in equalized assessed valuation was associated with an additional $14.42 per capita spent on city-provided services. This relationship is significant at the 5-percent level.

Fourth, form of government also appears to matter where expenditures are concerned. Cities with city managers spent an average of $23.93 per capita more on services than did mayoral cities. Since expenditures rather than cost data are being considered, we have not raised questions about efficiency in providing services.

Finally, type of city—independent or suburb—and population change were not significantly related to total city expenditures when the other factors had been considered. This is not to say that the type of city is not a factor for certain types of services. However, whether a city is a suburb or an independent city per se does not seem to be a critical factor in overall expenditure levels. However, the importance of this variable may be reduced by its correlation with the wage term since wages in the suburbs are likely to be higher.

POLICE PROTECTION EXPENDITURES

Table 5-1 revealed that police protection represented the second largest city government expenditure for the study cities, averaging $38.14 per capita in 1977. Decisions about expenditures for police protection involve many factors. Residents' perceptions of personal safety in the city are high on the list. These attitudes, in turn, are influenced by news media coverage of crime and related events. The police chief's personality and negotiating abilities are also important, since the council must ultimately be persuaded to adopt his budget proposal. When making a presentation, the chief relies on trends in crime statistics, comparisons with other cities of personnel and equipment, staffing ratios suggested by professional associations, and other assorted guides such as clearance ratios or response times.

With the recent growth in public employee collective bargaining, the decision-making process has gained another participant. Professional associations and unions meet with city officials to present their list of wage and salary requirements. These organizations are usually well prepared to state their case and, without question, have enhanced the financial position of municipal police officers. The role of collective bargaining in determining expenditures for police protection is especially important in light of the relatively large proportion of these expenditures represented by personal services.

The amounts spent for police protection, by city type, are provided in Table 5-3. The independent cities averaged $35.61 per capita, compared with an average of $40.48 for Chicago suburbs. This difference is statistically significant at the 10-percent level. Chicago differs widely from its suburbs, spending $101.68 per resi-

Table 5-3. 1977 Per Capita Police Protection Expenditures, by City Type

	Police Expenditures	*Employment*[a] *per 10,000*	*Average Monthly Earnings*
Independent ave.	$ 35.61	20.18	$1,250
(S.D.)	(10.69)	(4.52)	(218)
Chicago suburbs ave.	40.48	20.12	1,476
(S.D.)	(10.54)	(4.75)	(177)
St. Louis suburbs ave.	33.37	20.66	1,170
(S.D.)	(10.38)	(6.88)	(100)
Chicago	101.68	52.28	1,509
Z (Chicago suburbs vs. independents)	1.69*	0.04	4.64**

Source: U.S. Bureau of the Census, *Finances of Municipalities and Township Governments, 1977* (Washington, D.C.: Government Printing Office, 1979), Table 22.

[a] Full-time equivalent

*Significant at 10-percent level.

**Significant at 5-percent level.

dent. The relatively large expenditures in Chicago may result from several factors, including large concentrations of lower socio-economic classes plus a large influx of commuters. Since suburban residents work and shop in the central city, additional police personnel are required for traffic control and related activities. The daytime population in Chicago is larger than the resident population, possibly causing the per capita expenditures to be higher.

The fact that older central cities of medium size have relatively high police expenditures is confirmed by data for Aurora, Joliet, Peoria, Rockford, and Waukegan. Their per capita police expenditures were among the highest in the independent cities, as shown in Appendix Table 5A-1. Comparable expenditures are found in Evanston, Maywood, and Oak Park in the suburban group, relatively old suburbs on the fringe of Chicago. Northbrook (a relatively high-income community on the north shore) is an exception among the suburbs, reporting an expenditure of $57.63 per resident. Lombard and Calumet City reported the highest police expenditures at $64.95 and $62.81 per capita, respectively.

Police protection expenditures represent predominantly personal services, with wages and salaries requiring as much as 85 percent of the total departmental expenditure.[5] Given the importance of wages and salaries, it makes sense to examine the differences among cities in employment per 10,000 residents and average monthly earnings. Examining employment patterns allows at least a basic understanding of the inputs used in providing police protection and permits insights into expenditure variations resulting from wage differences. The earnings data shown in Table 5-3 are not adjusted for length of service and other factors.[6]

Virtually no difference in staffing ratio is found between the two city types. Independent cities averaged 20.18 police officers per 10,000 residents, compared with an average of 20.12 in the Chicago suburbs. These findings are not surprising if national staffing guidelines are followed. A relatively wide variation, though, is found within each group. Independent cities ranged from 27.42 officers per 10,000 in Joliet to 12.30 per 10,000 in Normal. However, in Normal the university also provides a security force, which is not included in the employment totals.

Among the suburbs, the highest staffing pattern was found in Oak Park, a middle-class suburb experiencing in-migration of minorities from the western edge of Chicago. Discussions with municipal officials indicated that one way the city was accomodating for the in-migration and stabilizing neighborhoods was by increasing the visibility of public services. One of the most visible services is police protection, so that may explain the relatively high employment ratio. At the other extreme is Park Forest, a relatively new middle-class suburb south of Chicago.

Major differences between the city groups are found in a comparison of Chicago and the suburbs. Chicago employed 52.28 police officers per 10,000 population, compared with the average of 20.12 in the suburbs. This difference is somewhat overstated, however, since the populations are determined by night-time residents. As explained earlier some of the police protection in the city of Chicago is necessary to accommodate daytime commuters.

Another major element explaining police expenditures is the wage paid to police officers. The most complete information available is the monthly payroll for full-time employees. We obtained the earnings data in Table 5-3 by dividing the number of full-time employees into the monthly payroll. Distribution by rank and seniority within the police departments affects these figures, but information in this detail is not readily obtainable. Furthermore, the earnings data do not include employee benefits, which may run upward of 45 percent of pay.[7]

A significant difference was found between independent cities and Chicago suburbs in average monthly earnings of police personnel. The independent cities paid police personnel an average $1,250 per month, compared with $1,476 in the suburbs. There was much less difference between earnings of Chicago police officers ($1,509) and those in the suburbs. The greater similarity between Chicago and the suburban cities may reflect a common labor market for police personnel. This explanation is certainly supported by the wide differences between the independent cities and the suburbs.

The comparisons in Table 5-3 suggest that higher expenditures for police protection in the suburbs largely reflect wage differences rather than differences in numbers of police officers. The cost of living in the suburbs is probably higher than in downstate cities, and in real terms the earnings may not be substantially different. Regardless of whether police personnel in the suburbs have higher earnings in real terms or not, employing the same number of officers per 10,000 residents is considerably more expensive in the suburbs. Police departments in these cities may also be better trained and have more equipment.

We should also point out that police protection expenditures of equal amounts in two cities may represent considerably different types of services. In a wealthy suburb, for instance, the police department may spend more time routinely patrolling the homes of vacationers or may be trained to handle special emergencies such as kidnapings. Police in cities containing predominantly lower socioeconomic populations probably spend a disproportionate share of their time investigating family disturbances and property crimes.

FIRE PROTECTION EXPENDITURES

Police protection and fire protection services are similar in some aspects. They are commonly housed in the same public safety building. Both provide emergency services to residents. A parity pay arrangement may exist whereby police officers and firefighters receive similar pay levels and increases. Usually police and fire departments are organized in a military structure involving ranks. Personnel in both departments have recently emphasized professionalism, with considerable attention paid to improved training. Finally, there has been a large movement in recent years toward collective bargaining for both groups of employees.

The decision-making process underlying expenditures for fire protection services differs in at least one important way, however. Companies underwriting fire insurance have grouped together to develop a city rating system whereby they can obtain an estimate of the potential risk from fire loss in each city. The Insurance Services Office periodically assigns a protection class rating for each city. The rating is based on a study of the city's water supply, fire personnel and equipment, fire service communications, and fire safety control.[8] Although the system was revised in July 1980, the expenditure data are for 1977, so we will explain the system in operation at that time. Cities were rated according to a system of 5,000 deficiency points, with the cities grouped into classes of 500 deficiency points each. A rating class of 1 meant the lowest risk (best fire protection availability), and a class of 10 implied virtually no protection at all.

This rating system created considerable controversy between the Insurance Services Office (ISO) and municipal officials, who did not agree on the components used in the rating process and the importance of each.[9] Municipal officials claimed that the ISO paid too much attention to traditional firefighting technology, which makes heavy use of manpower and equipment with a large pumping capacity. To obtain a more favorable rating according to these guidelines, a city would have to spend large amounts and even then would have no assurance that an improved rating would mean lower insurance rates for residents.

The Insurance Services Office took the position that the protection classifications were meant only as a guide for insurers and were not designed to evaluate a fire department or to increase the fire department budget. The ISO further claimed that it was not worthwhile for local officials to spend large sums to advance their rating by one or two classes, since many insurance companies charge the same rates for property in several classifications.

Regardless of the use of the rates or the merits of the methods used in computing them, it is quite clear that the assigning of protection class ratings entered into the municipal resource allocation process:

> The effect has been that the ISO has acted as an unelected local policymaker by forcing basic local fire protection decisions. In effect the insurance industry has taxed the citizens twice; once through paying for public fire protection, and again through insurance premiums.[10]

While the fire protection rating system probably enters the decision-making process, other factors cause variations in city fire protection expenditures. Perhaps the greatest difference results from variations in the protection provided through a special district, distinct from the city government. It is common for a special district to be established in rural areas and small communities so that many residents can share the cost of firefighting equipment. These districts provide limited services, mainly fire suppression, and commonly have a mutual assistance pact with other governments in the area so that, in the event of a major fire, they can rely on outside support. As an urban area expands, it requires more complete fire protection services and usually establishes a municipal department. Where there are legal obstacles to dissolving the original fire protection district, sometimes—but infrequently—a city is served by both a municipal department and a special district.

Fire protection expenditures in two cities also differ significantly due to variations in services even when the same governmental arrangement exists. Some cities employ a paramedic team within the fire department. Others provide an ambulance service. In still other cities, though, these functions are provided by the private sector. The quality and amount of service are reflected in expenditures for fire protection.

Although services cannot be measured directly, a reasonably clear estimate of the cost to provide them is available. Table 5-4 lists per capita expenditures for fire protection by city type. As can be seen, the Chicago suburbs averaged $24.40 per resident for fire

Table 5-4. 1977 Per Capita Fire Protection Expenditures, by City Type

	Fire Protection Expenditures	*Employees[a] Per 10,000*	*Average Monthly Earnings*	*ISO Protection Class*
Independent ave.	$28.05	15.3	$1,328	4.7
(S.D.)	(7.61)	(3.8)	(254)	
Chicago suburbs ave.	24.40	12.3	1,507	5.1
(S.D.)	(7.81)	(4.0)	(182)	
St. Louis suburbs ave.	25.65	15.7	1,310	5.3
(S.D.)	(6.00)	(3.6)	(144)	
Chicago	34.87	15.7	1,612	5.0
Z (independent vs. Chicago suburbs)	1.75*	2.7**	2.9**	

Source: U.S. Bureau of the Census, *Finances of Municipalities and Township Governments, 1977* (Washington, D.C.: Government Printing Office, 1979), Table 22; *1976 Municipal Yearbook* (Washington, D.C.: International City Management Association, 1976), Table 1/1.

*Significant difference at 10-percent.

**Significant difference at 5-percent.

[a] Full-time equivalent

protection in 1977, compared with an average of $28.05 per resident in the independent cities. The St. Louis suburbs spent an average of $25.65 per capita, very close to other Illinois cities of similar size. Chicago, on the other hand, spent $34.87 per resident.

The fact that suburbs spent less on fire protection leads one to ask whether this difference might not be a result of cost-sharing arrangements. If two cities in close proximity could share expensive equipment, both could have better service at lower cost. In practice, mutual assistance pacts are common among the suburbs.

Some insight into whether these mutual aid pacts contribute to lower expenditures can be gained by comparing the ratio of firefighters to residents (Table 5-4). The average Chicago suburb employs 12.3 firefighters per 10,000 residents, compared with an average of 15.3 per 10,000 in the independent cities. While this comparison is consistent with the idea of cost sharing in the suburbs, differences in city characteristics are also responsible for variations in staffing patterns. A city with numerous railroad crossings may need additional fire stations to obtain access to all areas in the city. The fire hazard could be higher in independent cities, which tend to have older, poorer housing, and could thus require a larger fire protection staff. While differences in staffing ratios result from all these factors, mutual aid pacts may indeed be a significant component.

As in the case of police protection, the main component of the fire department budget is personal services. Fire department activities are labor intensive, with wages and salaries representing as much as 80 to 85 percent, depending on how pension contributions are treated. Thus, even though the Chicago suburbs employ a lower ratio of firefighters to population, they pay higher wages, offsetting much of the cost savings. The average monthly earnings of firefighters in the Chicago suburbs was $1,507, compared with an average of $1,328 in the independent cities. Of course, differences in living costs among the cities could offset much of this difference in average monthly earnings, but without detailed information about living costs we could not test this proposition.

A more complete listing of city expenditures is given in Appendix Table 5A-2. Waukegan reported the highest fire protection expenditure within the independent cities, $38.14 per resident. Its adjoining city, North Chicago, had the lowest expenditure, $10.67 per capita. The suburban cities ranged from $42.44 per resident in Bolingbrook to a low of $9.76 in Lansing. The low expenditures reported by several cities may reflect the use of volunteers, who are paid according to the frequency they are called into service.

Because of its perceived importance in determining fire protection expenditures, the Insurance Services Office fire protection class is shown in Table 5-4. Although not designed as an evaluative measure, the rating has come to be used in that way. A comparison between the two city groups indicates that, on the average, the independent cities rate slightly better than the suburbs.

Police and fire protection represent major components of the municipal budget, as well as a source for much heated discussion in council meetings. The nature of the services makes effective protection essential, while the growth of employee organizations has made the negotiations process more demanding. Not only do local officials have to agree on wages with the employees or their representatives, but they also have to finance pension benefits mandated by the state legislature. In recent years, the growing burden of retirement benefits has become critical. Local officials have been forced to raise property taxes to finance the mandated benefits at the same time that residents are protesting higher property taxes. In some cities, the cost of the pension program has become staggering and represents as much as 35 to 40 percent of property tax collections.

EXPENDITURES FOR STREETS

If police and fire protection represent the crisis services provided by city governments, street maintenance is certainly among the most visible. When potholes are not filled or when snow is not removed within a few hours, the mayor's office is likely to be beseiged with phone calls from irate residents. Streets are also important because they can affect property values. When the public infrastructure in a neighborhood is not in good condition, the quality of the neighborhood declines and so can property values.

Deciding how much street repair to undertake and in which part of the city can cause conflict in council meetings. Perhaps more than any other city service, street maintenance represents direct evidence of a council member's efforts. Residents can see their money being spent and know that their neighborhood is benefiting directly.

In the study cities, streets represented a major expenditure category, with an average of $33.63 per capita spent in 1977. The amount spent for streets is a function of many factors, including the amount of funds provided by the State of Illinois through the motor fuel tax rebate program. A city council can hold the street program in abeyance until an agreement on other services has been reached. Ordinarily, streets are not in poor enough shape to require emergency expenditures that will consume the entire street budget. On the other hand, if additional funds are available at the end of the fiscal year, there is always a need for street improvements.

Expenditures are also related to the weather. A hard winter can cause higher expenditures for snow removal or can necessitate greater expenditures for resurfacing. This is not to suggest that city officials do not follow a long-range plan of street upgrading and improvement in many cases. Rather, it is to suggest that the amounts spent and the projects undertaken may vary from those planned, depending on unpredictable events such as the weather.

Local decisions about streets are also affected by the standards imposed by the Illinois Department of Transportation regarding the spending of motor fuel tax funds. The department establishes standards, based on expected usage, for street width, base, thickness of surface, and related characteristics. When motor fuel tax (MFT) funds are to be used, approval must be obtained from the Illinois Department of Transportation before the project can be undertaken. The approval requirement has caused delays during which the cost of construction has increased markedly, sometimes even threatening completion of the project.

The state considers the approval system necessary because state revenues are provided to local governments for their use. Standards are imposed to ensure that the transportation system meets basic requirements. Requiring state approval helps local governments make certain that the streets will withstand expected usage and be adequate for handling the expected traffic volume.

From the view of a local official, however, the approval process can be irritating. First, local officials may think they have a better perspective on the needs of the community and the services it can afford. A common complaint is that the state requirements surpass those actually needed and make the cost of the project excessive. Second, as cities become better staffed, or can obtain the services of consulting engineers, the need for close supervision by the state decreases.

Depending on the city's accounting system, expenditures for streets are usually shown in the year in which they occur. Thus,a a large street expansion program financed from borrowed funds may distort street expenditure comparisons in any particular year. For this reason, capital expenditures have been shown separately from total expenditures by the street department in Appendix Table 5A-3. The expenditures used in subsequent comparisons pertain to the streets under city government control, although they may include state highways within the city limits. In the past, Illinois cities in some instances have had to agree to assume responsibility for maintaining certain streets in return for improvements financed by the state. This arrangement often met with opposition from city officials, who felt they were being coerced into higher expenditures or being required to withstand local pressures from not having the streets upgraded.

Based on the comparison in Table 5-5, independent cities spent considerably more on streets, averaging $39.34 per resident, compared with an average of $30.64 in the suburbs. One might hypothesize that the lower suburban expenditures are a result of more recent growth in these cities and the likelihood that the streets are in better condition. New developments annexed to a city usually already have streets.

Further breakdown of street expenditures into salaries and employment shows that the independent cities employ a significantly higher number of employees per 10,000 residents than suburban cities. However, the average monthly earnings by street employees are not significantly different between the two city groups.

A major difference in staffing patterns is found between Chicago suburbs and the city of Chicago. Chicago employs 11.9 street

Table 5-5. 1977 Per Capita Street Expenditures, by City Type

	Expenditures	Employment[a] per 10,000 Pop.	Ave. Monthly Earnings	Miles per 10,000 Pop.	MFT Authorizations (1975–1977)
Independent ave.	$39.34	7.3	$1,131	29.5	$ 8.31
(S.D.)	(20.63)	(4.3)	(199)	(7.6)	(3.31)
Chicago suburbs ave.	30.64	5.3	1,197	21.2	11.17
(S.D.)	(14.08)	(2.3)	(284)	(5.4)	(4.02)
St. Louis suburbs ave.	23.96	9.3	1,240	34.5	11.03
(S.D.)	(7.95)	(3.6)	(209)	(7.9)	(5.19)
Chicago	26.85	11.9	1.464	10.7[b]	14.00[c]
Z (independent vs. vs. Chicago suburbs)	1.76*	2.04**	1.02	4.51**	2.91**

Source: U.S. Bureau of the Census, *Finances of Municipalities and Township Governments, 1977* (Washington, D.C.: Government Printing Office, 1979), Table 22; MFT authorizations and street mileage obtained from Illinois Department of Transportation (IDOT).
*Significant at 10-percent level.
**Significant at 5-percent level.
[a]Full-time equivalent
[b]Estimated by Illinois Department of Transportation
[c]Includes funds allocated to RTA

workers for each 10,000 residents, compared with fewer than half that number in the average Chicago suburb. One is immediately tempted to attribute the relatively large number of employees in Chicago to patronage, but another possible explanation is that the additional workers are needed to accommodate traffic from commuters in the central city. The average earnings of street employees in Chicago are substantially higher than in the suburbs, with Chicago employees averaging $1,464 per month compared with a suburban average of $1,197.

Insight into the need for street employees and expenditures can be obtained from an examination of the street density, that is, miles of streets per 10,000 residents. The average independent city had 29.5 miles of streets per 10,000 population in 1977, compared with an average of 21.2 miles in the Chicago suburbs. The city of Chicago, on the other hand, had an estimated 10.7 miles per 10,000 residents. The comparisons between Chicago and its suburbs are particularly interesting since Chicago spends less per capita on streets but pays higher wages to more employees—even when adjusted for population.

Much of the difference among cities in street employment can be related to the use of independent contractors. In some cities, particularly the smaller ones, streets are constructed by private contractors rather than by city crews. In larger cities, more of the repair work and new construction may be undertaken by city employees. Cities may also finance streets differently. For instance, developers may be required to construct streets and dedicate them to the city. Thus, the city does not incur the cost of constructing the streets and can therefore employ fewer workers.

Because of the importance of motor fuel tax rebates in the financing of municipal streets, we have included the average authorization from MFT funds between 1975 and 1977 in Table 5-5. Although cities are allocated these funds based on population, they are actually reimbursed for expenditures on approved projects. Thus, it is possible, and even likely, that major differences in amounts spent will be found during a particular period. The 1975-1977 data clearly illustrate such differences: the average independent city received annual authorizations of $8.31 per resident, whereas the average suburb received $11.17.

Again, much variation is found within each city group (Appendix Table 5A-3). In most instances, cities with large expenditures had capital or construction expenditures. Thus, the $82.09 per resident spent by Peoria includes construction costs of $37.77 per resident. In general, the capital expenditures by suburban cities, especially those in the Chicago area, are lower than those made by independent cities. If the thesis that newer cities face lower costs for replacement and maintenance is true, then one might expect relatively new cities—Park Forest, Schaumburg, or Bolingbrook—to have comparatively low expenditures for streets. In fact, this is correct. Schaumburg and Bolingbrook are among the lowest in total street expenditures, and Park Forest is well below the average of the Chicago suburbs. Likewise, many of the older cities—both suburban and independent—have relatively high expenditure levels. Aurora, Joliet, and Waukegan are among that group.

SEWAGE DISPOSAL AND SANITATION EXPENDITURES

Police protection, fire protection, and street maintenance are provided by nearly every city government, although in a few instances fire protection is provided by special districts. Sewage treatment and disposal, however, involves large capital expenditures and offers many opportunities for cost-sharing arrangements. As a result, cities sometimes cooperate by financing this service through a special district. In these instances, each city maintains the lines in the city, with the special district financing

Table 5-6. 1977 Per Capita Sewage and Sanitation Expenditures, by City Type

	Municipal Sewage Expenditure	*Sanitary District Levy*	*Other. Sanitation Expenditure*	*Total Sewage and Sanitation Expenditure*
Independent Ave.	$15.46	$13.23	$ 8.47	$29.93
(S.D.)	(17.94)	(8.07)	(4.42)	(17.07)
Chicago suburbs Ave.	8.81	19.45	9.69	33.06
(S.D.)	(12.52)	(7.92)	(6.29)	(12.18)
St. Louis Ave.	15.95	12.62	8.51	30.77
(S.D.)	(15.85)	(5.69)	(3.07)	(12.02)
Chicago	10.67	15.39	28.33	54.39
Z (independent vs. Chicago suburbs)	0.62	1.93*	0.82	0.73

Source: U.S. Bureau of the Census, *Finances of Municipalities and Township Governments, 1977* (Washington, D.C.: Government Printing Office, 1979), Table 22.
*Significant at 10-percent.

the treatment facilities. The special district levies a tax on all property in the district.

Because of the financing through special districts, we have adjusted expenditures of the cities to include the taxes paid by residents to the sewage, or sanitary, districts. In the subsequent analysis, the taxes levied by the district have been assumed to approximate the expenditures by the district and are added to the costs of the city for maintaining the collection system. This estimation of the cost to the city will be closest to the actual cost when the district encompasses the entire city and when the district is financed entirely from property taxes.

The decision-making process concerning expenditures for sewage treatment and disposal is heavily influenced by environmental regulations. A recent and growing concern about environmental standards has led to requirements for local governments to improve their treatment systems. These improvements have often been very expensive. While partial support from the federal and state government has been provided for improvements, this aid virtually always requires matching funds.

Municipal expenditures for sewage and sanitation are shown in Table 5-6. In 1977 the average suburban city government spent $8.81 per resident, considerably less than the average $15.46 per capita spent by the independents. However, the capital expenditures of two independent cities, Carpentersville and Quincy, were high enough to affect the group average significantly (Table 5A-4).

Relatively few suburban cities reported large capital expenditures, the single exception being Lombard, where $39.99 per capita was spent. Chicago's expenditures for sewage treatment and disposal were not substantially different from its suburbs'. The average independent city resident paid $13.23, whereas the suburban residents paid $19.45. Fifteen of the 23 independent cities were included in a sanitary district, while 28 of the 32 suburbs belonged to such districts. Special districts in the suburbs offer potential cost savings when capital facilities can be shared. The Metropolitan Sanitary District of Greater Chicago, serving most of Cook County, is a primary example of this cooperative effort.

If use can be related to population, financing the sewage districts at least partly from property taxes can mean that wealthier cities subsidize poorer cities. Highland Park, for instance, is a high-income suburb. Its share of the tax levy for the sanitary district was $47.47 per resident, compared with a payment of $10.53 per capita in Maywood. The explanation for this difference is that the per capita assessed valuation in Highland Park ($6,380) is substantially above that in Maywood ($2,689).

The city sewer system is not completely financed from property taxes, however. Many cities also collect sewerage charges. For instance, during 1977, 38 of the study cities collected an average of $11.63 per resident. In light of the average expenditures shown earlier, these charges represent a substantial portion of the revenues used in financing these services.

When expenditures by cities are combined with property tax levies by sanitary districts, the average cost per resident in the independent cities in 1977 was $29.93, compared with an average of $33.06 in the suburbs. The main difference was found between Chicago and the suburbs. The cost per resident in Chicago was $54.39, compared with the $33.06 in the suburbs.

OTHER SANITATION SERVICE EXPENDITURES

The Census Bureau groups expenditures for solid waste disposal or refuse collection and street-cleaning operations in a general category called "other sanitation." While these functions are provided in virtually every city, significant differences are found in the arrangements for their provision, particularly with regard to refuse collection. These differences cause substantial variations in city expenditures for similar services.

Municipal solid waste collection can be arranged in one of three ways. A municipal crew supported by a property tax levy can be used. Based on a recent survey of Illinois cities larger than 25,000, approximately 38 percent of the cities responding used this collection method.[11] A second alternative is for the city to contract with a private collector. Such a contract could be financed either from the general fund or a special tax. The 1978 survey revealed that 33 percent of the Illinois cities responding used this approach. A third method is to allow competition among private collectors, with the city council regulating the maximum rate allowable. In this last instance, the city may charge a license fee for the privilege of collecting within the city limits. In 1978, 29 percent of the Illinois cities used this competitive arrangement for solid waste collection.

Seventeen of the 47 cities responding to the survey indicated that refuse collection was financed from a tax levy, while the remainder employed a service charge. Census of Governments data show that 22 cities in this study charged for sanitation service, collecting an average of $4.12 per capita. The services differed, especially in the number of collections per week. Sixty-two percent of the cities provided one collection per week, and the remaining 38 percent provided collection service twice each week. The types of refuse collected also varied.

Table 5-6 shows the city government expenditures for sanitation services. As the data indicate, major differences were not found between the city groups. The average independent city spent $8.47 per capita, while the average suburb spent $9.69 per resident in 1977. Within the city groups, however, major differences were found. An expenditure of only 24 cents per capita was reported in Park Forest, compared to the $27.61 per resident reported in Wilmette (Table 5A-4). The precise reason for these variations is not known, but we can reasonably assume that they are related to differences in the collection arrangements and services provided.

PARKS AND RECREATION EXPENDITURES

The provision of parks and recreational services frequently involves a special district. Bond and debt limitations in effect prior to the introduction of home rule offer one explanation for the popularity of these districts. Special districts, offer several advantages. First is the expanded taxing power they afford. Second, with a single-purpose government, residents interested in a particular service need not compete with other demands for municipal funds. And, not least of all, the prospect of serving on a district board or governing agency also offers citizens an opportunity to participate in government, to promote their stature in the community, and to advance their professional careers.

Special districts are not without their limitations, however. In particular, coordination problems can arise when multiple districts serve the same population. Residents in the same city may reside in different park districts having substantially different tax rates. Since many park and recreation activities are open to the public, residents in a city with more than one park district may pay different costs for similar services. This example is not limited to park districts; it applies to any service provided by special districts financed from general property taxes instead of user charges.

In the Chicago area, the Forest Preserve of Cook County provides open areas and recreational opportunities to Cook County residents. Residents pay taxes to this district in the same way they pay taxes to a municipal government or other government in their locality.

City government expenditures for parks and recreational activities are shown in Table 5-7. The average independent city spent $11.69 per resident in 1977, compared with an average of $7.28 per capita in the Chicago suburbs. Expenditures by Chicago were $4.48 per resident. However, that city is also served by the Chicago Park District, a separate government entity. Expenditures by the City of Chicago primarily represent the costs of maintaining beaches.

Seventeen of the 23 independent cities (74 percent) were served by park districts, compared with 28 of the suburban cities (88 percent). The average tax collection by park districts in the independent cities was $13.38 per capita, compared with $19.48 per resident in the suburbs. The taxes levied by the Forest Preserve of Cook County were included as part of the park district levies for the suburbs.

We approximated the total cost to residents of park and recreational activities by summing municipal expenditures and park district tax levies. The average for the independent cities is $18.53 per resident, compared with $20.70 in the Chicago suburbs (Table 5-7). Given the variations among cities, this difference is not significant at the usual levels. In a few instances, cities reported large capital expenditures that made substantial differences in the averages.

A major difference, however, was found between expenditures for parks in Chicago and those in the suburbs. As shown in the table,

Table 5-7. 1977 Per Capita Expenditures for Parks, Libraries, and General Governments, by City Type

	Municipal Park & Rec. Expenditures	*Park District Levy*	*Total Municipal and Park District Levy*	*Library Expenditures*	*Administrative Expenditures*
Independent ave.	$11.69	$13.38	$18.53	$ 8.73	$14.90
(S.D.)	(11.41)	(4.43)	(9.17)	(5.18)	(9.85)
Chicago suburbs ave.	7.28	19.48	20.70	14.24	18.41
(S.D.)	(9.96)	(7.63)	(8.55)	(10.73)	(10.27)
St. Louis suburbs ave.	14.00	7.42	16.07	6.51	17.14
(S.D.)	(4.40)	(3.99)	(4.10)	(1.93)	(9.48)
Chicago	4.48	35.36	39.84	7.30	25.04
Z (independent vs. Chicago suburbs)	1.20	3.45**	0.89	2.48**	1.29

Source: U.S. Bureau of the Census, *Finances of Municipalities and Township Governments, 1977* (Washington, D.C.: Government Printing Office, 1979), Table 22.

**Significant at 5-percent.

the major per capita expenditure in 1977 was made by the Chicago Park District, a government distinct from the city (although its board is appointed by the mayor). The park district has been a site of patronage, which may be a partial explanation for Chicago's higher expenditures.[12] Expenditures for parks in Chicago will be better understood when we compare Chicago with other cities having populations over 1 million (Chapter 6).

LIBRARY EXPENDITURES

While library districts are not nearly as common as park districts, a potential attraction of such a special government is that residents outside the city limits can have access to library facilities where they otherwise might not. In addition to being financed from property taxes, libraries also collect fees for services and benefit from private philanthropic contributions.

Table 5-1 shows that 50 cities in the present study reported an average expenditure of $11.68 per resident for libraries. Table 5-7 shows that the average independent city spent $8.73 per resident for library services in 1977, compared with an average of $14.24 per resident in the suburbs. Chicago spent $7.30 per capita, or about half the suburban expenditure. Not all revenues used to support library services are obtained from property taxes, however. In our sample, 38 cities reported receiving an average of 88 cents per capita from fees involving library services. These fee revenues represent a relatively small proportion of the total library expenditures. Libraries, in turn, represent a relatively small portion of the total municipal expenditures.

EXPENDITURES FOR CITY ADMINISTRATION

Not to be overlooked in an examination of city expenditures are the moneys spent to finance an administrative staff to collect revenues, establish priorities for services, and otherwise manage daily operations. Conducting the city business requires a multitude of groups and activities, including the city council, the executive offices, and ancillary services such as planning and zoning. The Census Bureau subdivides these activities into general control, financial administration, general government, and general public building activities. *General control* is handled by the city council and office of the mayor or manager, as well as the staff or agencies concerned with personnel administration, law, recording, planning, zoning, and similar activities. *Financial administration* is handled by municipal agencies involved with assessment and collection, auditing, accounting, budgeting, purchasing, and related functions. *General government* is a broad classification including activities that cannot be conveniently grouped into the other categories. The *general public buildings* category includes expenditures on public buildings, which are not allocated to particular functions. Precisely what is included in this category depends to a great extent on the city's system of accounting. Comparisons of expenditures for construction or maintenance of general public buildings, therefore, should be undertaken with caution.

In Table 5-7, the four Census Bureau categories of general control, general government, financial administration, and public buildings have been lumped together because different organizational structures within a city government may cause expenditures to be recorded in different departments. The average independent city spent $14.90 per resident for administrative activities, compared with an average of $18.41 per capita in the Chicago suburbs. Major differences among cities were encountered (data not shown). In the independent group, Bloomington reported an expenditure of $53.38 per capita, and Quincy reported a low of $5.30 per capita. The suburbs ranged from $5.35 per capita in Lansing to $46.16 per capita in Naperville. Overall, however, the difference in the administrative expenditures between the two city groups was not significant.

EXPENDITURES FOR SEMICOMMERCIAL OPERATIONS

In addition to the traditional municipal services previously described, city governments provide a group of services that are financed largely by charges and fees. These services, commonly termed semicommerical operations, include parking facilities, airports, hospitals, and similar activities. A common approach is to finance the service through a revenue bond issue retired from the sales of services. In some cases the city bills the project for administration expenses and receives a transfer to the corporate fund to cover these costs. The essential difference between the semicommercial or enterprise operations and the common municipal services lies in the manner of financing. Semicommercial operations are more nearly self-supporting; residents receiving the services pay for them in proportion to use.

Water Supply

The financing of water distribution within a city commonly involves an enterprise fund. Fifty-five of the cities in this study spent an average of $38.76 per resident on this service. The vast majority of the revenue was derived from charges to residents and, in some cases, from the sale of water to residents outside the city limits. Since water and sewage charges are frequently on the same bill, it is difficult to separate the receipts, given published information. Fifty-three cities in our sample reported average sewer/water receipts of $42.26 per resident during 1977. Thus, it would appear that the receipts pretty well cover the cost of providing services.

Residents usually purchase water based on a fee schedule with different fees for household, commercial, and industrial users. The fees are established to pay current operations, amortize outstanding debt, and reimburse the general fund for administrative costs. Improvements to the water or sewage system are financed from revenue bonds, which are then retired from sales. In periods of high interest rates, local officials often find it advantageous to finance these improvements with general obligation bonds, intending to retire the issues from sales revenues. This approach offers the advantage of borrowing at reduced interest, since the city's taxing resources are pledged to pay off the debt.

The sale of water and sewage disposal services offers another advantage. A city government can use these services as an enticement to an industrial or commercial firm considering the city as a possible location. The cost savings accruing to a firm from connecting to the city system can be substantial, and these services are being used increasingly as an economic incentive to rebuild the city economy.

Parking Facilities

The second most frequently reported semicommercial operation involves parking facilities. In our sample, 48 cities reported expenditures for parking operations in 1977, with an average of $5.27 spent per capita. Parking programs within the cities differ widely. On-street parking is popular in some areas, while greater use of municipal lots or parking garages predominates in others. Much of the support for parking facilities is derived from revenues generated by parking meters; the study cities reported an average of $3.16 per resident collected from this source. Depending on the success of the parking facility, it may have to be subsidized by the general fund, or there may be a transfer to the general fund for administrative costs.

Municipal parking facilities have become important in recent years, as it is common for a central business district to compete with outlying shopping centers, which provide free parking. If the central business district is congested and cannot easily accomodate shoppers, the downtown merchants may pressure the city council to purchase land for additional parking. The local merchants' position is strengthened by the fact that their presence contributes sales tax revenues used in financing city services. Thus, the additional parking works to the advantage of both the city government and the downtown business community. In some instances merchants pressure the city government to allow free parking on certain days or during certain seasons so that residents are not encouraged to avoid the central business district in favor of a shopping center or a neighboring city.

Hospitals

In 1977, five of the study cities reported expenditures for hospitals. Alton, Champaign, Moline, and Park Ridge reported an average expenditure of $281.21 per resident, and Chicago reported $0.61 per resident. Hospital facilities are frequently provided by private agencies, special districts, or counties. While in some instances the city makes a contribution to the operation of the hospital, it is rare in Illinois for a city to finance a hospital completely.

When a city is involved in providing hospital services, the hospitals are generally managed by a board of directors or trustees responsible to the city council and appointed by the council. In the daily operation of the hospital, however, the city officials exert very little influence. Borrowing to support an expansion, for instance, is usually done with revenue bonds to be paid from future hospital-generated revenues.

Airports

In Illinois, airports can be financed in many different ways. In Champaign-Urbana, for example, the airport is financed by the state government through the University of Illinois. In Decatur, the airport is part of the park district. In other areas, the airport is constructed and maintained by an airport authority. Eight cities in the study reported municipal expenditures for airports. The average expenditure for airports was $4.33 per resident, which was offset by revenues from airport services amounting to $4.21 per resident, as reported by six of the eight cities with such expenditures. Airport expenditures may involve purchase and acquisition of land or buildings. These are generally financed from bonds, so that the expenditure of $4.21 per resident includes more than current operations. In fact, the average expenditure for current operations by the eight cities was $3.30 per resident. This discussion, of course, is limited only to expenditures by the city government.

ECONOMIC DEVELOPMENT ACTIVITIES

In recent years, cities have become much more involved in assisting the economic development of the community. As the downtown ages and deteriorates or the industrial base erodes, city governments find it to their advantage to help private developers rebuild the city's economic base. Since the city's long-range ability to finance public services depends on a growing tax base, city support for development activities is almost a necessity.

Detailed data on the extent to which city governments are involved in private development activities are virtually nonexistent. However, at least conceptually, there are several avenues open to a municipal government. The most obvious example of city involvement in stimulating private development is the industrial park or bond program. Cities can purchase property and then lease or sell the property to a developer. In many instances, the property is improved by extending city water and sewer services. When useful, a rail spur or street access is provided, depending on the intended use of the area. In some cases, a general-purpose building is erected so that a business can relocate quickly and begin operations. The city's involvement, of course, is as an intermediary, with city expenditures expected to be recovered from additional taxes, resale of the property, or lease revenues.

Similar programs are used for rehabilitating downtown areas. Special taxing districts can be created to finance the needed improvements. If a major retailer is considering locating in the city, it is common for the city government to assist by expanding services or arranging a property purchase.

Since the mid-1970s city governments have become involved in mortgage revenue bond programs to attract middle-class residents back into the central city and to upgrade the housing stock by making housing accessible when interest rates are high. By using revenue bonds, cities were able to provide lower-cost loans to qualified applicants. These programs met with opposition from the U.S. Treasury Department, and since 1980 the use of mortgage revenue bonds has been severely limited.

There can be little doubt that city governments will continue to become more directly involved in urban development activities. As residents pressure local officials to keep residential taxes down, it will become even more important to maintain a healthy economic climate in the city. Businesses have come to expect city support as a price for relocating and, without question, the competition among cities for attracting business activity will increase. This will be especially true in states, such as Illinois, that have a history of lagging economic growth.

AGGREGATE CITY EXPENDITURES

A comprehensive profile of the expenditures by city governments is shown in Table 5-8. The expenditures are grouped into five types, including the park and sanitary district levies shown in earlier tables. This comparison among cities must be undertaken with care since in several instances unusually large expenditures are included. For instance, earlier we noted that Quincy received a large federal environmental protection grant. These funds are part of the $422.9 per resident shown in the municipal expenditures column. The semicommercial activities of the cities also vary widely, and the hospital expenditures by Champaign and Moline, for instance, significantly increase the averages in the independent cities. Springfield and Naperville operate large utilities, and Bolingbrook reported large expenditures for the provision of water services.

Perhaps what is best to be gained from Table 5-8 is an appreciation of the many services provided by city governments and the relative importance of each. The variations in types of services and the arrangements under which they are provided make a study of municipal finance difficult unless a researcher can gather data from many different sources and reorganize the data to make the expenditures at least roughly comparable. Even given the time and effort needed to make these adjustments, there are still difficulties in making conclusions about the efficiency with which services are provided. Unfortunately, the casual observer or critic of municipal practices usually has neither the time nor the inclination to develop a meaningful data base for making these comparisons.

Table 5-8. Municipal Per Capita Expenditure Summary

	Municipal Expenditures	Parks and Sanitation Districts	Semicommercial	Interest on Gen. Debt	Grand Total
Independent					
Aurora	$205.90	$29.08	$ 62.31	$12.06	$309.35
Bloomington	230.09	12.64	91.72	6.14	340.59
Carpentersville	222.98	13.45	18.82	2.40	257.65
Champaign	148.72	27.07	219.22	11.88	406.89
Danville	146.22	19.56	4.28	7.45	177.51
Decatur	127.23	31.36	47.32	11.91	217.82
DeKalb	92.13	20.34	27.14	1.77	141.38
Elgin	183.59	42.43	63.81	8.64	289.83
Freeport	124.48	13.13	17.09	7.20	154.70
Galesburg	198.68	25.51	40.12	2.58	266.89
Joliet	179.82	13.70	66.53	10.76	270.81
Kankakee	193.34	12.40	5.22	10.73	221.69
Moline	221.80	1.56	344.37	6.98	574.71
Normal	112.43	6.21	48.51	8.55	175.70
North Chicago	62.15	17.52	21.48	—	101.15
Pekin	167.51	12.75	11.10	0.96	192.32
Peoria	216.83	38.05	0.48	6.26	261.62
Quincy	422.99	13.59	47.76	19.89	504.23
Rockford	153.95	32.09	21.40	9.05	217.30
Rock Island	201.55	1.35	60.90	13.89	277.69
Springfield	214.06	23.91	555.39	8.88	802.24
Urbana	120.95	24.63	3.28	7.50	156.36
Waukegan	198.87	60.72	23.31	1.00	283.90
Average	$180.27	$21.44	$ 78.33	$ 8.02	$287.06
(S.D.)	(70.12)	(13.71)	(129.69)	(4.62)	(158.55)
Suburban Chicago					
Addison	$140.20	$35.63	$ 13.92	$ 9.41	$199.15
Arlington Heights	131.45	36.84	37.23	28.42	233.94
Berwyn	95.11	16.30	26.02	1.39	138.82
Bolingbrook	135.97	—	233.76	—	369.73
Calumet City	134.83	32.45	32.68	4.37	204.33
Chicago Heights	161.38	35.92	24.67	15.96	237.93
Cicero	136.42	38.13	43.58	1.06	219.19
Des Plaines	221.77	56.51	76.05	7.09	361.42
Dolton	104.22	28.13	31.81	2.83	166.99
Downers Grove	197.79	47.72	73.35	6.48	325.34
Elmhurst	175.01	34.86	43.71	7.02	290.60
Elmwood Park	124.50	16.40	35.24	1.34	177.48
Evanston	198.57	20.57	24.85	7.29	251.28
Glenview	126.58	43.81	31.98	3.93	202.37
Harvey	158.08	27.24	89.64	2.98	277.94
Highland Park	178.65	91.23	37.25	5.16	312.29
Lansing	97.81	29.36	46.77	1.84	175.78

Table 5-8. *(continued)*

	Municipal Expenditures	Parks and Sanitation Districts	Semicommercial	Interest on Gen. Debt	Grand Total
Lombard	$209.93	$33.23	$ 33.27	$13.22	$289.65
Maywood	141.20	20.97	35.86	1.15	199.18
Morton Grove	135.70	50.40	44.11	2.64	232.85
Mt. Prospect	137.14	40.08	26.62	8.00	211.84
Naperville	236.52	39.49	309.87	7.37	593.25
Niles	182.16	74.15	47.82	0.50	304.63
Northbrook	163.44	59.88	36.87	7.66	267.85
Oak Lawn	159.47	35.71	52.79	7.06	255.03
Oak Park	197.25	28.87	36.99	19.34	282.45
Palatine	115.96	40.76	21.12	2.00	179.84
Park Forest	117.47	13.47	27.68	1.27	159.89
Park Ridge	144.00	41.68	407.90	14.04	607.62
Schaumburg	116.87	59.57	21.66	0.83	198.93
Skokie	141.12	51.09	28.65	2.88	223.74
Wheaton	127.07	42.45	59.76	1.87	231.15
Wilmette	146.16	63.21	41.38	2.78	253.53
Average	$151.21	$40.19	$ 64.69	$ 6.22	$261.70
(S.D.)	(35.58)	(17.27)	(85.51)	(6.22)	(103.87)
Suburban St. Louis					
Alton	$147.36	$ —	$257.29	$33.36	$438.01
Belleville	139.41	5.28	1.58	11.59	157.86
East St. Louis	169.95	13.03	0.95	9.53	193.46
Granite City	118.04	28.60	3.32	6.74	156.70
Average	$143.69	$15.64	$ 65.79	$15.31	$236.51
(S.D.)	(21.44)	(11.88)	(127.67)	(12.20)	(135.41)
Chicago	$363.05	$50.31	$ 42.38	$14.76	$470.50
Z (independent vs. Chicago suburbs)	1.83*	4.55**	—	1.22	—

*Significant at 10-percent.
**Significant at 5-percent.

EXPENDITURE TRENDS

With the renewed interest in imposing limitations on tax levies and local government spending, the news media have paid much attention to the growth in local government spending. These comparisons are often made with little concern to the impact of inflation, population growth, or the source of the revenues used to finance the services. This section examines the increase in municipal expenditures from 1962 to 1977 and illustrates the extent to which inflation has contributed to these expenditure changes.

To study the impact of inflation on municipal expenditures, a price index reflecting municipal spending patterns is needed. We used a municipal price index for 1962 to 1977,[13] a weighted aggregate of price relatives with fixed weights based on expenditure patterns of Illinois cities larger than 20,000 (excluding Chicago) in 1976. Detailed comparisons of the price increases, by department or function, are shown in Table 5-9. In each case 1962 = 100. For example, the police index indicates that the same collection of inputs for police protection that $100 would have purchased in 1962 would have cost $298 in 1977. This does *not* say that the cost of police protection, however measured, has increased by 198 percent during this period. It is altogether possible that the productivity of the inputs at the two time periods is different. New, improved training methods or more sophisticated equipment may have permitted police officers to perform more services in 1977 than in 1962. In this instance, the index would overstate the impact of price increases since fewer resources were needed in 1977 to provide similar services.

The price increases show substantial variation in the impact of inflation among the city departments. For total city expenditures, the amount necessary to purchase the same inputs in 1977 was 2.43 times the 1962 level. The price increases for the city service inputs were considerably greater than those reflected by the Consumer Price Index, the commonly cited measure of inflation in the private sector. The obvious explanation is the heavy labor concentration within the municipal expenditure patterns. In the private

Table 5-9. Price Indices for Illinois Municipal Purchases (1962 = 100.0)

Function	*1967*	*1972*	*1977*
Police	132.0	188.6	298.0
Fire	129.9	187.0	303.0
Streets	117.2	151.6	221.3
Water-Sewer	111.4	160.5	223.3
Other sanitation	117.5	157.8	226.2
Libraries	118.2	159.0	215.3
General control	120.4	175.4	237.3
Parks	117.5	165.7	228.6
Total expenditures	121.1	170.1	243.0
Consumer Price Index	110.3	138.2	212.8

Source: Computed from data provided in Norman Walzer and Peter J. Stratton, *Inflation and Illinois Municipal Expenditure Increases* (Springfield: Illinois Cities and Village Municipal Problems Commission, 1978).

sector, prices for services have increased more rapidly than prices in the non-service industry groups.

Municipal expenditures in 1962 and 1977 are compared by function in Table 5-10. To illustrate the importance of price increases, the current dollar expenditures are shown along with the real expenditures (price increases removed). Overall, per capita expenditures in suburban cities increased from $51.99 in 1962 to $195.24 in 1977, or 276 percent. Per capita expenditures for police protection increased from $9.47 in 1962 to $40.48 in 1977, or 328 percent. When inflation is removed, the real expenditure (1962 dollars) for police in 1977 was $16.66 per capita, or an increase of 76 percent. Likewise, the 397-percent increase for fire protection is reduced to 105 percent when real dollars are computed. Finally, in real terms, the total expenditure by suburban cities was $80.35 per capita in 1977, an increase of 54.5 percent over the 1962 level. The important point to be obtained from this comparison is that while current dollar expenditures have increased markedly during this period, real increases have been substantially lower.

Although expenditure increases differed by department, it appears that the total municipal expenditure increase was greater in the independent cities than in the suburbs. One explanation might be the great importance of federal aid in the independent cities. With more outside support, services could be expanded without increasing property taxes. This is especially important in light of the greater number of services provided by the municipal government in these cities.

The notion that independent cities were able to increase expenditures without increasing their reliance on the property tax, as suggested in Chapter 3, has been borne out. In 1962 the independent cities received 41 percent of their revenues from the property tax, compared with the suburbs' 38 percent. However, by 1977, the independent cities received 26 percent of their revenues from property taxes, compared with 32 percent in the suburbs. Although both city types were able to reduce their reliance on property taxes, the independent cities were able to do so to a greater extent. These findings support the idea that the additional expenditures were financed to a considerable extent with intergovernmental revenues, particularly from the federal government.

Another factor affecting the expenditure growth is the governmental structure through which services are provided. The greater importance of special districts in the Chicago suburbs may be one explanation for the slower expenditure growth in these cities when compared with the independents. This explanation is especially

Table 5-10. Trends in Municipal Expenditures, 1962-1977

	Suburban Chicago			Independent		
Expenditure Categories	*1962*	*1977*	*% Increase*	*1962*	*1977*	*% Increase*
Police						
Current dollars	$ 9.47	$ 40.48	327.5%	$ 6.99	$ 35.61	409.4%
Real dollars	9.47	16.66	75.9	6.99	14.65	109.6%
Fire						
Current dollars	5.16	25.65	397.1	7.24	28.05	287.4
Real dollars	5.16	10.56	104.7	7.24	11.54	59.4
Streets						
Current dollars	11.57	30.64	164.8	12.10	39.34	225.1
Real dollars	11.57	12.61	9.0	12.10	16.19	33.8
Sewer & sanitation						
Current dollars	5.96	33.06	454.7	6.25	29.93	378.9
Real dollars	5.96	13.60	128.2	6.25	12.32	97.1
Libraries						
Current dollars	3.49	14.24	308.0	3.08	8.33	170.5
Real dollars	3.49	5.86	67.9	3.08	3.42	11.0
General control						
Current dollars	2.86	13.48	371.3	1.62	10.52	549.4
Real dollars	2.86	5.55	94.1	1.62	4.33	167.3
Parks						
Current dollars	3.18	39.84	1152.8	2.36	18.53	685.2
Real dollars	3.18	16.40	415.7	2.36	7.63	223.3
Total general expenditures						
Current dollars	51.99	195.24	275.5	54.64	251.37	360.05
Real dollars	51.99	80.35	54.5	54.64	103.44	89.31

Source: U.S. Bureau of the Census, *Finances of Municipalities and Township Governments, 1977* (Washington, D.C.: Government Printing Office, 1979), and *Governments in Illinois, 1962* (Washington, D.C.: Government Printing Office, 1964).

plausible given the suburbanization process prevalent during the period under study. Many new special districts were created to accommodate demands for services.

SUMMARY

Expenditure levels of municipalities vary widely. Wealthier cities tend to spend more per capita, as do those receiving more intergovernmental aid. Form of government also seems to make a difference in expenditure levels—even when variations resulting from cost of living differences, as measured by earnings, have been considered. These findings are consistent with what one might have expected at the onset of the study.

This chapter highlights the differences between suburbs and independent cities in expenditures by function and attempts to show how these differences may be explained in terms of governmental organization and cooperative arrangements for providing services. Relatively little difference between the two city types was found in city expenditures for common city functions. However, quite different arrangements for providing services were found. The suburbs generally relied more heavily on special districts to provide sewage treatment facilities and parks, for example. Suburbs also differed significantly from independents in employment patterns and earnings.

Chicago also differed considerably from the surrounding suburbs in expenditures levels, wages, and staffing patterns. Any of these differences can be traced to Chicago's role as a major retail and employment center for the SMSA. Likewise, differences between the suburbs and independent cities may be traced to differences in economic functions and the greater ability to achieve cost savings by cooperating with surrounding cities in the suburban areas. Mutual aid pacts are an obvious example.

When expenditures are examined between 1962 and 1977, definite differences in the two city groups are seen. In constant dollars, the expenditures by the Chicago suburbs increased an average of 55 percent, while those of the independent cities increased by nearly 90 percent. Two possible explanations for these differences are likely. First, because the independent cities serve as the hub of their particular region, they are in a position similar to Chicago's. Residents outside the city limits travel to the central business district to shop and work, thus placing extra demands on services in the central cities. Second, the suburbs rely much more heavily on special districts in the provision of services. Because of this, the city governments are relieved of some of the responsibility for services and the expenditure increase can be smaller.

On the other hand, however, many suburbs have changed from mainly bedroom communities to cities with a full range of services. Thus, while special districts have helped take the burden off the city government, many city governments in suburban areas have had to expand considerably. In the future, the older suburbs will be faced with even higher expenditures to accomodate the influx of minorities and residents in lower socioeconomic positions. In some instances, the economic base in the suburban community is not broad enough to accomodate the required expenditure growth. This will become more critical as shopping centers tend to widen the disparity in sales tax receipts.

Finally, the independent cities, based on the analysis in Chapter 4, appear to have received more intergovernmental aid than the suburbs. This is partly a result of the change to funding formulas that emphasize socioeconomic conditions and housing status. The higher expenditure growth is, without question, at least partially accommodated by the higher intergovernmental receipts. The generally lower socioeconomic status of residents in the independent cities is also a probable contributing factor to the higher expenditures.

At several points in this chapter, we have commented that because Chicago serves as the hub of the SMSA, residents in the suburbs have imposed added costs of services on the city of Chicago. Up to this point, however, we have not addressed the question of how Chicago is financed, how it compares with other cities of similar size, and what the impact of different arrangements for financing services in Chicago might have on the suburbs.

Chicago's size and importance in the SMSA demand that it be treated separately. Accordingly, the following chapter examines Chicago in detail and compares it with cities of similar size. We will pay particular attention to the importance of financing arrangements that have developed to compel suburban residents to help finance central city services.

NOTES

1. See Helen F. Ladd, "Municipal Expenditures and the Rate of Population Change," in *Cities Under Stress: The Fiscal Crises of Urban America,* ed. by Robert W. Burchell and David Listokin, ed. (Piscataway, N.J.: Rutgers, The State of University of New Jersey, 1981), pp. 351-367.
2. Readers unfamiliar with the multiple-regression procedure are referred to the Appendix to chapter three.
3. Thomas Muller, *Growing and Declining Urban Areas: A Fiscal Comparison* (Washington, D.C.: Urban Institute, 1976); Ladd, "Municipal Expenditures."
4. A more complete examination of the impact of intergovernmental aid, by type, is provided in Seymour Sacks, George Palumbo, and Robert Ross, *"The Determinants of Expenditures: A New Approach to the Role of Intergovernmental Grants,"* in Burchell and Listokin, *Cities Under Stress,* pp. 369-385.
5. For a more complete breakdown on the composition of police department expenditures in Illinois cities, see Norman Walzer and Peter J. Stratton, *Inflation and Illinois Municipal Expenditures Increases* (Springfield; Illinois Municipal Problems Commission, 1977), esp. pp. 23-28.
6. Norman Walzer and M. David Beveridge, *Expenditures for Fringe Benefits in Illinois Cities* (Springfield: Illinois Municipal Problems Commission, 1976).
7. Ibid.
8. For a more complete discussion of the components of the grading schedule, see *Grading Schedule for Municipal Fire Protection* (New York: Insurance Service Office, 1974).
9. Porter W. Homer, John W. Lawton, and Costis Toregas, "Challenging the ISO Rating System," *Public Management* (July 1977), pp. 2-6.
10. Ibid.
11. Norman Walzer and Vickie Winters, "License Fees and User Charges in Illinois Cities," *Illinois Municipal Review* (June 1979), pp. 12-13.
12. A thorough discussion of the growth in the Chicago Park District is available in Donald Foster Stetzer, *Special Districts in Cook County: Toward a Geography of Local Government* (Chicago: University of Chicago, Department of Geography, Research Paper No. 169, 1975), pp. 90-95.
13. Norman Walzer, "A Price Index for Municipal Purchases," *National Tax Journal,* Vol. 23, No. 4 (1970), pp. 441-447; or Walzer and Stratton, *Inflation and Illinois Municipal Expenditure Increases.*

Appendix: Table 5A-1. 1977 Per Capita Police Protection Expenditures

	Total Per Capita Police Expenditures	FTE[a] Police Employment Per 10,000	Average Monthly Earnings
Independent			
Aurora	$ 56.71	23.52	$1,550
Bloomington	32.07	19.76	1,263
Carpentersville	34.58	13.54	1,298
Champaign	36.63	20.89	1,425
Danville	41.46	26.20	1,003
DeKalb	30.56	19.04	1,327
Decatur	25.09	15.51	1,223
Elgin	36.90	19.75	1,464
Freeport	19.74	13.26	1,003
Galesburg	37.37	19.49	1,231
Joliet	51.79	27.42	1,426
Kankakee	36.97	25.75	1,327
Moline	31.95	19.52	629
Normal	21.03	12.30	1,262
North Chicago	20.64	14.31	891
Pekin	34.14	21.70	1,210
Peoria	49.32	25.56	1,493
Quincy	26.40	18.04	1,222
Rock Island	29.72	21.82	1,164
Rockford	47.86	19.66	1,422
Springfield	39.85	27.34	1,082
Urbana	24.84	17.14	1,338
Waukegan	53.44	22.72	1,506
Average	$ 35.61	20.18	$1,250
(S.D.)	(10.69)	(4.52)	(218)
Suburban Chicago			
Addison	$ 44.11	23.24	$1,260
Arlington Heights	29.61	15.00	1,638
Berwyn	28.64	15.52	1,486
Bolingbrook	34.25	20.75	1,298
Calumet City	62.81	18.43	1,441
Chicago Heights	44.48	25.55	1,235
Cicero	42.29	—	1,052
Des Plaines	44.57	20.60	1,539
Dolton	30.30	16.21	1,556
Downers Grove	24.28	15.02	1,177
Elmhurst	35.87	18.44	1,471
Elmwood Park	28.31	16.07	1,386
Evanston	47.22	27.39	1,440
Glenview	38.20	19.97	1,464
Harvey	46.58	28.24	1,250
Highland Park	48.98	21.38	1,721
Lansing	38.99	14.25	1,687

Appendix: Table 5A-1. *(continued)*

	Total Per Capita Police Expenditures	FTE Police Employment Per 10,000	Average Monthly Earnings
Lombard	$ 64.95	18.28	$1,413
Maywood	45.33	24.41	1,301
Morton Grove	41.92	21.08	1,495
Mt. Prospect	30.04	14.65	1,745
Naperville	35.35	20.93	1,464
Niles	51.33	25.47	1,859
Northbrook	57.63	25.99	1,682
Oak Lawn	34.95	18.45	1,598
Oak Park	56.30	31.95	1,433
Palatine	45.45	22.99	1,444
Park Forest	25.74	11.23	1,736
Park Ridge	27.00	14.43	1,559
Schaumburg	37.91	21.81	1,497
Skokie	45.81	20.39	1,466
Wheaton	33.74	18.72	1,410
Wilmette	33.04	16.98	1,517
Average	$ 40.48	20.12	$1,476
(S.D.)	(10.54)	(4.75)	(177)
Suburban St. Louis			
Alton	$ 34.14	20.66	$1,248
Belleville	24.08	16.00	1,146
East St. Louis	47.63	30.38	1,039
Granite City	27.62	15.58	1,247
Average	$ 33.37	20.66	$1,170
(S.D.)	$ (10.38)	(6.88)	(100)
Chicago	$101.68	52.28	$1,509
Z (independent vs. Chicago suburbs)	1.69*	0.04	4.64**

Source: U.S. Bureau of the Census, *Finances of Municipalities and Township Governments, 1977* (Washington, D.C.: Government Printing Office, 1979), Table 22.

*Significant at 10-percent level.

**Significant at 5-percent level.

[a] Full-time equivalent.

Appendix: Table 5A-2. 1977 Per Capita Fire Protection Expenditures

	Total Expenditures	FTE[a] per 10,000	Ave. Monthly Earnings	ISO[b] Protection Class
Independent				
Aurora	$33.85	—	$1,110	4
Bloomington	27.22	15.9	1,389	5
Carpentersville	FPD	—	—	7
Champaign	26.78	13.7	1,427	3
Danville	28.65	17.3	1,126	5
DeKalb	23.53	14.5	1,565	5
Decatur	22.09	13.3	1,356	4
Elgin	36.13	12.9	1,578	4
Freeport	30.16	17.1	1,140	5
Galesburg	22.64	13.5	1,359	5
Joliet	33.17	17.1	1,788	5
Kankakee	41.52	23.2	1,278	5
Moline	24.52	15.0	652	4
Normal	15.48	8.1	1,271	7
North Chicago	10.67	5.6	1,057	6
Pekin	37.73	18.6	1,359	4
Peoria	33.08	15.7	1,825	4
Quincy	25.44	17.8	1,127	5
Rock Island	22.37	13.7	1,306	4
Rockford	29.27	18.1	1,470	3
Springfield	33.75	19.8	1,230	4
Urbana	20.86	13.7	1,306	5
Waukegan	38.14	16.0	1,496	4
Average	$28.05	15.3	$1,328	4.7
(S.D.)	(7.61)	(3.8)	(254)	
Suburban Chicago				
Addison	FPD	—	—	5
Arlington Heights	26.98	12.5	1,633	5
Berwyn	22.69	11.9	1,384	5
Bolingbrook	42.44	14.6	1,340	7
Calumet City	18.49	—	1,110	6
Chicago Heights	27.88	15.7	1,305	6
Cicero	22.59	12.9	1,094	6
Des Plaines	33.33	15.6	1,679	5
Dolton	11.12	6.0	1,481	6
Downers Grove	21.32	6.5	1,364	5
Elmhurst	19.52	8.9	2,021	6
Elmwood Park	18.52	9.6	1,440	5
Evanston	26.41	15.8	1,493	3
Glenview	22.36	13.1	1,505	4
Harvey	30.03	16.7	1,282	5
Highland Park	27.76	13.2	1,590	4
Lansing	9.76	4.5	1,613	6

Appendix: Table 5A-2. *(continued)*

	Total Expenditures	*FTE per 10,000*	*Ave. Monthly Earnings*	*ISO Protection Class*
Lombard	$12.68	6.6	$1,321	6
Maywood	23.47	11.5	1,404	6
Morton Grove	25.98	13.4	1,536	4
Mt. Prospect	30.83	16.7	1,528	5
Naperville	14.38	9.0	1,582	7
Niles	35.98	17.9	1,590	3
Northbrook	36.39	15.9	1,688	5
Oak Lawn	28.18	16.0	1,462	6
Oak Park	30.73	14.7	1,622	3
Palatine	23.35	12.5	1,595	6
Park Forest	13.36	7.0	1,725	4
Park Ridge	22.25	10.9	1,622	5
Schaumburg	27.93	15.0	1,502	6
Skokie	32.95	18.5	1,468	3
Wheaton	15.08	4.0	1,685	6
Wilmette	26.09	13.9	1,554	4
Average	$24.40	12.3	$1,507	5.1
(S.D.)	(7.81)	(4.0)	(182)	
Suburban St. Louis				
Alton	$32.05	18.4	$1,304	5
Belleville	18.19	12.3	1,179	5
East St. Louis	28.52	19.3	1,245	5
Granite City	23.83	12.9	1,511	6
Average	$25.65	15.7	$1,310	5.3
(S.D.)	(6.00)	(3.6)	(144)	
Chicago	$34.87	15.7	$1,612	5
Z (independent vs. Chicago suburbs)	1.75*	2.7**	2.9**	

Source: U.S. Bureau of the Census, *Finances of Municipalities and Township Governments, 1977* (Washington, D.C.: Government Printing Office, 1979), Table 22; Fire protection classes obtained from *1976 Municipal Yearbook* (Washington, D.C.: Government Printing Office, 1976), Table 1/1.

*Significant difference at 10-percent level.

**Significant difference at 5-percent level.

[a]Full-time equivalent.

[b]Insurance Services Office.

Appendix: Table 5A-3. 1977 Per Capita Street Expenditures

	Expenditures			*Ave.*		*MFT*
	Total	*Capital*	*FTE*[a] *per 10,000*	*Monthly Earnings*	*Miles/ 10,000*	*Authorizations (1975–1977)*
Independent						
Aurora	$62.67	$31.60	5.7	$1,288	25.2	$ 5.88
Bloomington	51.56	30.55	5.1	1,235	39.5	10.85
Carpentersville	16.47	1.77	5.5	1,214	22.4	14.02
Champaign	18.63	7.36	4.1	1,245	17.5	5.71
Danville	31.70	0.53	7.0	1,035	41.2	9.59
DeKalb	16.71	—	6.9	1,279	22.9	3.58
Decatur	35.00	21.29	4.1	966	40.1	2.42
Elgin	47.51	39.39	8.5	1,153	24.3	9.57
Freeport	25.99	2.16	4.5	922	30.9	10.86
Galesburg	81.51	58.27	6.9	1,358	39.8	12.13
Joliet	57.82	10.50	4.2	1,556	26.2	8.00
Kankakee	33.58	3.33	21.1	1,191	37.3	8.94
Moline	45.12	21.88	3.4	1,072	31.8	3.96
Normal	23.64	12.09	5.4	1,114	28.4	10.31
North Chicago	20.38	12.69	9.6	698	10.2	9.16
Pekin	29.52	6.32	4.0	1,256	35.4	8.19
Peoria	82.09	37.77	7.2	1,418	27.6	5.97
Quincy	13.57	—	6.6	782	30.3	4.66
Rock Island	23.70	12.87	14.9	1,028	29.2	7.95
Rockford	36.70	14.51	3.5	1,191	31.3	14.81
Springfield	57.19	28.17	13.5	987	31.7	4.48
Urbana	26.67	8.16	6.1	1,033	30.2	9.05
Waukegan	67.09	41.05	11.1	984	24.7	10.99
Average	$39.34	$19.16	7.3	$1,131	29.5	$ 8.31
(S.D.)	(20.63)	(15.79)	(4.3)	(199)	(7.6)	(3.31)
Suburban Chicago						
Addison	$38.66	$16.16	5.2	$ 882	19.5	$14.84
Arlington Heights	33.49	8.00	6.7	1,475	18.6	12.44
Berwyn	13.95	2.42	1.6	1,029	15.8	17.83
Bolingbrook	18.31	3.06	8.4	1,130	14.2	15.85
Calumet City	33.10	2.61	3.4	895	13.3	9.16
Chicago Heights	22.09	7.01	6.3	794	22.0	7.29
Cicero	23.56	11.10	5.5	589	22.4	12.00
Des Plaines	39.28	0.68	7.5	1,325	23.5	9.63
Dolton	33.62	9.12	3.8	1,349	17.7	10.22
Downers Grove	38.19	12.44	4.9	859	30.8	6.13
Elmhurst	69.72	46.51	6.7	870	30.3	11.28
Elmwood Park	34.82	16.45	8.0	1,031	14.4	7.23
Evanston	42.76	26.05	5.1	1,209	15.4	16.04
Glenview	26.87	13.19	7.2	1,456	23.6	8.20
Harvey	31.94	18.34	5.5	1,097	23.0	8.26
Highland Park	44.77	13.05	7.9	1,653	32.1	9.58
Lansing	13.45	$ 2.29	9.0	1,126	17.9	3.93

Appendix: Table 5A-3. *(continued)*

	Expenditures		*FTE per*	*Ave. Monthly*	*Miles/*	*MFT Authorizations*
	Total	*Capital*	*10,000*	*Earnings*	*10,000*	*(1975–1977)*
Lombard	$45.73	$25.39	3.1	$1,681	24.4	$17.09
Maywood	24.91	8.76	1.8	900	18.7	13.09
Morton Grove	23.11	8.55	4.6	1,833	22.3	11.42
Mt. Prospect	12.11	0.88	4.5	1,247	16.1	9.23
Naperville	62.92	31.23	3.7	1,090	29.1	9.79
Niles	32.84	12.30	9.9	1,402	17.6	18.28
Northbrook	25.65	4.57	8.3	1,488	34.3	8.92
Oak Lawn	53.07	38.16	3.0	1.424	21.3	2.02
Oak Park	19.07	11.03	3.2	1,426	18.0	7.70
Palatine	14.58	0.85	3.0	1,309	18.7	12.78
Park Forest	21.67	5.10	4.2	1,195	16.8	17.84
Park Ridge	30.10	17.46	5.8	948	19.6	10.52
Schaumburg	7.70	24.87	1.0	1,106	19.1	11.26
Skokie	20.30	8.94	3.5	952	20.2	9.98
Wheaton	32.93	10.91	6.9	1,371	25.3	16.65
Wilmette	25.72	17.35	4.6	1,369	22.5	12.18
Average	$30.64	$13.17	5.3	$1,197	21.2	$11.17
(S.D.)	(14.08)	(10.89)	(2.3)	(284)	(5.4)	(4.02)
Suburban St. Louis						
Alton	$26.02	$ 5.22	5.3	$1,498	45.4	$18.60
Belleville	16.73	2.08	7.3	991	31.7	6.86
East St. Louis	18.82	3.64	13.3	1,200	33.9	9.71
Granite City	34.28	10.73	11.1	1,271	26.8	8.95
Average	$23.96	$ 5.42	9.3	$1,240	34.5	$11.03
(S.D.)	(7.95)	(3.77)	(3.6)	(209)	(7.9)	(5.19)
Chicago	$26.85	$10.50	11.9	$1,464	10.7[b]	$14.00[c]
Z (independent vs. Chicago suburbs)	1.76**	1.58	2.04*	1.02	4.51*	2.91*

Source: U.S. Bureau of the Census, *Finances of Municipalities and Township Governments, 1977* (Washington, D.C.: Government Printing Office, 1979), Table 22; MFT authorizations and street mileage obtained from Illinois Department of Transportation.

*Significant at 5-percent level.

**Significant at 10-percent level.

[a] Includes funds allocated to RTA.

[b] Estimated by IDOT.

[c] Full-time equivalent.

Appendix: Table 5A–4. 1977 Per Capita Sewage and Sanitation Expenditures

	Municipal Sewage Expenditure		Total Sanitary District	Other Sanitation	Total Sewage and
	Total	Capital	Levy	Expenditure	Sanitation
Independent					
Aurora	$ 3.34	$ 3.34	$12.99	$11.81	$ 28.14
Bloomington	22.38	14.67	12.64	12.99	48.01
Carpentersville	153.38 [a]	135.93[a]	—	10.77	164.15 [a]
Champaign	3.32	—	10.18	—	13.50
Danville	5.34	0.38	19.56	9.93	34.83
DeKalb	—	—	5.31	7.91	13.22
Decatur	16.65	14.55	12.23	1.47	30.35
Elgin	1.57	0.10	3.82	7.06	12.45
Freeport	20.20	—	—	5.15	25.35
Galesburg	—	—	25.51	11.18	36.69
Joliet	—	—	—	10.85	10.85
Kankakee	37.73	7.55	—	9.19	46.92
Moline	71.60	50.48	—	7.16	78.76
Normal	13.17	6.21	6.21	5.88	25.26
North Chicago	—	—	10.45	1.97	12.42
Pekin	8.28	—	—	7.38	15.66
Peoria	1.60	—	15.37	15.17	32.14
Quincy	329.53[a]	328.84 [a]	—	8.36	337.89[a]
Rock Island	29.92	20.91	—	19.46	49.38
Rockford	1.84	—	12.69	8.26	22.79
Springfield	14.52	9.72	8.98	2.91	26.41
Urbana	6.71	1.77	8.06	1.80	16.57
Waukegan	4.64	0.25	34.48	9.76	48.88
Average	$ 15.46	$ 10.83	$13.23	$ 8.47	$ 29.93
(S.D.)	(17.94)	(14.17)	(8.07)	(4.42)	(17.07)
Suburban Chicago					
Addison	$ 24.16	$ 0.52	$ —	$ 0.77	$ 24.93
Arlington Heights	9.33	9.33	17.83	—	27.16
Berwyn	—	—	13.14	10.64	23.78
Bolingbrook	1.31	0.04	—	10.48	11.79
Calumet City	3.00	—	17.17	2.66	22.83
Chicago Heights	5.39	0.23	19.29	9.34	34.02
Cicero	2.46	0.17	19.24	21.69	43.39
Des Plaines	4.19	—	27.69	12.04	43.92
Dolton	—	—	14.27	8.67	22.94
Downers Grove	—	—	10.84	—	10.84
Elmhurst	11.33	—	—	12.31	23.64
Elmwood Park	0.73	—	13.21	13.58	27.52
Evanston	2.19	0.01	16.58	13.15	31.92
Glenview	4.29	—	20.29	2.13	26.71
Harvey	4.49	0.24	13.83	9.66	27.98

Appendix: Table 5A-4. *(continued)*

	Municipal Sewage Expenditure		*Total Sanitary District Levy*	*Other Sanitation Expenditure*	*Total Sewage and Sanitation*
	Total	*Capital*			
Highland Park	$ 5.69	$ 5.06	$47.47	$ 1.95	$ 55.11
Lansing	2.47	—	15.11	11.57	29.15
Lombard	52.75	39.99	—	—	52.75
Maywood	0.54	—	10.53	9.48	20.55
Morton Grove	5.90	1.69	22.73	12.91	41.54
Mt. Prospect	2.48	—	18.11	16.65	37.24
Naperville	48.93	22.16	—	0.66	49.59
Niles	6.32	2.51	33.05	10.38	49.75
Northbrook	6.83	0.55	27.31	2.63	36.77
Oak Lawn	9.80	4.11	16.54	11.46	37.80
Oak Park	8.47	5.91	14.16	15.53	38.16
Palatine	3.81	—	17.28	8.41	29.50
Park Forest	2.61	0.30	11.13	0.24	13.98
Park Ridge	2.16	0.65	18.66	9.75	30.57
Schaumburg	9.93	1.15	28.38	12.46	50.77
Skokie	—	—	26.18	10.31	36.49
Wheaton	6.64	0.08	15.36	1.61	23.61
Wilmette	7.38	3.61	19.31	27.61	54.30
Average	$ 8.81	$ 4.92	$19.45	$ 9.69	$ 33.06
(S.D.)	(12.52)	(9.72)	(7.92)	(6.29)	(12.18)
Suburban St. Louis					
Alton	$ 12.28	$ 3.15	$ —	$11.42	$ 23.70
Belleville	38.98	23.29	—	9.35	48.33
East St. Louis	9.60	—	8.60	4.18	22.38
Granite City	2.92	—	16.64	9.10	28.66
Average	$ 15.95	$ 13.22	$12.62	$ 8.51	$ 30.77
(S.D.)	(15.85)	(14.24)	(5.69)	(3.07)	(12.02)
Chicago	$ 10.67	$ 4.86	$15.39	$28.33	$ 54.39
Z (independent vs. Chicago suburbs)	0.62	1.28	1.93*	0.82	0.73

Source: U.S. Bureau of the Census, *Finances of Municipalities and Township Governments, 1977* (Washington, D.C.: Government Printing Office, 1979), Table 22.

*Significant at 10-percent level.

[a]Excluded from average.

Appendix: Table 5A-5. 1977 Per Capita Expenditures for Parks and Libraries

	Municipal Park and Recreation		Park District	Total Municipal and Park District	
	Total	Capital	Levy		Libraries
Independent					
Aurora	$10.10	$ 2.22	$12.90	$23.00	$ 7.47
Bloomington	31.78	11.44	—	31.78	11.44
Carpentersville	0.28	0.04	11.20	11.48	—
Champaign	29.18	15.81	13.99	43.17	19.74
Danville	15.79	1.66	—	15.79	—
DeKalb	—	—	14.47	14.47	—
Decatur	0.30	—	19.13	19.43	8.43
Elgin	31.53	20.17	—	31.53	—
Freeport	1.55	—	13.13	14.68	6.78
Galesburg	18.57	6.99	—	18.57	.72
Joliet	—	—	10.21	10.21	5.89
Kankakee	0.86	—	9.39	10.25	5.51
Moline	11.33	2.36	—	11.33	10.16
Normal	11.88	1.08	10.70	22.58	6.69
North Chicago	—	—	4.89	4.89	2.16
Pekin	—	—	12.75	12.75	7.81
Peoria	1.01	0.64	22.68	23.69	8.70
Quincy	—	—	7.31	7.31	7.93
Rock Island	16.97	—	—	16.97	6.89
Rockford	0.10	—	16.43	16.53	8.66
Springfield	17.16	8.79	14.93	32.09	23.30
Urbana	—	—	14.28	14.28	8.69
Waukegan	0.41	—	19.05	19.46	8.97
Average	$11.69	$ 6.47	$13.38	$18.53	$ 8.73
(S.D.)	(11.41)	(6.84)	(4.43)	(9.17)	(5.18)
Suburban Chicago					
Addison	$ —	$ —	$23.20	$23.20	$ 7.82
Arlington Heights	0.41	—	14.72	15.13	25.59
Berwyn	6.57	0.10	—	6.57	3.43
Calumet City	1.50	—	11.14	11.29	—
Chicago Heights	—	—	12.68	12.68	6.10
Cicero	—	—	14.26	14.26	3.18
Des Plaines	—	—	22.15	22.15	13.67
Dolton	—	—	10.43	10.43	8.56
Downers Grove	4.72	0.03	24.39	29.11	54.30
Elmhurst	0.22	—	22.65	22.87	10.68
Elmwood Park	6.43	—	—	6.43	9.14
Evanston	35.19	2.74	—	35.19	14.09
Glenview	—	—	18.63	18.63	12.31
Harvey	—	—	10.07	10.07	4.92
Highland Park	2.67	1.45	33.88	36.55	13.77

Appendix: Table 5A-5. *(continued)*

	Municipal Park and Recreation		*Park District*	*Total Municipal and*	
	Total	*Capital*	*Levy*	*Park District*	*Libraries*
Lansing	$ —	$ —	$10.61	$10.61	$ 5.35
Lombard	6.51	0.74	21.61	28.12	9.63
Maywood	14.25	6.03	7.91	22.16	6.10
Morton Grove	—	—	21.68	21.68	15.14
Mt. Prospect	0.22	—	17.60	17.82	27.19
Naperville	—	—	26.08	26.08	14.68
Niles	—	—	33.13	33.13	—
Northbrook	—	—	25.98	—	18.44
Oak Lawn	—	—	18.36	18.36	8.38
Oak Park	18.14	2.43	11.29	29.43	22.82
Palatine	—	—	19.31	19.31	—
Park Forest	23.49	7.71	—	23.49	9.35
Park Ridge	0.49	—	18.52	19.01	30.52
Schaumburg	—	—	20.95	20.95	—
Skokie	0.24	—	18.60	18.84	14.60
Wheaton	2.61	0.32	16.24	18.85	14.82
Wilmette	0.06	—	39.25	39.31	—
Average	$ 7.28	$ 2.39	$19.48	$20.70	$14.24
(S.D.)	(9.96)	(2.75)	(7.63)	(8.55)	(10.73)
Suburban St. Louis					
Alton	$15.72	$ 0.28	$ —	$15.72	$ —
Belleville	9.00	1.30	5.87	14.87	5.05
East St. Louis	17.28	5.73	4.44	21.72	5.78
Granite City	—	—	11.96	11.96	8.70
Average	$14.00	$ 2.44	$ 7.42	$16.07	$ 6.51
(S.D.)	(4.40)	(2.90)	(3.99)	(4.10)	(1.93)
Chicago	$ 4.48	$ .07	$35.36	$39.84	$ 7.30
Z (Chicago suburbs vs. independent)	1.20	1.81*	3.45**	0.89	2.48**

Source: U.S. Bureau of the Census, *Finances of Municipalities and Township Governments, 1977* (Washington, D.C.: Government Printing Office, 1979), Table 22.

*Significant at 10-percent level.

**Significant at 5-percent level.

Chapter 6

Chicago and Other Large Cities

The city of Chicago provides employment, shopping, and cultural activities to the entire Standard Metropolitan Statistical Area, spanning more than 3,700 square miles and including more than 7 million residents. While many suburbs have gained at least partial independence in recent years by broadening their economic base, there is little doubt of the important role Chicago continues to play in the economic region. As shown earlier, large percentages of the suburban residents are employed in Chicago, and in many instances the economies of these cities are directly linked with economic conditions in Chicago.

Historical growth and development patterns in the Chicago metropolitan area have produced a maze of overlapping governments that numbered more than 1,200 distinct units in 1977. As a result of this fragmentation, wealthy residents seeking high-quality services at reasonable tax rates can migrate to the suburbs and avoid many of the social problems associated with aging cities. Suburban residents can commute to the central city to earn a living and return in the evening to a quiet, clean, mid-sized community away from congestion, crime, and pollution.

This suburbanization process is, of course, not unique to Chicago. Most large central cities have been plagued with population losses, economic declines, and rising costs of local public services. In fact, Chicago may have suffered to a smaller degree from these trends than New York or other large cities. Political arrangements with the state government in Illinois and Cook County have allowed Chicago to pass part of the cost of services to the suburbs and, in this way, to retain access to some of the wealth leaving the city limits.

Nevertheless, Chicago exhibits many signs of deterioration and distress common in old central cities. Until relatively recently, Chicago was generally thought to be in sound fiscal condition, having relatively low debt and a high credit rating. In late 1979, though, fiscal problems surfaced, causing bond rating firms to lower the appraisal of the city's creditworthiness. This, in turn, caused a marked increase in property taxes, along with other attempts to improve Chicago's fiscal condition. Simultaneously, difficulties arose with financing the Chicago School District and the Cook County Hospital. Although these agencies are separate governmental entities, the alleviation of their fiscal problems has directly involved the Chicago city government in many ways.

In this chapter, we describe Chicago's financing of services in detail, and we compare Chicago to other cities having populations of 1 million and more. As is commonly the case, the time lag that exists between published data and current happenings reported in the news media causes some of the analysis to be dated. Whenever possible, we have brought the information up to date with at least a brief analysis of subsequent events.

SOCIOECONOMIC STRUCTURE OF METRO AREAS

In recent years, major shifts in population and economic resources have occurred in metropolitan areas. Suburban areas have usually benefited economically from these shifts, while central cities have undergone a general economic decline. These movements have had a major impact on methods of financing services in central cities nationwide. Chicago is no exception.

Population Trends

Table 2-2 indicated that, nationwide, central cities represented 42.6 percent of the SMSA population in 1976, compared with 56.8 percent in 1950. A more detailed comparison of the six largest SMSAs (Table 6-1) shows a similar population decline. In every one of the six cities, 1975 population was a smaller proportion of

Table 6-1. Population Trends and Comparisons, Six Largest Cities (Millions)

City/SMSA	*1950*	*1960*	*1970*	*1975*
Chicago City	3.621	3.550	3.367	3.099
Chicago-Gary SMSA	5.178	6.221	6.978	7.015
City population as percent of SMSA population	69.9%	57.1%	48.3%	44.2%
Detroit City	1.850	1.670	1.511	1.335
Detroit SMSA	3.016	3.750	4.435	4.424
City population as percent of SMSA population	61.3%	42.3%	34.1%	30.2%
Houston City	0.596	0.938	1.233	1.375
Houston SMSA	0.807	1.430	1.999	2.286
City population as percent of SMSA population	73.9%	65.6%	61.7%	59.4%
Los Angeles City	1.970	2.479	2.816	2.727
Los Angeles SMSA	4.368	6.039	7.042	6.987
City population as percent of SMSA population	45.1%	41.0%	40.0%	39.0%
New York City	7.892	7.782	7.895	7.482
New York City SMSA	9.556	9.540	9.974	9.561
City population as percent of SMSA population	82.6%	81.6%	79.2%	78.3%
Philadelphia City	2.072	2.003	1.949	1.816
Philadelphia SMSA	3.671	4.343	4.824	4.807
City population as percent of SMSA population	56.4%	46.1%	40.4%	37.8%

Source: U.S. Bureau of the Census, Census of Population, *Final Population Counts* (Washington, D.C.: Government Printing Office), respective years.

the SMSA population than was the 1950 population. Detroit had the largest relative loss, followed by Chicago and Philadelphia. Four of the six cities also showed a decline in the actual number of residents in the central city. Chicago lost slightly more than half a million residents, or 14.4 percent of its 1950 population.

Income and Housing Characteristics

The ability of cities to provide public services is directly correlated with their tax base. Services provided are influenced, to a large extent, by residents' socioeconomic status. Table 6-2 lists 1975 per capita income. As the table shows, Chicago's $4,984 per capita income is comparable to an unweighted average of $5,151 for the six cities.

A simple comparison of income is limited, however, since major

Table 6-2. Income and Housing Characteristics (Central Cities)

	Income		*Housing*	
	1975 Urban Intermediate Budget	*1975 Per Capita Income*	*Pre-1939 Housing*	*Lacking Some or All Plumbing*
Chicago	$15,712	$4,984	67%	3.5%
Detroit	15,701	4,661	62	2.4
Houston	14,020	5,726	17	1.8
Los Angeles	15,186	5,650	32	1.5
New York	17,498	5,222	62	2.4
Philadelphia	15,689	4,660	70	1.8
Average	$15,634	$5,151	51.7	2.3

Source: U.S. Bureau of the Census, *County and City Data Book, 1977* (Washington, D.C.: Government Printing Office, 1978), Table 4, and U.S. Bureau of the Census, *Statistical Abstract of the United States, 1975* (Washington, D.C.: Government Printing Office, 1975), Table 694.

variations in costs of living are likely among these cities. The U.S. Department of Labor, Bureau of Labor Statistics, publishes a data series on what it costs a family of four to maintain a certain standard of living in large SMSAs. These estimates are included for the six cities in the first column of Table 6-2. The importance of adjusting for living costs is illustrated by a comparison between Houston and New York. In Houston in 1975, the per capita income was $5,726 and the intermediate standard of living budget for a family of four was $14,020. In New York, the per capita income was $5,222, but an intermediate standard of living required $17,498.[1] Among the six cities, Chicago was fourth highest in per capita income and second highest in cost of living.

The condition of the housing stock in a city is also an important indicator of its ability to provide services. Improving the condition of housing was the focus of major legislation, including the Housing and Community Development Block Grant enacted in the early 1970s. The two housing measures in Table 6-2 describe housing conditions: percent constructed prior to 1939 and percent lacking plumbing facilities.[2]

In the city of Chicago, 3.5 percent of the housing units lacked some or all plumbing facilities, a percentage that is substantially higher than in other large cities. Detroit and New York were next, each reporting 2.4 percent. The presumption is, of course, that units with plumbing deficiencies are older and likely to be in blighted neighborhoods. The age of the housing stock in Chicago (67 percent pre-1939) is comparable with the other central cities in the Northeast, but much older than housing in Los Angeles or Houston.

Population Characteristics

Empirical studies have shown a relationship between socioeconomic characteristics and costs of providing public services. Indeed, one of the major reasons for the rising costs of services facing large cities has been the inmigration of residents from a lower socioeconomic class who have located in the the city's slums. The population composition and density (population per square mile) in the large cities are shown in Table 6-3. When compared to the unweighted average for the six SMSAs, Chicago is above average in both the percentage of black residents and the overall population density.

The percentage of black residents in central cities receives considerable attention in studies of urban expenditures. The probability of a black family being poor or residing in a deteriorated neighborhood is much higher than that for a white family. In 1970, the most recent year for which data are available, nearly one-third (32.7 percent) of Chicago's population was black, compared with an average of 29.0 percent in the six central cities. For the entire Chicago SMSA, the black population comprised 17.6 percent of the

Table 6-3. Population Composition and Density, 1970 (Central Cities)

	Overall Population Density	*Percent Black*	*1970 Black Med. Family Income*	*1970 Black/White Income Ratio*
Chicago	13,911	32.7%	$7,883	77.0
Detroit	9,675	43.6	8,639	86.1
Houston	2,744	25.3	6,391	64.7
Los Angeles	5,879	17.9	7,198	68.4
New York	24,964	21.1	7,146	73.9
Philadelphia	14,131	33.5	7,373	78.8
Average (unweighted)	11,884	29.0	7,438	74.7

Source: U.S. Bureau of the Census, *County and City Data Book, 1977* (Washington, D.C.: Government Printing Office, 1978), Tables 3 and 4.

whole, but in the suburbs it was 3.5 percent.

The median black family income in Chicago was $7,883, compared with the six-city average of $7,438 (Table 6-3). Chicago ranked second behind Detroit, which reported an average of $8,639. Detroit was also highest in relative standing, with the median black family income representing 86.1 percent of the income reported by whites. Chicago ranked third, with black incomes 77 percent of those of white families, and was close to Philadelphia, where black incomes were 78.8 percent.

In terms of population density, another critical population characteristic, the large central cities differed markedly. Density is related to many factors, including the amount of land devoted to commercial and industrial use and the time period during which the city was developed. Cities such as Los Angeles and Houston, which were built primarily after the automobile gained popularity, had a much lower density than the other four cities: 5,879 and 2,744 persons per square mile, respectively, in 1970 (Table 6-3), compared with New York's 24,964, Chicago's 13,911, and Philadelphia's 14,131 persons per square mile.

Shifts in Sales and Employment

Within major metropolitan areas, there has been a shift in retail sales and employment from the central city to the suburban areas. Chicago has experienced the same relative decline in retail sales as central cities in the other large SMSAs. Table 6-4 shows that in 1958 sales in Chicago were $5,486 million, or 65.3 percent of

Table 6-4. Retail Sales, by City and by SMSA (Millions of Dollars)

	1958			*1977*		
	City	*SMSA*	*Percent*	*City*	*SMSA*	*Percent*
Chicago	$5,486	$ 8,398	65.3%	$ 8,960	$25,208	35.5%
Detroit	2,274	4,448	51.1	2,969	15,846[a]	18.7
Houston	1,299	1,545	84.1	7,150	10,491[a]	68.2
Los Angeles	4,433	9,039	49.0	10,288	25,889	39.7
New York	9,898	13,582	72.9	17,224	24,812	69.4
Philadelphia	2,528	4,943	51.1	4,327	14,787	29.3

Source: U.S. Bureau of the Census, *1977 Census of Retail Trade, Geographic Area Series* (Washington, D.C.: Government Printing Office, 1978), Tables 4 and 6.

[a] Houston and Detroit SMSAs changed definitions during this period with the addition of Brazoria, Fort Bend, Liberty, Montgomery, and Waller Counties to Houston and Lapier, Livingston, and St. Clair Counties to Detroit.

the $8,398 million in sales for the SMSA as a whole. By 1977, sales in the city were $8,960 million, 35.5 percent of the $25,208 million spent in the SMSA. Without doubt, regional shopping centers in the suburban areas account for part of this shift in sales. The long-term public finance implications are that the central city will not be able to rely as heavily on sales tax receipts in the future and may have to rely on other taxes or charges for services. Considering the shift in sales, the availability of broad home rule powers for developing alternative tax bases is especially important.

Accompanying the decline in sales in Chicago was a loss in employment during the late 1960s and early 1970s. Table 6-5 shows, for example, that total employment in the city of Chicago decreased by 12.4 percent from 1966 to 1975, compared with a gain in suburban Cook County of 67.7 percent and an increase of 62.3 percent in the collar counties. The heaviest actual losses were in the manufacturing industry, with the suburban portions of the county clearly experiencing the benefits of industry moving out from the city and from new industry locating in Cook County.[3] The percentage increase in the collar counties was approximately the same as for the suburban portion of Cook County.

The central city lost employment in each category except in finance, insurance, and real estate, and in service and miscellaneous employment. Employment increased 61.8 percent in the general service category, but the increase is small when compared with the corresponding increase of about 300 percent in both the suburban portion of Cook County and the collar counties.

Employment in nearly every important category increased in suburban Cook County and the collar counties between 1966 and 1975. Not much difference in growth was found between suburban Cook County and the collar counties except in the wholesale and retail trade categories. Wholesale trade employment increased 130 percent in the collar counties, compared with 92.6 percent in the suburbs of Cook County. Retail trade employment showed an opposite emphasis, increasing 127.4 percent in Cook County, but only 68.6 percent in the collar counties.[4] Population movements and changes in the locations of shopping centers partially account for these trends.

Assessed Valuation

While changes in retail sales affect how much revenue a city obtains from sales taxes, assessed valuation more directly underlies a city's ability to provide services. Through the years, property

Table 6-5. Employment Trends (Thousands of Employees)

	Chicago			Cook County (excl. Chicago)			Chicago SMSA (excl. Cook Co.)		
Industry	*1966*	*1975*	*Percent Change*	*1966*	*1975*	*Percent Change*	*1966*	*1975*	*Percent Change*
Manufacturing	583.5	375.9	-35.6%	241.3	279.7	15.9%	127.9	145.9	14.1%
Mining and quarries	2.3	0.9	-60.9	2.5	2.1	-16.0	1.2	1.2	—
Contract construction	54.6	35.3	-35.3	24.5	33.3	35.9	15.1	20.8	37.7
Transportation	59.4	46.6	-21.6	25.5	41.0	60.8	5.0	7.6	52.0
Communication and utilities	37.2	36.6	- 1.6	8.7	14.5	66.7	7.8	12.4	59.0
Wholesale trade	144.1	127.6	-11.5	33.8	65.1	92.6	11.0	25.3	130.0
Retail trade	242.8	190.8	-21.4	72.9	165.8	127.4	53.5	90.2	68.6
Finance, insurance, and real estate	111.8	134.6	20.4	14.0	32.6	132.9	8.2	17.6	114.6
Service and miscellaneous	180.2	291.6	61.8	32.8	132.1	302.7	21.8	86.2	295.4
All industries	1415.3	1239.9	-12.4	456.7	766.1	67.7	250.9	407.1	62.3

Source: Where Workers Work in the Chicago SMSA (Chicago: Illinois Bureau of Employment Security, 1975), Table 1.

taxes have been a mainstay of local government revenues. For a city to continue to be able to finance quality services, the property tax base must grow. The earlier comparisons of employment and population might lead one to expect that during the past decade the per capita assessed valuation in the central city has been declining *as a percentage of the entire SMSA*. This has indeed been the case in three of the large SMSAs. Table 6-6 shows that the *total* assessed valuation in Chicago represented 45.0 percent of the SMSA in 1966, whereas in 1976 the assessed valuation in the city was 42.5 percent of the total SMSA.

Table 6-6. Trends in Assessed Valuation (Locally Assessed Real Property)

City or SMSA	*1966*	*1976*	*Percent Change*
Chicago			
City, per capita	$2,235	$3,947	76.6%
SMSA, per capita	2,834	4,103	44.8
Total city/total SMSA	45.0%	42.5%	-5.6
Per capita city/per capita SMSA	78.9%	96.2%	21.9
Detroit			
City, per capita	2,003	3,089	54.2
SMSA, per capita	2,094	5,193	148.0
Total city/total SMSA	37.2%	18.2%	-51.1
Per capita city/per capita SMSA	95.7%	59.5%	-37.8
Houston			
City, per capita	1,064	5,892	453.8
SMSA, per capita	1,305	3,420	162.1
Total city/total SMSA	51.6%	76.0%	47.3
Per capita city/per capita SMSA	81.5%	172.3%	111.4
Los Angeles			
City, per capita	2,074	3,375	62.7
SMSA, per capita	1,955	3,333	70.5
Total city/total SMSA	43.0%	39.5%	-8.1
Per capita city/per capita SMSA	106.1%	101.3%	-4.5
New York			
City, per capita	4,068	5,621	38.2
SMSA, per capita	4,073	5,282	29.7
Total city/total SMSA	80.2%	83.2%	3.7
Per capita city/per capita SMSA	99.8%	106.4%	6.6
Philadelphia			
City, per capita	2,218	3,011	35.8
SMSA, per capita	1,975	3,788	91.8
Total city/total SMSA	48.4%	57.9%	19.6
Per capita city/per capita SMSA	89.0%	79.5%	-10.7

Source: U.S. Bureau of the Census, *Taxable Property Values and Assessment/Sales Price Ratios* (Washington, D.C.: Government Printing Office, 1978), Table 18.

The comparisons in Table 6–6 show that the *per capita* assessed valuation increased more rapidly in Chicago than in the SMSA as a whole: a 76.6 percent increase versus a 44.8 percent increase.

Table 6–6 also compares the relative wealth of the central city and the Chicago SMSA. In 1966, the per capita assessed valuation in the city was 78.9 percent of that in the SMSA; by 1976, however, there was little difference between the per capita assessed valuation in the central city ($3,947) and that in the SMSA ($4,103). One explanation for the relative increase in Chicago is the way real property is classified. Residential property, which is assessed at substantially lower rates than commercial property, constitutes a larger portion of assessed valuation in suburbs than it does in the central city. Commercial property, on the other hand, constitutes a larger share of the tax base in the city. The value of office buildings and other facilities used by daytime residents of the city may noticeably affect the tax base also. In Illinois, detailed information about property classes is not available for each city.

Comparing the relative growth of central cities and SMSAs reveals wide variations. The value of both total real property assessments and per capita assessments decreased more in the city of Detroit, for instance, than in the Detroit SMSA. Los Angeles followed a similar pattern, but there the percentage changes were less dramatic. Houston, reveals a very different pattern: the real per capita wealth of the city constituted a much higher proportion of the SMSA in 1976 than it did a decade earlier.

The comparison of assessed valuations makes quite clear that Chicago's experience is not much different from that of other large cities. In fact, per capita real property assessments in the city of Chicago increased more rapidly than in most of the others. While, Chicago declined in importance in the aggregate, in per capita terms the city increased relative to the SMSA from 1966 to 1976.

GOVERNMENTAL STRUCTURE

Chapter 5 made clear that governmental structure affects the financing of city services. The importance of overlapping governments is clear in a study of large cities. Fiscal difficulties created by the outmigration of high-income residents are magnified in the large, old central cities, so that very substantial fiscal disparities are created between central cities and suburbs. Once the outmigration process has begun, it tends to accelerate as higher tax rates are needed in the central cities to offset the shrinking tax base.

A major problem facing central cities is that of benefit spillovers. That is, suburbanites work and shop in the central cities but do not pay property taxes to the city government. Public officials in central cities can minimize the effect of benefit spillovers in one of at least three ways. First, they can annex property adjoining the outskirts of the city. If the annexations are successful, the increased wealth can help provide services. However, the suburbanization movement reflected, at least in part, an attempt to avoid high city tax rates, and it may be difficult to annex rapidly enough to retain the fiscal base in the central city. This is especially true in states where city incorporation is a relatively easy process.

A second approach to reducing benefit spillovers is to transfer city services to a separate government unit with wider boundaries. A township or county government already in existence is a likely possibility for providing services; alternatively, a new government specifically designed to provide the service may be created. Transferring the service to an existing government may require a petition to the legislature. In such cases, legal complications are common, especially when boundaries do not coincide. Thus, creating a new special district—such as a sanitary, water, park, or library district—may actually be easier. Spreading the cost of service over a larger area reduces the effects of a shrinking tax base in the central city, but central city officials lose some control over the service and the taxes to support it.

The third possibility for reducing the externalities problem involves developing a system of taxes and user charges that effectively bill suburban residents for city services. Chicago, for instance, taxes businesses based on the number of employees. Presumably, this tax covers at least a portion of the services provided to commuters. The disadvantage to user charges or taxing employers, however, is they may adversely affect the business climate in the central city. A tax on employers, for example, may hasten the exodus of businesses to the suburbs. Local payroll or income taxes based on where income is earned might be useful but, at least in Illinois, such taxes are not allowed by state statute and home rule municipalities may not impose them unless the statutes so authorize.

A unique program was developed in St. Paul-Minneapolis, where each year a portion of the assessed valuation increase is redistributed so that governments share in the prosperity of the region. This type of program requires cooperation among the governments involved, however, so it may be difficult to institute in a large metropolitan area that contains a complex maze of overlapping and competing governments.

The governmental structures of the six large SMSAs are shown in Table 6-7. One is immediately impressed by the relatively large number of governments in the Chicago SMSA (1,214 in 1977) compared with the other metropolitan areas. Although the number of governments is great, adjustments for population make Chicago much more representative. For example, Chicago reported one government for each 5,779 residents, compared with one for each 4,685 residents in Houston and one for each 5,564 in Philadelphia.

A common claim is that the presence of many competing, over-

Table 6-7. Units of Local Government, by SMSA, 1977

	Chicago	Detroit	Houston	Los Angeles	New York	Philadelphia
Total number	1,214	349	488	232	362	864
Pop./gov't.	5,779	12,696	4,685	30,116	26,413	5,564
No. with property-taxing power	1,166	327	450	228	346	570
Percent	96.0	93.7	92.2	98.3	95.6	66.0
Type						
Counties	6	6	6	1	4	7
Municipalities	261	107	86	78	106	140
Townships	113	102	—	—	38	199
School districts	315	108	53	95	135	189
Special districts	519	26	343	58	79	329
Cemeteries	5	—	—	5	—	—
Education (sch. bldg. dist.)	—	—	—	—	—	91
Fire protection	146	—	—	—	63	27
Highways	6	—	—	—	—	3
Health	11	—	—	4	—	1
Hospitals	5	5	3	2	—	7
Housing and urban renewal	5	—	4	2	—	13
Libraries	61	—	—	2	—	—
Natural resources	44	8	24	3	—	3
Parks and recreation	166	1	—	5	—	2
Sewerage	48	3	1	2	—	104
Utilities	10	2	15	25	—	14
Other	4	5	2	—	1	26
Multiple-function	8	2	294	8	1	38
Special Districts						
Overlying central SMSA city	9	4	71	12	1	6

Source: U.S. Bureau of the Census, *Governmental Organization* (Washington, D.C.: Government Printing Office, July 1978), Table 15.

lapping governments leads to inefficiency and wasteful government spending. Citizens are unable to determine which governments are responsible for providing services, and in some cases small governments provide services only at very high costs. Theoretically, one cannot always be sure whether the presence of many governments does cause higher expenditures. On one hand, the presence of benefit spillovers (meaning that not all those benefitting from a service are within the boundaries of the small government) may mean that fewer services are provided. On the other hand, since special districts are responsible for only one service, they may show little concern for the aggregate property tax bill imposed on residents.[5] At the very least, the presence of overlapping governments may lead to frustration among taxpayers as they try to determine which governments are responsible for providing services.

A comparison of the numbers of governments in the SMSAs should differentiate between units with taxing ability and those without. In the Chicago SMSA, for example, 1,166 of the units (96.0 percent) could levy property taxes in 1977. This percentage is similar to most SMSAs shown in Table 6-7, with the exception of Philadelphia, where only 66 percent could levy these taxes. Districts without taxing ability and all others obtain revenues from user charges, intergovernmental aid, and other sources.

In the Chicago SMSA, 695 of the government units were counties, townships, cities, or school districts. The remaining 519 were special districts, in most cases providing a single function.[6] With the number of governments involved, a resident may pay taxes to eight or nine separate governments. Likewise, residents in the same neighborhood may pay markedly different taxes on equal assessments. This situation easily leads to resentment against property taxes; often the municipal government receives most of the criticism because it is the most visible.

A measure of the complexity of municipal decision making in an SMSA is the number of special districts overlapping the central city. In 1977, Chicago was about average with 9, compared with 4 in Detroit, 12 in Los Angeles, 1 in New York, and 6 in Philadelphia. Houston was the exception with 71. In Chicago, a voter pays taxes to the county, township, school district, city, and up to 9 additional units of government. Because special districts include park districts, sanitary districts, and so on, the average voter is probably included in only one unit of each type.

The number of duly organized governments with or without taxing powers is one dimension of the local decision-making structure.

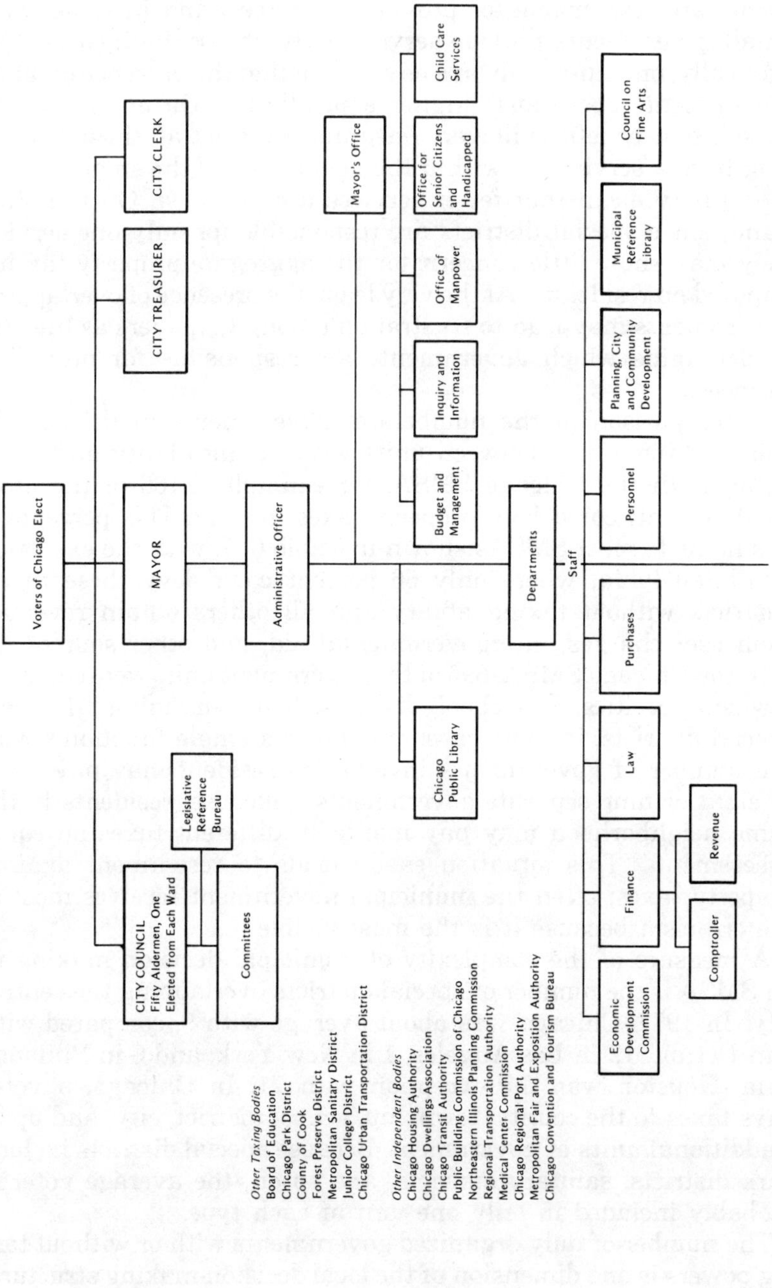
Voters of Chicago Elect
MAYOR
CITY TREASURER
CITY CLERK
CITY COUNCIL Fifty Aldermen, One Elected from Each Ward
Legislative Reference Bureau
Committees
Administrative Officer
Mayor's Office
Budget and Management
Inquiry and Information
Office of Manpower
Office for Senior Citizens and Handicapped
Child Care Services
Chicago Public Library
Departments
Staff
Economic Development Commission
Finance
Comptroller
Revenue
Law
Purchases
Personnel
Planning, City and Community Development
Municipal Reference Library
Council on Fine Arts
Other Taxing Bodies
Board of Education
Chicago Park District
County of Cook
Forest Preserve District
Metropolitan Sanitary District
Junior College District
Chicago Urban Transportation District
Other Independent Bodies
Chicago Housing Authority
Chicago Dwellings Association
Chicago Transit Authority
Public Building Commission of Chicago
Northeastern Illinois Planning Commission
Regional Transportation Authority
Medical Center Commission
Chicago Regional Port Authority
Metropolitan Fair and Exposition Authority
Chicago Convention and Tourism Bureau

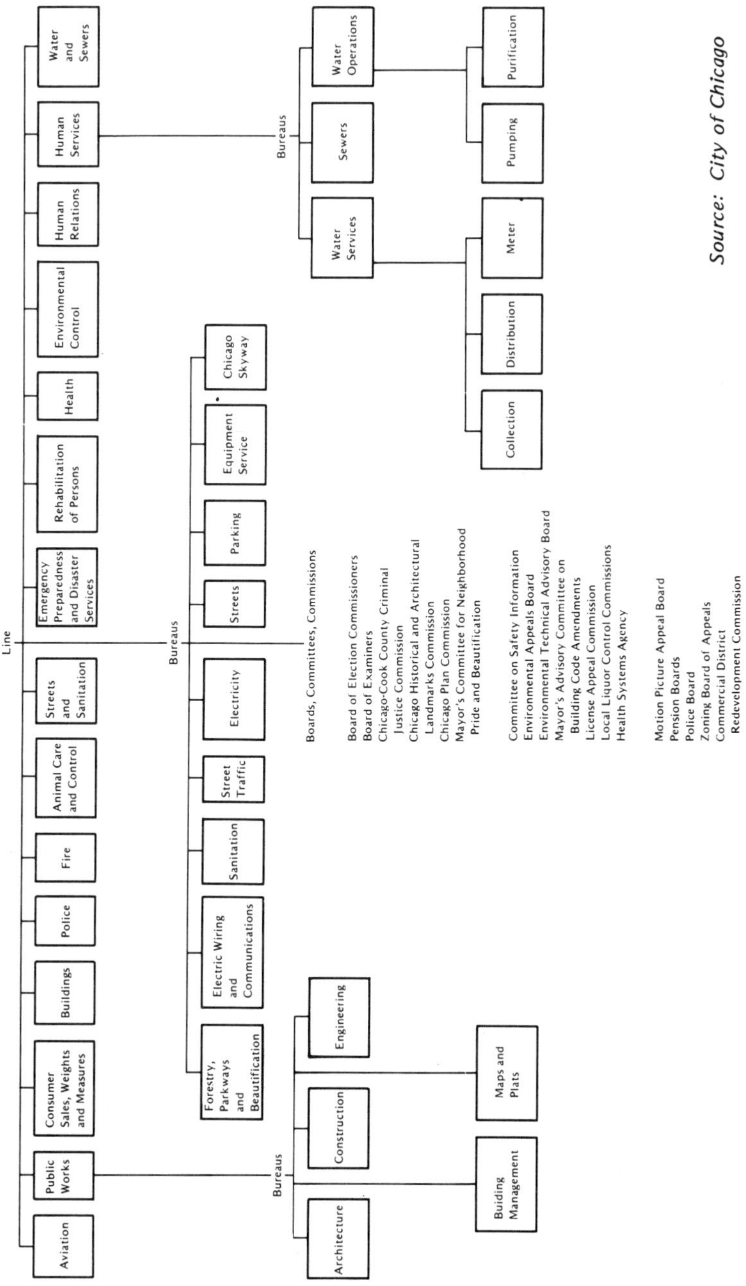

Source: City of Chicago

Figure 6–1. Organization chart, City of Chicago, January 1, 1978.

Many governing boards, agencies, and community action groups also influence municipal decisions. Figure 6-1 lists the departments, agencies, and bureaus in the Chicago city government. Space does not permit a complete description of the responsibilities of these agencies—and even if the data were assembled, the relative decision-making strength of each agency would be hard to assess. Nevertheless, the impact of these groups should be recognized when a study of expenditures and revenues is undertaken.

RESPONSIBILITY FOR SERVICES

How cities are financed is affected by which agencies are responsible for providing services. To facilitate later comparisons, the agencies or governments responsible for providing services in Chicago are compared with other cities here.[7] Service arrangements are particularly important when a single government is studied because taxpayers receive services that are financed by taxes paid to many governmental units. If only the city government is examined, a city providing relatively few services may appear to be in better fiscal position or more efficient than cities with more responsibilities.

Nearly all major cities provide the same set of urban services: police and fire protection, street maintenance, civil defense, parks and recreation facilities, health and safety inspections, financial administration, and general control. Other services—such as welfare, education, hospitals, and urban renewal housing projects—are sometimes provided by the city government and sometimes by other governments. In a comparison of revenue collections or city government expenditures, adjustments must be made for these differences.

The city of Chicago has virtually no legal responsibility for providing educational services. In Illinois the elementary and secondary eduation systems are financed by property taxes raised by school districts and state grants based on a resource equalizer formula. The school board is appointed by the mayor of Chicago, however.[8] This approach is much different from that used in New York, where the local school systems are a part of and financed by the municipal government.

In Chicago, educational services are also provided by parochial schools financed by tuition and private contributions. The higher education system includes state universities, private colleges or universities, and a junior college system operating as a special district. Because of these special districts, the city's education expenditure is practically nil.

Because of its greater responsibilities for financing education, New York City spent $351.38 for education in 1977, compared with Chicago's $5.63 per person. The reason for the disparity is that taxes raised in New York to fund the educational system appear as city revenues, whereas those raised in Chicago appear as revenues for the school district or the junior college district. New York received approximately $172 per resident in state support for educational purposes in 1977 and collected $21.06 per resident from charges. The remaining $158 per resident apparently was collected from other sources to provide the city's total expenditure of $351 per capita.

A second major difference between the cities' expenditures is in the way welfare programs are financed. Within Illinois, the welfare system is administered by the state, county, and township governments. In New York and California, on the other hand, the city governments pay a substantial portion of the welfare expenditures. In 1977, for instance, New York City paid approximately $472 per resident for welfare programs. Since approximately $420 per capita was obtained from the state, New York City was responsible for approximately $52 per resident, compared with the $7.66 per person paid by the city of Chicago. Chicago received an average of $3.43 per capita from the state for welfare-related programs.

Cities' service responsibilities also differ in regard to health care and hospitals. In Chicago, hospitals are funded by the county and private agencies; in New York, the city itself funds hospitals to a great extent. In 1977, for instance, New York spent an average of $112 per capita for hospitals. Charges for hospitals brought in an average of $29 per resident, and intergovernmental support from the state represented an additional $17 per capita. These data suggest that local resources of approximately $66 per resident were needed to finance the hospital services. Chicago spent approximately $17.87 per resident for health and hospital programs, $5.40 of which the state provided for these services. Not enough detail was available to determine the amount of revenue obtained from private sources and federal categorical grants. If such "outside" income is substantial, of course, demands on the local tax base will be fewer.

Chicago also receives services from the Metropolitan Sanitary District of Greater Chicago (MSDGC), which was established in 1889 to treat and dispose of sewage, to control storm runoffs, to maintain canals connecting Lake Michigan with inland waterways, and to protect Lake Michigan from pollution.[9] The sanitary district boundaries extend beyond the city limits, so other municipalities within Cook County receive services. The special district has its own taxing powers and operates independently. If the city of Chicago were to finance the sewage treatment completely as part of the city government operations, its expenditures would be substantially greater.

Chicago is also included in a park district coterminous with the city. Governed by a five-member Board of Commissioners (appointed by the mayor to serve five-year staggered terms),[10] the park district reflects a series of consolidations of smaller districts that once operated independently. Chicago residents pay taxes to the park district, whereas residents of other major cities pay similar amounts to their city governments.

Chicago is served by yet another special district, the Forest Preserve District of Cook County, which encompasses the entire county. The Forest Preserve protects the undeveloped area in the county and provides park related services. Operating like other units of government, the Forest Preserve levies its own taxes and issues bonds within fairly tight statutory limitations. The Census Bureau classifies the Forest Preserve as a dependent agency of the county government. Whatever its administrative status, it provides services to residents in Chicago and relieves the city of a need to make higher municipal expenditures.

The Regional Transportation Authority (RTA), established in 1974, provides public transportation in the six counties of the Chicago SMSA. Voting patterns during the referendum (suburbs against; city in favor) creating the RTA reflected the view that the financially troubled Chicago Transit Authority, another government agency, would reap financial benefits. However, since commuters represent a sizable portion of the daily ridership of the mass transportation system, the RTA method of financing was an attempt to assign a portion of the cost of transportation services to them by creating a region wide transportation system. During 1977, the RTA was financed from several sources, including 3/32 of the state sales tax collected in the area, $14 of each motor vehicle registration fee collected by the state from Chicago automobile owners, $5 million in contributions from governments in Cook County (usually interpreted as meaning $3 million from Chicago and $2 million from Cook County), plus funds from a 5-cent-per-gallon gasoline tax initiated in 1977. The RTA also received funding from federal sources, such as the Urban Mass Transit Administration, and other sources, including taxes on parking facilities.[11] Within the RTA, at least two-thirds of the revenues raised by a tax levy must be spent for services in the geographic area in which the funds were raised. For purposes of this distribution, seven areas are considered: Chicago, suburban Cook County, and each of the remaining five counties.[12] While the establishment of a more coordinated transportation system might seem desirable, there is no concensus about how to improve service in the region.

While we cannot hope to describe in detail the structure of governments providing services in Chicago in a few short pages, the number and types of governments do determine how a city fares in financial comparisons. To describe the governments providing services to Chicago residents, we list a classification system employed by the Bureau of the Census, Governments Division, in Table 6-8. The major distinction in city government is between

Table 6-8. Census Classifications of Governments in Chicago Area

Dependent Agencies	
Calumet Skyway	Municipal Tuberculosis Sanitarium
Department of Urban Renewal	Municipal Contagious Disease Hospital
Chicago Public Building Commission	Port of Chicago Department
Chicago Public Library	Water supply (Department of Water and Sewers)
Parking facilities	
Municipal airports (Midway, O'Hare Field, and Meigs Field)	
Dependent Activities	
Subway system (owned by city but operated by Chicago Transit Authority)	
Joint Agencies or Activities	
Northeastern Illinois Metropolitan Planning Commission	
Independent Governmental Units	
Chicago School District	
City Colleges of Chicago (Junior College District #508)	
Housing Authority of Chicago	
Chicago Park District	
Chicago Regional Port District	
Metropolitan Sanitary District of Greater Chicago (provides sewage service to city of Chicago)	
Chicago South Suburban Mass Transit District	
Chicago Transit Authority	
Chicago Urban Transportation District	
Metropolitan Fair and Exposition Authority	
Suburban Cook County Tuberculosis Sanitarium District	
Housing Authority of the County of Cook	
Dependent Agencies or Activities of Cook County Government	
Cook County Forest Preserve District	
Health districts	

Source: Unpublished data from U.S. Bureau of the Census, Governments Division, Governmental Organization Branch, 1975.

independent and dependent agencies. The independent agencies operate largely outside the city's influence, but the board of trustees or other governing agency may have been appointed by the mayor.

In developing financial arrangements with other governments, Chicago has had a decided advantage because the same political party controls both the city and the county. This means that agreements may be more easily reached in situations where cooperation is needed between the city and county. The voting power of Chicago legislators in the state legislature has also been very important in arranging financing for Chicago.

In addition, Chicago has had excellent working relations with employee groups. Until 1977, the city was not plagued with employee work stoppages and labor problems. Under the administration of Mayor Richard Daley, unionized employees worked without a written contract. A common view is that the workers, in exchange for their cooperation, received substantial wage and benefit increases. This situation could change, however, now that Daley is no longer mayor and collective bargaining legislation may be on the horizon. Organized labor could well exert greater influence on the city management, as has happened in other large cities. Certainly the Chicago firefighters' attempt to obtain a written contract early in 1980 was a move in this direction.

REVENUE COMPARISONS

All the variables discussed so far—variations in governmental structure, population characteristics, and tax resources—might be expected to have an effect on the types and amounts of revenues collected in each particular city. In practice, the variations among the large cities are striking. For instance, New York City collected $1,915 per capita in revenues during fiscal year 1977, compared with $396 per capita in Chicago and or $310 in Houston. As discussed earlier, one explanation for the large revenues in New York is that the city provides education, hospitals, and a significant portion of the welfare costs. In Houston, on the other hand, a relatively large number of special districts provided services that a city might otherwise provide. Subtracting the local revenues raised in New York to provide welfare, hospitals, and education would considerably reduce the revenues needed to provide common services. In 1976, for instance, one estimate was that $1.125 billion of the $2.994 billion in property taxes collected by New York were dedicated to school uses.[13]

On the average, New York City received nearly half its revenue from other governments. Detroit was the only other large city receiving anywhere near so large a proportion (Table 6-9). Chicago and Philadelphia received about one-third, and Houston received less than 20 percent of its revenues from intergovernmental sources. It might be expected that older, more distressed cities would receive a greater proportion of their revenues from intergovernmental sources. Given the direction that federal grant programs took in the Carter years, cities such as Detroit and New York would qualify for higher funding. The cutbacks proposed by Reagan are another story.

The popular, nationwide movement in the last several years to control government spending and to limit growth in property taxes makes a comparison of taxes among the six cities interesting (see Table 6-9). The property tax represented 49 percent of the taxes collected by Chicago, or $103.12 per resident. Compared with other large cities, Chicago's property tax assessments were very competitive.

Although the sales tax provided approximately 7.5 percent of the revenue in Chicago, the dollar amount per capita was lower than in the other large cities with sales taxes. The $29.88 per resident collected in Chicago was only about 25 percent of the $116 per capita collected in New York City, for instance. Much of the difference is explained by the fact that the respective city tax rates were 1 percent in Chicago and 4 percent in New York. Additional differences may involve trading patterns within the SMSA. At present, Chicago is involved in a major redevelopment project in the downtown shopping district. While the trend is clearly for suburbs to play a greater role in shopping patterns in the future, presumably the downtown development projects will help the city get back some of the sales.

Chicago receives substantial revenue from its gross receipts tax on utilities. As of this writing, there is an 8-percent tax on electric, telephone, and telegraph receipts and a 5-percent tax on gas company receipts imposed in two forms—a Municipal Public Utility Tax and a Chicago Compensation Public Utility Tax. The former is imposed at 5 percent on gas, telephone, and telegraph companies and 4 percent on electric companies. The compensation tax is imposed at 4 percent on electric companies and 3 percent on telegraph and telephone companies, but not on gas companies.[14]

Chicago is comparable with cities over 1 million in its reliance on the property tax and taxes in general. Compared with its surrounding suburbs, however, Chicago raised a much greater amount

Table 6–9. 1977 Per Capita Revenues of Cities over 1 Million

Revenue Source	*Ave. of Cities of 1 Million and Larger*		*Chicago*		*Detroit*		*New York City*		*Philadelphia*		*Los Angeles*		*Houston*	
	Dollars	*%*	*Dollars*	*%*	*Dollars*	*%*	*Dollars*	*%*	*Dollars*	*%*	*Dollars*	*%*	*Dollars*	*%*
Population (1975)			3,099,391		1,335,085		7,481,613		1,815,808		2,727,399		1,326,809	
General revenue	730.99		$396.43		$671.88		$1915.36		$667.86		$424.65		$309.76	
Intergov't. revenue	292.46	40.00	136.71	34.49	330.33	49.16	907.51	47.38	217.82	32.61	115.15	27.12	47.26	15.26
From state	184.18	25.20	44.96	11.34	158.51	23.59	779.85	40.72	78.09	11.69	37.39	8.80	6.26	2.02
From federal	101.97	13.95	78.33	19.76	159.53	23.74	125.36	6.54	135.36	20.27	75.33	17.74	37.89	12.23
Gen. Rev. Shar.	25.13	3.43	21.76	5.49	30.46	4.53	38.93	2.03	29.43	4.41	15.71	3.70	14.48	4.67
From local	6.32	0.86	13.42	3.39	12.30	1.83	2.30	0.12	4.37	0.65	2.44	0.57	3.11	1.00
Own sources	438.52	59.99	259.72	65.51	341.55	50.83	1007.85	52.62	450.05	67.39	309.50	72.88	262.50	84.74
Taxes	337.22	46.13	211.29	53.30	246.75	36.73	806.40	42.10	359.69	53.86	216.17	50.91	183.04	59.09
Property	164.23	22.46	103.12	26.01	125.49	18.68	437.14	22.82	96.06	14.38	109.73	25.84	113.83	36.75
Gen. sales	58.81	8.04	29.88	7.54	—	—	116.00	6.06	—	—	42.21	9.94	47.18	15.23
Selective sales	30.66	4.19	49.83	12.57	22.75	3.39	59.58	3.11	4.69	.70	29.22	6.88	17.92	5.79
Utilities	23.85	3.26	39.87	10.06	22.75	3.39	14.57	0.76	—	—	26.39	6.21	15.69	5.07
Other taxes	103.11	14.11	28.46	7.18	98.50	14.66	193.68	10.11	258.94	38.77	35.00	8.24	4.10	1.32
Vehicle licenses	2.61	0.35	11.59	2.92	0.10	0.01	3.99	0.21	—	—	—	—	—	—
Current charges	66.27	9.06	30.60	7.72	77.34	11.51	134.22	7.01	53.09	7.95	54.48	12.84	47.89	15.46
Misc. gen rev.	35.03	4.79	17.82	4.50	17.46	2.60	67.24	3.51	37.27	5.58	38.85	9.15	31.56	10.19

Source: U.S. Bureau of the Census, *City Government Finances in 1976–1977* (Washington, D.C.: Government Printing Office, 1979), Table 8.

per capita, $103.12 per resident, than the $66 per capita raised in the suburbs. There is little question, however, that the economic bases in the Chicago area differ from city to city. Homeowners in the suburbs probably pay a greater share of the property taxes than their counterparts in the independent cities or in Chicago simply because the latter cities have a higher nonresidential tax base. What is somewhat surprising is that Chicago obtains less per capita from the sales tax than middle-size cities in Illinois.

EXPENDITURE COMPARISONS

Revenues are collected to provide services. Table 6-10 compares major expenditures of the six large cities in detail. Functional, rather than aggregate, expenditure comparisons are most useful since the researcher can impose some adjustment for services provided. In 1977, the average city larger than 1 million spent $85.99 per capita for police protection; Chicago spent $101.68 per resident. Among the six cities, Houston spent the least by far: only $51.83 per resident. When Houston is excluded, Chicago's police expenditures resemble those of the other large cities, especially New York City and Philadelphia.

Staffing patterns and average monthly earnings of city employees can also explain variations among cities. On the average, the six major cities employed 42.7 full-time equivalent police officers per 10,000 residents (Table 6-11). While Philadelphia employed the greatest number of full-time equivalent police personnel, Chicago ranked second, nearly double Houston's count at 27.4 per 10,000.

The average earnings of full-time police officers in Chicago were also comparable with those in other large cities. The $1,509 per month in Chicago in 1977 was slightly below the six-city average of $1,587. New York City was high with an average of $1,992 per month, and Houston was low at $1,243. No account has been taken of employee benefits or differences in employee rank, which could materially affect the averages.

Relatively less variation was found among the cities' fire protection expenditures, which ranged from $30.30 in Philadelphia to $39.92 per capita in New York City. Chicago was similar to the other cities, spending $34.87 per resident, compared with an average of $34.56 per capita among all the cities. Chicago employed 15.7 full-time firefighters per 10,000, slightly above the average for the group. Average earnings for firefighters in Chicago were competitive with those in Detroit, above those in Houston and Philadel-

Table 6-10. 1977 Per Capita Expenditures in Cities over 1 Million

	Ave. of Cities of 1 Million or Larger		Chicago		Detroit		New York City		Philadelphia		Los Angeles		Houston	
Expenditure Categories	*Dollars*	*%*	*Dollars*	*%*	*Dollars*	*%*	*Dollars*	*%*	*Dollars*	*%*	*Dollars*	*%*	*Dollars*	*%*
Direct gen. expend.	$602.08		$373.68		$503.50		$1,534.77		$587.25		$327.58		$285.72	
Police protection	85.99	18.49	101.68	27.21	89.97	17.87	95.03	6.19	94.01	16.01	83.43	25.49	51.83	18.14
Fire protection	34.56	7.75	34.87	9.33	31.80	6.32	39.92	2.60	30.30	5.16	35.06	10.70	35.38	12.38
Highways, total	25.41	6.84	26.85	7.19	31.29	6.21	21.26	1.39	21.22	3.61	28.79	8.79	23.07	8.07
Health & hospitals	49.14	6.84	17.87	4.78	65.05	12.92	143.16	9.33	55.70	9.48	0.91	0.28	12.16	4.26
Sewerage	29.06	6.47	10.67	2.86	50.34	10.00	23.19	1.51	37.50	6.39	8.79	2.68	43.87	15.35
Other sanitation	23.81	4.70	28.33	7.58	25.73	5.11	35.22	2.29	27.33	4.65	14.38	4.39	11.89	4.16
Parks and recreation	19.81	4.22	4.48	1.20	34.19	6.79	16.80	1.09	28.12	4.79	19.79	6.04	15.50	5.42
Libraries	7.83	1.66	7.30	1.95	7.70	1.53	9.55	0.62	9.41	1.60	6.34	1.94	6.70	2.34
Financial adm.	9.95	2.13	6.46	1.73	13.35	2.65	11.51	0.75	10.22	1.74	9.50	2.90	8.63	3.02
General control	17.40	3.09	4.73	1.27	16.50	3.28	26.14	1.70	39.85	6.79	11.50	3.51	5.65	1.98
General public bldgs.	8.98	1.84	13.85	3.71	7.80	1.55	10.39	0.68	12.21	2.08	8.21	2.51	1.39	0.49
All other	290.15	36.95	116.59	31.20	129.78	25.78	1,102.60	71.84	221.38	37.70	100.88	30.80	69.65	24.38

not correct figures

Source: U.S. Bureau of the Census, Governments Division, *City Government Finances in 1976–1977* (Washington, D.C.: Government Printing Office, 1979), Table 8 and *City Government Employment in 1977* (Washington, D.C.: Government Printing Office, 1979), Table 4.

Table 6–11. 1977 Full-Time Monthly Payroll and Employment Per 10,000 Population

Function		*Average*	*Chicago*	*Detroit*	*New York*	*Philadelphia*	*Los Angeles*	*Houston*
Financial adm.	Payroll (F.T.)	$1,335	$1,362	$1,909	$1,106	$1,251	$1,352	$1,030
	Employment (F.T.)	4.2	2.6	3.1	4.7	7.7	2.8	4.3
General control	Payroll	1,263	1,042	1,584	1,165	1,245	1,452	1,090
	Employment	8.1	3.9	5.6	5.8	19.8	10.0	3.6
Police	Payroll	1,587	1,509	1,676	1,992	1,498	1,604	1,243
	Employment	42.7	50.6	47.2	39.3	53.1	38.5	27.4
Fire	Payroll	1,773	1,612	1,700	2,266	1,453	2,186	1,420
	Employment	15.5	15.7	14.3	15.8	17.1	12.2	17.7
Sewerage	Payroll	1,304	1,392	1,470	1,101	1,535	1,411	912
	Employment	3.1	2.8	2.3	2.6	3.7	1.9	5.5
Other sanitation	Payroll	1,131	1,237	978	1,133	1,116	1,394	927
	Employment	12.5	10.1	17.0	13.7	22.3	4.5	7.6
Parks	Payroll	1,047	1,161	1,106	1,216	1,124	879	794
	Employment	9.3	1.6	10.9	4.8	11.6	18.3	8.4
Libraries	Payroll	1,068	893	1,558	—	1,186	868	834
	Employment	4.1	4.5	3.1	—	5.1	4.7	3.2
Highways	Employment	7.7	11.9	4.6	8.0	6.7	7.2	7.9
Total	Payroll	1,436	1,433	1,498	1,734	1,342	1,463	1,145
	Employment	98.9	91.8	103.7	86.7	140.4	93.0	77.7

Source: Unpublished information provided by U.S. Bureau of the Census, Governments Division.

phia, but substantially below those in New York and Los Angeles. The relatively high wages in New York are related to the expenditure for services because of the importance of personal services in city budgets. The expenditures for fire protection in cities larger than 1 million closely approximated those in middle-sized Illinois cities, which reported $26.13 per capita for fire protection (see Chapter 5). There do not appear to be major differences in the employment ratios between the two city size groups.

On the average, the cities larger than 1 million spent $25.41 per resident for highways and employed 7.7 full-time employees per 10,000 residents. Among the cities, Chicago was substantially above average with 11.9 employees. Many factors—including street density, quality of maintenance, and condition of streets—determine the need for employees. A possible explanation of the higher number of highway employees in Chicago is patronage since Chicago has been criticized in the news media for using more personnel than necessary for various tasks performed.[15] Differences in reporting public works functions could also account for some of these variations. However, Chicago does not spend noticeably more for streets than the other five cities.

The Chicago Park District—as mentioned before, a separate government unit with a governing board appointed by the mayor—is responsible for providing parks and recreational facilities. The city parks and recreation department also provides these services. To compare the city expenditures for parks and recreation, the taxes levied by the Chicago Park District and Forest Preserve were added to the city expenditure data in Table 6-10. Although taxes collected represent a gross estimate of the expenditures involved, their addition makes the Chicago expenditures more comparable with those of other large cities. The expenditure of $23.58 per capita (not shown) spent by the city and by the park and forest preserve district was lower than the amount spent in Detroit and Philadelphia but greater than amounts spent in other cities. Substantial differences in types of services provided could easily account for these expenditure variations among the cities.

Chicago's expenditures for financial administration and general control compare quite favorably with those of the other five cities. With a total expenditure of $11.19 per capita for financial administration and general control, Chicago was the lowest of all cities; Philadelphia was highest with $50.07 per resident. Even though we can make only limited comparisons (because land and construction costs are included within these broad categories), Chicago does not appear to have unusually high administration costs.

The comparisons in this and the preceding chapters indicate that the major expenditure differences between the large and mid-sized cities are in police protection. It seems reasonable that extra police protection is needed to handle the commuter rush in the central city. Police protection may also be one of the benefits subject to spillovers. And, as mentioned before, differences in population characteristics could also affect police expenditures.

DEBT COMPARISONS

Cities borrow funds for two major purposes: to finance long-term projects (which will benefit future generations or for which current revenues are inadequate), and to meet existing needs (borrowing on a short-term basis when revenues are inadequate). A continued reliance on short-term debt can be an indication that the city government is attempting to provide more services than the tax base will allow, which in turn may portend significant fiscal problems. In this section we will compare the debt structure of Chicago with that of other large cities.

Table 6-12 shows that cities larger than 1 million exhibited wide variations in debt outstanding in 1976-1977. Due to the fiscal crises in New York City and the resulting borrowing, the New York data are considered atypical and have been excluded from the averages.

Municipal debt is of several types: utility debt and general debt. Utility debt is used to finance utilities and is not repaid from the city tax base. General debt includes full faith and credit borrowing plus nonguaranteed debt. The full faith and credit obligations, of course, are backed by the taxing power of the city. Because of the possible lower interest rates, in some instances general debt is used to finance revenue-producing operations. Thus the full faith and credit debt does not always represent an outstanding claim against municipal resources, although it certainly does represent a *potential* claim. The nonguaranteed debt is usually in some form of revenue bonds paid from the receipts of the enterprise being financed.

In addition to these types of debt, governments sometimes use a special arrangement to finance the construction of a building. One example is that of the Chicago Building Commission, which constructs buildings and leases them to the city government. The effects of this arrangement on city finance are somewhat similar to those arising from special districts. The debt of the public

Table 6–12. 1977 Per Capita Debt Structure of Cities with Populations Larger Than 1 Million

Debt Category	*Average (excl. NY)*	*Chicago*	*Detroit*	*New York City*	*Philadelphia*	*Los Angeles*	*Houston*
Gross debt outstanding	$684.58	$436.07	$512.13	$1989.01	$861.89	$975.05	$637.76
Long-term	642.03	365.89	453.54	1806.92	800.39	952.58	637.76
By purpose							
General debt	384.37	311.67	332.66	1440.44	639.52	217.15	420.87
Utility debt	127.40	54.21	120.88	366.48	160.88	735.43[a]	173.62
By financing method							
Full faith & credit	263.58	99.20	219.10	1556.51	621.90	49.79	327.91
Utility debt only	43.63	—	9.80	359.72	127.67	0.08	37.16
Nonguaranteed	238.80	266.69	243.44	250.41	178.49	902.79[a]	266.59
Utility debt only	83.74	54.21	111.05	6.76	33.21	735.34[a]	136.47
Short-term	53.19	70.19	58.60	182.09	61.49	22.47	—
Interest on general debt	23.81	14.76	21.31	96.91	50.35	12.88	19.73
Full faith & credit/ Assessed valuation	7.4%	2.5%	7.0%	27.7%	20.7%	1.4%	5.6%
Utility only	1.3%	—	0.3%	6.4%	4.2%	0.002%	0.6%

Source: U.S. Bureau of the Census, Governments Division, *City Government Finances in 1976–77* (Washington, D.C.: Government Printing Office, 1979), Table 5.

[a] Excluded from average

building commission does not always appear as city debt, and payments by the city for use of the buildings are treated as rent payments rather than as interest expense. In some instances, using a separate government is a result of debt limits imposed on governments. In the case of Chicago however, the 1970 constitution removed these debt limits.

In Chicago, the city government's share of the lease payments supporting the Public Building Commission debt are included in the city government debt. In 1976, the lease payments to the Public Building Commission were $142.6 million, or $46 per resident.[16]

Chicago had substantially less outstanding debt than any other large city in 1977, with $436.07 per capita compared with an average (excluding New York City) of $684.58 per resident. In each instance, long-term debt represented the major share of the city's debt; in Chicago, it represented 84 percent. In fact, New York was the only city with any major short-term debt outstanding. Chicago's $70.19 per capita short-term debt outstanding may have been an indication of things to come, however. Of the $365.89 per capita in long-term debt in Chicago, most was general debt, with $47 per person for the financing of airports alone. The utility debt, which represented $54.21 per resident, was incurred to improve the water systems.

The nonguaranteed debt in Chicago ($266.69 per resident) included parking facilities, ports, and similar ventures. According to the data in Table 6-12, Chicago was below average in general obligation debt but above average in nonguaranteed debt in 1977. The advent of tax-exempt bonds for housing has changed the debt structure, however.[17] On July 1, 1978, Chicago issued housing bonds of $100 million and in March, 1979, issued another $150 million.

As mentioned earlier, heavy short-term borrowing is sometimes a signal that a city is trying to provide more services than its fiscal resources will support. Chicago's short-term debt, at $70.19 per capita, exceeded that of the other cities except New York. Nevertheless, the difference between Chicago, Detroit, and Philadelphia was not major. A look at earlier data for short-term debt in Chicago shows that it was actually declining—from $96.44 per capita in 1974 and $93.99 per capita in 1975.

A fairly common way to analyze city debt is to find what percentage of assessed valuation full faith and credit debt represents. This figure facilitates an estimate of the city's ability to finance its outstanding obligations. Table 6-12 shows that in Chicago general obligation debt represented 2.5 percent of assessed valuation in 1977, a percentage substantially lower than that in the other cities except for Los Angeles. Since Chicago faces no tax rate limits involving the repayment of this debt, it was not surprising that it had a very good bond rating in 1977. One might simply note, however, that the ratio of indebtness to assessed valuation has been increasing during the past decade. In 1967, for instance, net bonded indebtness constituted 1.40 percent of assessed valuation, but during the last ten years—in 1973—it hit a high of 2.25 percent. In spite of the increase, though, these ratios are well within the usual debt limitations imposed by state governments.

Since more than one government has access to the same property tax base, an examination of the overlapping debt in the city of Chicago is in order. In FY 1977, a total of $1,096.3 million in outstanding debt was issued by the city of Chicago, the Board of Education, the City College District, the Park District, the Sanitary District, Cook County, and the Forest Preserve District. The city of Chicago's share of this debt was $950.3 million or 87 percent.[18] Thus, the claims against the assessed valuation in the city (Table 6-12) represented 87 percent of the total debt outstanding against the tax base of the city.

The importance of the outstanding debt can be partially measured by the service cost, namely, the interest expense. In 1977, Chicago spent $14.76 per resident for interest on general debt, compared with an average for the five cities of $23.81 per capita. Only Los Angeles spent less on interest, $12.88 per capita. In terms of total revenues of $396 per resident,[19] the interest cost in Chicago was obviously not heavy. The data show that cities larger than 1 million had considerably more outstanding debt than the mid-sized cities in Illinois. By comparison with the largest cities, however, Chicago had relatively low debt levels.

In 1979, Chicago suffered a serious cash flow problem, which led to a lowering of its bond rating and triggered corrective actions to improve the city finances. A combination of overstating accrued tax liabilities, lagging reimbursements from the federal government, and attempts to hold property taxes down led to a serious deterioration of the city's fiscal position. These difficulties happened to coincide with the financial problems faced by the Chicago School District. Although the two units of government are separate and their financial difficulties arose largely from different factors, news media coverage of the problems made it difficult to separate the two. The following section briefly reviews the current fiscal situation in Chicago, to bring the earlier discussion up to date.

OVERALL FISCAL HEALTH

The complicated nature of municipal accounting systems makes it difficult to evaluate a city's fiscal position accurately. Bond rating firms are usually in the best position to evaluate the financing practices in a city, but it is difficult for anybody to predict potential fiscal problems accurately. This is especially true when liability for taxes is involved and when estimates must be made of the percentages of taxes that will ultimately be collected. Even so, there were early signs, even in 1977, that Chicago might be headed for fiscal difficulties.[20]

In assessing the fiscal health of large cities, one must consider recent trends in addition to current expenditures, revenues, and debt levels. Particularly important are budget deficiencies or surpluses and the annual growth rate of expenditures or revenues.[21] Early detection of a situation in which expenditures are increasing at a faster rate than revenues may avert financial problems. Many indices can be compiled showing ratios of expenditures to revenues—or perhaps debt as a percentage of assessed valuation—and each measure has its merits. We have selected measures focusing on trends in expenditures, revenues, and tax burdens. This information pertains to conditions in the large cities prior to 1977.

Table 6-13 shows four measures of the financial position and budget performance of the large cities. The first measure, overall cash position (OCP), is an index of the city's overall liquidity. The cash position includes "total cash—restricted or unrestricted—as reported by the government, plus non-pension fund investments minus short-term loans."[22] For comparison, the cash position is shown as a percent of the general fund. Based on existing information, Chicago's cash position was more liquid than New York's, roughly similar to Philadelphia's, but substantially below that of the other three cities. Going by the rule of thumb that the OCP should be approximately 50 percent of the general fund, Chicago showed signs of being relatively illiquid, even as early as 1975. In fact, Dearborn described Chicago's overall cash position as relatively low and falling when compared with 30 major cities.[23]

A second index of fiscal condition is the reported budget balance (surplus or deficit) as a percent of annual expenditures. Chicago had a budget surplus of approximately 3 percent, whereas three cities—Detroit, New York, and Philadelphia—reported deficits. Since this comparison was based on a single year, its generality

Table 6–13. Financial Picture of Cities over 1 Million

	Overall Cash Position[a]	Reported Balance (Deficit) as Percent of Annual Expenditure	Accumulated Budget Performance (last three years)[b]	Estimated 1975 Tax burden as Percent of Income[c]
Chicago (1975)	3%	3%	5%	10%
Detroit (1975)	42	(3)	2	10
Houston (1975)	92	9	3	5
Los Angeles (1976)	103	12	4	12
New York (1976)	-8	(21)	(7)	18
Philadelphia (1975)	2	(2)	(5)	10

Source: Philip M. Dearborn, *Elements of Municipal Financial Analysis, Parts I and II* (New York: First Boston Corporation, 1977).

[a]Net cash and investments as percent of general fund.

[b]Represents budget excess (deficiency) as percent of three-year expenditures.

[c]Includes income, real estate, sales, and auto-related taxes.

is limited. An especially bad year in revenue receipts or unexpected expenditures can easily distort the data; comparing trends for several years removes many of these distortions. The accumulated budget performance measure shown in Table 6–13 adjusts for the single-year limitation and, as shown, those cities (with the exception of Detroit) with deficits in 1975 or 1976 also had net deficits over the longer period. Chicago had a budgetary surplus equal to 5 percent of expenditures during this period, making it appear to be financially stable.

In FY 1976, Chicago had a budgetary deficit of about $3.16 per resident, or approximately 1 percent of expenditures. In FY 1977, a budgetary surplus of approximately 5 percent was reported. Then, in 1979, the city was faced with unusually large expenditures because of the record snowfall and the postponing of payments of some costs incurred in 1978. Because of these and other factors, the city had a $21.2 million deficit in the corporate fund and an $81.4 million accumulated deficit in the internal service accounts at the close of 1979. These accounts had been established to purchase equipment and similar items and were reimbursed by transfers from the departments using the services. The accumulated deficits resulted from the departments' inability to meet the costs. Thus, from the close of 1978, when the corporate fund had an unreserved balance of $8.3 million, to the close of 1979, when the fund had a deficit of $21.2 million, there was a $29.5 million loss from the municipal coffers. However, the balance at the end of 1978 contained an estimated $15 million of unpaid bills, bills which had not been processed.

The above discussion amply shows how complicated a system of municipal accounting can become. Postponing payment of bills, overestimating unpaid taxes, and billing city agencies through intraservice accounts can cause a city to appear in a much better position than it really is. Ultimately, the city must face the effects of these practices; unfortunately, the cost can be a reduced credit rating. In September 1979, Chicago's rating was reduced, with the effect, of course, being higher borrowing costs.

To correct these problems, Chicago instituted several measures. First was the practice of fully discharging prior-year obligations. Second was the generation of sufficient revenues to pay the costs of services provided in 1980. The budget called for $854.3 million to be spent, from which $36.2 million would be used to reduce prior-year deficits of $21.2 million in the corporate fund and $15 million in the intraservice funds. The 1980 budget called for a 1-percent increase in the appropriation ordinance and marked "the lowest rate of proposed increased expenditures in 16 years."[24] The extra revenue needed to accomplish city objectives is to be obtained from increased receipts from the sales, parking, and other taxes, increased fees, and a new gas utility tax. The additional tax on gas utilities has not only raised the utility tax structure in the city 8 percent on gas, electricity, and telephone use; it also was expected to generate an estimated $35 million. The financial problems facing Chicago have continued to increase and the city council, at this writing, is considering another round of tax increases.[25]

SUMMARY

Throughout the nation, large cities have undergone significant losses in tax base, as well as changes in population composition whereby middle-income and wealthy residents have been replaced by growing segments of minorities and disadvantaged populations. These changes have placed considerable pressure on local revenues, particularly property taxes, to finance essential public services. Crime is increasing, streets need repair, and the costs of providing even minimal services continue to climb. The increased demands being placed on local revenues have forced the central cities to look for additional revenues, a fact that compounds the problem by forcing even more outmigration of population and industry.

Chicago conforms well to this national pattern. The population has barely held its own during the first half of the 1970s. There has been an outmovement of industry, most industrial employment has declined, and retail sales taxes are no longer able to prevent large increases in property taxes. The disadvantaged populations represent a growing share of the central city population, and the costs of providing effective public services to these population segments are steadily rising.

Chicago has been blessed, however, by the presence of other governments to help provide services. Higher education is provided by state and private agencies. Elementary and secondary education is provided by special districts. Parks and recreational services are provided by the Chicago Park District and the Forest Preserve of Cook County, both taxing districts separate from the city government. Sewage treatment facilities are financed by a sanitary district. Welfare payments are financed by a combination of the state, county, and city governments. Each of these separate districts must raise revenues to provide services, but the taxes do not appear directly in the city government accounts.

As a result of these arrangements with other governments, the city of Chicago has not had to face some of the expenditure increases associated with welfare, education, and other relatively high-cost services. In 1977, Chicago spent only $7.66 per capita on welfare-related expenditures, much less than the $52 per capita required in New York. This is not to say that Chicago residents were not taxed for these services; rather, the city of Chicago was not directly involved in providing the services. Likewise, some of the financial problems of the Chicago school system had only an indirect impact on the city government. Of course, the Chicago Transit Authority has had financial problems for a long time and, as this is written, bills are being debated in the General Assembly to find ways of alleviating the fiscal difficulties faced by the Regional Transit Authority (an ironic turn of events, especially since the RTA was originally designed to help finance transportation in Chicago).

While Chicago was long viewed as an efficiently managed city with relatively low service costs, a good credit rating, and relatively few labor problems, the budget deficits that appeared in 1979 required two years of significant property tax increases on the local property tax base, and attempts to hold taxes down caused the city to face cash flow problems. While the immediate steps taken to remedy the situation are well underway, there is no way of knowing to what extent they will prevent the city from facing similar problems in the future. A continued exodus of wealth and tax base from the city certainly would lead one to expect a repeat performance.

As if the declining tax base and influx of residents requiring high-cost services are not enough, central cities are entering the 1980s with the prospect of declining intergovernmental aid. The federal government, as part of its budget cuts, has put cities on notice that federal aid will not be as plentiful in the future. At present, cities will have more decision-making authority over grant funds but the total pie will be smaller. On the bright side, however, the enterprise zone approach proposed by the Reagan administration may provide assistance in rebuilding parts of the inner city. If it is effective, portions of central cities may be improved in the long run.

NOTES

1. For an explanation of the methodology used in constructing this index and comparisons among SMSAs, see U.S. Bureau of Labor Statistics, *Annual Urban Family Budget and Comparative Indexes for Selected Urban Areas* (Washington, D.C.: Government Printing Office), Bulletin 1570-5.
2. The Census Bureau used to publish a percentage dilapidated measure, but found the statistic to be unreliable. In 1970, the index was discontinued. For further discussion, see Aaron Josovitz, "Housing Statistics: Published and Unpublished," *Monthly Labor Review* (December 1969), pp. 50–55.
3. A more complex discussion of movements of firms within the Chicago metro area can be found in Marianne Nealon, "The Movement of Firms in the Chicago Area,"Metro Area Memo, (Chicago: First National Bank, August 1978).
4. For a discussion of national employment shifts, see Brian J. L. Berry and John D. Kasarda, *Contemporary Urban Ecology* (New York: Macmillan, 1977), esp. chap. 12 and 13.
5. A more detailed discussion of the relationships between number of governments and tax effort is available in Norman Walzer, *Financing Local Services* (Urbana: University of Illinois Cooperative Extension Service, 1979), esp. chap. 6.
6. An excellent analysis of the special districts in Cook County (the core county) is provided in Donald Stetzer Foster, *Special Districts in Cook County: Toward a Geography of Local Government*, (Chicago: University of Chicago, Department of Geography, Research Paper no. 169, 1975).
7. An excellent paper comparing Chicago with other large cities in terms of service distribution was prepared by Woods Bowman, "Paying Big City's Bills" (Chicago: The Center for the Study of Democratic Institutions, 1977), mimeo. Also, a comparison of finances in large central cities and their suburbs is available in "Composite Finances in Selected City Areas" (Washington, D.C.: Bureau of the Census, Governments Division, 1974), unpublished paper. A general comparison of big-city finances is available in *Moody's Analytical Overview of 25 Leading U.S. Cities* (New York: Moody's Investor's Service, 1977).
8. In the recent Chicago School District fiscal crisis, the city purchased school bonds in exchange for a share of the school district's taxing power. Thus the city government is involved in financing educational services although the council does not spend the funds directly.

9. A more detailed discussion of the development and operation of the MSDGC is available in *The Key to Our Local Government* (Chicago: Citizens Information Service of Illinois, 1978); or Stetzer, *Special Districts in Cook County,* pp. 60–67.
10. Foster, pp. 94–102.
11. A more detailed description of the operation of the RTA is available in *The Key to Our Local Government,* pp. 160–168.
12. In 1979, the method of financing the RTA was changed to authorize an additional 1-percent sales tax in Cook County and an increase of 0.25 percent in the collar counties. The 5-percent tax on motor fuel sales was eliminated.
13. School taxes are not counted in the general tax effort for purposes of General Revenue Sharing allocations. Consequently, the Census Bureau prepares an estimate of school taxes when education is provided as part of a general purpose government. The estimate shown for New York was obtained from the RS-12C form for 1976.
14. 1978 Municipal Utility Tax Survey (Springfield: Illinois Municipal League, 1978), p. 3.
15. The Better Government Association and the Chicago *Tribune* established a task force in 1974, which stated that the costs of providing municipal services in Chicago exceeded those in other large cities. The findings were released in a series of *Tribune* articles in November and December 1974. A statement, dated November 25, 1974, criticizing noncomparabilities in the data and defending the city's position was prepared by Budget Director Edward Bedore.
16. The Census Bureau classifies cities having a fiscal year ending December 31, 1976, as having a 1977 fiscal year. For a more complete profile of the net outstanding debt for Chicago, see *Report of the Comptroller of the City of Chicago,* FY ended December 31, 1976, Schedule V-13, p. 139.
17. See *Tax-Exempt Bonds for Single-Family Housing,* a study prepared by the Congressional Budget Office for the Subcommittee on the City of the Committee on Banking, Finance and Urban Affairs, House of Representatives, 96th Cong., 1st Session, April 1979; *Mortgage Revenue Bond Advisory Committee's Report on the City of Chicago Mortgage Revenue Bond Program* (Chicago, December 1978); *The Chicago Plan Report as of December 9, 1978* (Chicago: First Federal Savings and Loan Association, 1978).
18. *Report of the Comptroller,* Schedule V-13, p. 139.
19. A more detailed comparison of debt trends in Chicago and cities over 1 million can be found in *Moody's Analytical Overview,* pp. 28–36.
20. A more detailed discussion of the situation in Chicago is available in Pierre de Vise, "Chicago in the Red—Not the Pink," *Illinois Issues (March 1980), pp. 32–*33; a comparison of the fiscal position of large cities is available in *Moody's Analytical Overview.*
21. A detailed comparison of the finances of large cities has been prepared by Philip M. Dearborn, *Elements of Municipal Financial Analysis, Part I: Measuring Liquidity,* and *Part II: Budget Performance* (New York: First Boston, 1977). Another review of the fiscal condition of large cities can be found in *City Financial Emergencies* (Washington, D.C.: Advisory Commission on Intergovernmental Relations, 1973).
22. Dearborn, *Elements of Municipal Financial Analysis, Part I,* p. 4.
23. Ibid., p. 8.
24. See *Official Statement, City of Chicago, General Obligation Tax Anticipation Notes* (January 1980), pp. 32–33.
25. "CTA Crisis Is to Become More Taxing," *Chicago Tribune,* July 21, 1981, Section 1, p. 8.

Chapter 7

Changing Profiles of Municipal Finance

Modern cities have developed largely for economic reasons. Many economic activities are carried on more cheaply because of the internal and external economies of scale that can be achieved when economic activity is near the population concentrations that make up a city.

These economies of scale, in turn, do much to explain the rapid economic growth that has characterized this century. In the early twentieth century, large central cities arose. But changes in technology and the improvements in transportation—notably automobiles and trucks and the construction of major highways from the central cities—facilitated suburban growth. The period since the Second World War has certainly been an era of suburbanization.

The hypothesis advanced early in this book is that the urbanization and suburbanization processes have created two very different types of cities in states like Illinois. The outmigration of wealthy and middle-class residents from the central cities provided opportunities for middle-sized cities in the surrounding area, especially those along rail lines, to prosper. The suburbs did not have to provide employment in order to attract residents. They merely had to provide a basic set of services and a pleasant living environment with affordable housing. Residents were financially able to construct new, high-quality housing, and collecting property taxes to provide needed services was not a major problem. In fact, the relatively low suburban tax rates, compared with those in the central city, may have been a prime factor in central city residents' interest in relocating.

Of course, not all suburbs contain only wealthy residents seeking to avoid the congestion, pollution, and high taxes associated with the central city. Some of the older suburbs with less desirable characteristics and more modest housing attracted people from the lower middle classes who wished to escape the problems of the central city but who did not have the income and financial status to be able to afford living in the richer areas.

The urbanization process also created another type of city—the free-standing city—which serves as the hub of a smaller, less metropolitan region. In Illinois, many of these cities are central cities of smaller SMSAs and face some of the same types of problems as large cities do, but to a much lesser degree. The housing is dated, the tax base is eroding, and the public infrastructure is in need of significant repair. More prosperous residents of many of these free-standing cities are building new homes on the cities' outskirts to get farther away from the blighted business district. Shopping centers are following these residents, and consequently the downtown areas are suffering economic decline. In some instances, the shopping centers are outside the city limits, so the city does not even obtain sales tax receipts from them.

To test the hypothesis that free-standing cities differ markedly from suburbs, we divided Illinois cities of roughly comparable size into two groups: Chicago suburbs and independent cities. Statistical tests of significant differences were applied, and the findings generally confirmed our hypothesis. Residents in the Chicago suburbs are better off financially, live in better housing, and have more wealth available for providing public services. Because much of the suburban development has been recent and because in many instances the residents have relocated from Chicago in search of communities with precisely these characteristics, this finding is not all that surprising.

Also of interest, however, is the great diversity within the suburban category. Some of the older suburbs are beginning to take on many of the characteristics of the independent cities, such as deteriorating housing stock and growing numbers of minorities. These changes are indicative of a dissemination of minorities from the central city—in this case, Chicago. It is quite clear that both the population composition and the economic characteristics of the suburbs adjacent to Chicago will change considerably during the next few years. One can easily imagine that a continuation of these trends will widen the disparity among suburban cities.

Urbanization, suburbanization, and economic growth have important, but less-well-understood, implications for the character and finance of local government. It does seem clear that the same growth of cities that produces private economies of scale also produces important diseconomies of scale in the public sector. The interdependence resulting from specialization causes social problems. Residents who are not currently self-supporting tend to be concentrated in central cities. And concentration of population increases the demand for governmental services of many kinds.

Unfortunately, government services are not self-financing in the sense that those who wish to consume them must pay the full cost. Compulsory extractions, called taxes, are levied against people, property, or income that are within the legal jurisdiction of the governmental unit involved. As the process of suburbanization divides the economic city into several governmental cities, the possibility increases that taxpayers and beneficiaries may not live in the same governmental jurisdiction. It is widely alleged that many of the financial problems of American cities result from central cities being burdened by the cost of providing services to high-income nonresidents and problem-prone residents.

A major focus of this book has been how the suburbs differ from the independent cities in their methods of financing services (and what types of expenditures they make). There are several possible explanations for differences between the two city types:

Socioeconomic characteristics of city residents and resulting differences in types of services desired.
Variations in tax base, which largely determine the types of revenue sources and the amounts of revenues that can be collected.
The amount of intergovernmental aid provided to cities and the allocation process employed.
The intergovernmental arrangement for providing services.

Initially, one might expect that wealthier cities would have lower tax rates, since a larger tax base would produce large sums at low tax rates. Our findings paint a much more complicated picture, however. While the independent cities have slightly higher city property tax rates than the suburbs, this is partly because they provide a greater share of public services to their residents. On the other hand, suburban residents receive services from a county, a township, a city, school districts, and usually several special districts. A close examination of independent cities shows that property taxes represent approximately 25 percent of the aggregate property taxes paid by their residents. City property taxes in the suburban group, however, represent only 19 percent of the total property taxes collected. This difference is statistically significant.

An examination of the aggregate taxes paid by urban residents shows that property tax payments for services are higher for suburban residents. Suburban residents pay not only a higher dollar amount but also a higher percentage of their incomes in property taxes than do residents of independent cities.

The differences in the share of services provided by city governments may reflect the potential for cooperation among cities that are located in proximity. For example, mutual aid pacts can be made for such things as fire protection. And special districts can be set up for park services, sanitation services, libraries, and so on, so that residents of neighboring cities can share services.

While special districts may offer cost advantages in providing services, they also disperse control over property taxes. Residents may pay higher property taxes to a set of small overlapping governments than to a few larger governments, for several reasons. First, special districts rely more heavily on property taxes than do general-purpose governments, which have access to other revenue sources. Second, at least in Illinois, an early reason for the growth of special districts was that they could bypass property tax rate limitations. And the larger the number of governments that can levy taxes, the larger the tax collections can be. Third, officials elected to the governing boards of the special districts have less opportunity to see the size of the overall tax burden and may be more prone to spend more on the service over which they have control. In fact, it is sometimes claimed that one benefit of special districts is that they eliminate the need to compete with demands for other services in a general government budgeting process.

For these reasons and probably other reasons, then, residents in the suburbs are paying higher aggregate property taxes. Suburban residents are still paying lower taxes than Chicago residents, however, and relocation to the suburbs remains attractive, at least on the basis of taxes.

When the two city types are compared in terms of intergovernmental aid, it is quite clear that the independent cities receive significantly more federal aid and rely much more heavily on this revenue source for financing public services. In 1977 in the average Chicago suburb, federal intergovernmental revenues represented 5.2 percent of the revenues collected by the city. In the independent cities, however, the average was 13.7 percent. The two major state programs, income tax rebates and motor fuel tax payments, are based on population. It would appear, then, that the independent cities have qualified for more federal aid, which has borne part of the cost of providing local services. In the suburbs, more of the services are being financed through special districts, which rely more heavily on property tax revenues.

Discerning differences between expenditure patterns of the two city types was more difficult. Looking only at total dollar expenditures by the city government, we saw relatively little difference between the two: only $29.06 per capita, with the independent cities spending the higher amount. This difference was not statistically significant at the 5-percent level.

We found similar results when we undertook a more detailed examination of expenditures, considering other factors that might affect spending. Specifically, variables such as earnings, intergovernmental aid, assessed valuation, and presence of a city manager were found to be significantly associated with expenditure variations among the sample cities. Two characteristics, population change and type of city (independent or suburb), were not significantly related to total spending.

Some statistically significant differences among the cities were found when spending patterns were examined according to type of service, however. When we did not find statistically different expenditure levels, in some instances we did find differences in wages paid and employment patterns. Suburban cities in the Chicago area paid higher wages in several instances, particularly for police officers and firefighters. In other cases, the differences in earnings were not great. Some of these differences might be attributed to cost-of-living variations among the cities.

What did become evident in the comparisons of expenditures by city type was the importance of sanitary and park districts. In the Chicago suburbs, residents received services costing $40.19 per capita from these districts. Since the estimate of the cost of services provided by these districts is based on property tax collections, the same arguments about economies of scale which were presented in the property tax discussion above apply.

Wide variations were found among the cities' semicommercial activities. Interestingly, however, the variations were more between cities within each group than between the two city types. On average, the two city types differed in this expenditure category by less than $12 per capita.

Our final comparison of expenditures was the rate of growth during the 1962–1977 period. The growth rate differed markedly between the two city types, with independent city expenditures increasing at a substantially faster rate. An equally important finding was the impact inflation has had on municipal government expenditures. When price increases are removed, the expenditure increases are found to be substantially lower.

While the main focus in this book has been on middle-size cities, the importance of Chicago in Illinois municipal finance required that we pay at least some attention to financing large cities. When we compared Chicago with Detroit, Houston, Los Angeles, New York, and Philadelphia, we found several major differences. For instance, the city of Chicago does not have major responsibility for providing many of the relatively high-cost urban services that New York City must provide. Education, welfare, hospitals, parks, and sewage treatment facilities represent relatively small expenditures in the Chicago city budget because these services are primarily financed through separate governments.

An examination of remaining expenditures showed that Chicago was quite comparable with the other five cities. The one possible exception was police protection, for which Chicago's expenditures were considerably above average. In total dollar expenditures, however, Chicago was considerably below the three northeastern cities—Detroit, New York, and Philadelphia—but above Houston and Los Angeles, the two sunbelt cities. If expenditures of the special districts were added to those of the city of Chicago, the total expenditures for the older central cities would be fairly comparable.

Chicago also compared quite favorably with the other large cities in revenues collected. Property taxes represented a slightly higher proportion of revenues in Chicago, but the dollar amount collected per capita was very competitive. The importance of sales taxes in Chicago was surprisingly lower than in other cities; its relative importance as a revenue source, however, was similar from city to city.

It is quite clear that the financing of services in Chicago is related to property tax payments by residents in the Cook County suburbs. Several of the special districts established to finance services in Cook County are countywide. This arrangement undoubtedly has provided some advantages to the central city. Without it, the city's tax base would have decreased substantially as residents migrated to the surrounding suburbs. With the present arrangement, the tax base in the suburban portions of Cook County can be tapped for services that are provided by a special district or county government.

OUTLOOK FOR THE NEAR FUTURE

Since the mid-1970s, municipal finance in Illinois and in the United States as a whole has been in a state of flux. Attempts to impose stricter tax limitations continue. Challenges to home rule authority appear on the ballot in large cities fairly regularly. Periodically, the Illinois General Assembly considers restricting the revenue-raising powers of municipal governments by reducing the tax base. Clearly, municipal officials both in Illinois and throughout the country are in for a period of belt-tightening.

As if the limitations on local revenues are not enough, the federal government has placed state and local officials on notice that intergovernmental revenues may decrease in the future or at least have smaller than expected increases. The public service employment section of CETA is currently under review, for possible elimination. In addition, state governments did not receive their portion of general revenue sharing in 1981, and future appropriations will be decided annually. Other funding programs are being consolidated, and the amounts scheduled for such funding are being consistently reduced.

There are some bright spots on the horizon, however. The Reagan administration intends to consolidate some of the categorical grants into block grants and to provide more decision-making authority to local governments. The red tape associated with federal grants has long been an irritant for local officials, so greater discretionary authority should be good news. Of course, the need to make more difficult choices about which projects to finance at the local level will not be politically pleasant.

As the 1980 Census of Population data become available, it is becoming clear that many of the suburbs close to Chicago are changing in their population composition. As early as 1977, it was apparent that many of these cities were experiencing population losses. One might expect the 1980 Census to emphasize this fact even more, and perhaps to pinpoint some of the difficulties that these cities will face in the near future.

Our analysis of suburban economies in Chapter 2 revealed that, in many instances, the suburbs did not have large tax bases. Residents work in Chicago or a neighboring city and rely on the suburb for essential public services. In recent years, however, these cities have found it necessary to broaden their economic bases to raise enough funds to provide the wider range of services that residents have come to expect. The need for increased expenditures to repair and rebuild the city's physical plant and to provide some of the services mandated by the federal and state governments is therefore going to cause many suburbs to pursue economic development policies much more aggressively in the future. Movements in this direction will noticeably change the economies of these cities and probably make them much more similar to the independent cities. This similarity will certainly come about as the suburbs become older and their housing stock deteriorates.

The older suburbs close to Chicago—such as Evanston and Oak Park—are already facing these problems as economically disadvantaged populations make their way into them. During the next decade, we will probably experience a continuation of these trends in the second tier of suburbs.

The problems faced by suburbs may be intensified as public officials in central cities take advantage of programs to draw middle- and upper-class residents back within the city limits. Chicago was a leader in the development of housing revenue bonds to help residents finance homes at reduced interest rates. A reverse movement of middle-class residents would inevitably place greater pressure on low-income residents, whose homes might be replaced by condominiums, to find housing elsewhere. The fact that lower-skilled jobs are also moving to the suburbs will certainly put pressure on central city residents to relocate there as well. With time, housing in the older suburbs may become more accessible to current residents of the central city. This hypothetical scenario, of course, is not applicable only to Illinois or the Chicago metro area but rather to most large metropolitan areas throughout the United States.

MUNICIPAL FINANCE: A LOOK INTO THE FUTURE

This research endeavor should be concluded with some comments on the issues that Illinois cities will face during the next decade or so. Specific projections by necessity are imprecise, but several trends are evident.

Population Changes

Population growth or decline is a critical factor in the financing of Illinois cities. Accurate population projections for municipalities are difficult to obtain. Growth in a broad metropolitan region may involve widely divergent growth rates in each city, with major differences in the levels and types of services required. (Such differences are especially evident in environmental services such as sewage treatment and water distribution.) Major capital investment decisions evolve only after long periods of deliberation, and cooperation among levels of government is often required.Thus, there can be a long time lag between population change and expenditure changes.

While population growth creates demands for local services, shifts in the age composition of the population are equally important. The average age of the population will increase as a result of the decrease in birth rates in the 1970s. The baby boom that followed World War II caused a bulge in the population distribution, which involved considerable frustrations for local officials responsible for financing public services. During the 1950s and 1960s the growing need for school facilities was met by a major building program, but during the 1980s many of these schools will no longer be needed and some will be closed. Baby boom children have begun their professional careers and established households, which increases the need for municipal services. With a relative shift in services from school districts to municipalities, the pressures of financing schools may ease while they increase in other governments.

In recent years, municipal officials have played an important role in building and expanding the employment base of the city. Population movements to the suburbs have caused building booms in some cities, while facilities in neighboring areas go unused. Local officials in both cases are developing policies designed to attract business and to strengthen the local economy.

The problems faced by officials differ depending on whether a city is a suburb in a large urban complex or a free-standing, independent city. In the former case, the degree of growth will be affected partly by the growth pattern of the metropolitan area. People can change jobs without changing places of residence. In the independent cities, policy makers must be more concerned about shaping the city's future because of the close correlation between the legal and economic city. The loss of a major industry has a more significant effect on population size in a free-standing city because alternative employment may not be within driving distance. Residents thus may have to leave the city to find work.

The future of a city also depends on the state's economic growth. A trend toward relocation in the South is underway; as a result, Northeastern and Midwestern states are growing at a rate slower than the national average. Illinois has certainly not been immune to this trend. During the 1960s, the Illinois population increased 10.2 percent, but from 1970 to 1975 the estimated growth was only

0.8 percent. Even though the state growth has slowed, however, the proportion of residents living in urban areas may continue to increase. In other words, the urbanization process could continue. One estimate is that population increases in Illinois will lag behind those in the rest of the nation until about 1990, at which point Illinois will meet or exceed the national average growth rate for at least the subsequent 10-year period. From 1975 to 2000, the population of Illinois is expected to increase by slightly more than 13.5 percent, while the national population is expected to increase by approximately 23 percent. Such an increase will represent a gain of nearly 1.5 million residents during the 25-year period.[1]

As important as the overall state population growth is the shift in population by region within the state. The major urban area in Illinois, the northeastern portion, will probably continue to be a relative growth area, although one might expect a continuation of the general movement toward the northern and western suburbs, unless rising energy prices and high interest rates lead to a reversal of the trend toward dispersal of population in urban areas.

Changes in Services

The increased number of two-income families permitted many families to own a second automobile and other luxuries. Higher incomes usually mean that more and better public services are demanded, even though residents' willingness to pay property taxes may not change. Higher family incomes also mean larger purchases, which should mean higher sales tax receipts for a city and higher income taxes for the state. Whether cities with increasing demands for services are the same as those receiving the additional revenues is another question. Particularly in the suburbs, the presence of regional shopping centers may cause a wide disparity in fiscal capacity.

Earlier discussions emphasized that municipal expenditures are becoming heavily influenced by mandates from the state and federal governments. These mandates are especially prevalent in environmental services such as waste treatment facilities. Federal and state governmental agencies have intervened to set standards for local services, and they have increased local expenditure requirements substantially. Over the past decade, civil rights legislation has increased the operating costs of local governments since personnel must spend more time complying with new regulations. These outside influences, which are usually beyond local control, involve additional paperwork and reporting requirements.

The recent requirement in Illinois that the state government reimburse local governments for mandates will help them stem these cost increases.

Distinct from the need for additional public services, attempts to have the city government help new employers and stimulate housing construction in the city is expected to continue. At least in Illinois, cities have a whole new arsenal of weapons to fight urban blight and downtown deterioration. Tax-increment financing, commercial revenue bonds, and industrial development bonds are expected to come into greater use. Depending on actions of the federal government, housing revenue bonds may be used more and more, particularly by cities losing middle-income residents. The older suburbs may find these tools important as they strive to stabilize their populations and economic base. The independent cities with older housing and more deteriorated physical facilities are also likely to find these financing instruments useful.

While revenue bond financing and other tax-increment financing methods are attractive because they represent little cost to the city government, policy makers should be alerted to the growing responsibility a city undertakes when it commits resources to developing the private sector. This added responsibility may prove to be very effective for maintaining a healthy economic environment in the city, but it also represents new areas of responsiblity for municipal officials—responsibilities with which they may be unfamiliar.

Changing Attitudes Toward Taxes

Continued demands by citizens for tax relief, tax reform, or both —especially in property tax administration—may require significant adjustments by cities. While cities have decreased their reliance on the property tax over the past decade, the tax remains a major source of local revenue. Public officials are well aware of taxpayers' feelings, and considerable evidence has been found that property tax rates are being held down to avoid incurring the wrath of residents. In interviews, local officials in the study cities frequently disclosed, for instance, that they would not increase property taxes even if they had to reduce services. In most cases, cutting back means postponing capital improvements or delaying the purchase of new equipment.

In some instances, municipal officials have succeeded in transferring traditional municipal services, such as refuse collection, to the private sector, where taxpayers are charged directly. In the spirit of resistance to tax increases, one might expect more cities to rely on a private collection system since this exchanges a municipal tax for a direct purchase agreement between the user and the collector.

SUGGESTED POLICY OPTIONS

Municipal officials interviewed during the course of this research offered several policy suggestions. Most of these suggestions require cooperation by the General Assembly, but tax limitation pressures may make this the right time at least to consider a realignment of state-local fiscal interrelationships.

Reimbursement of State Mandates

In cases where local governments are limited in revenue sources, state reimbursements need to be provided to local units for mandates involving significant costs. Mandates, especially for such things as pensions, increase local government expenditures. Many times such mandates are imposed with little or no input from the local governments affected. Although statewide standards and mandates are necessary, the legislature or other state agencies must seriously evaluate mandates before imposing them. One of the most significant tests to determine whether a mandate is truly necessary is to require the mandating agency to fund it. Illinois began a reimbursement program in 1981 and the initial experiences have been favorable.

Pension Reform

The rising costs of public employee pensions are going to be one of the most serious problems facing municipal officials during the 1980s in Illinois and in other states. Even though local pension systems vary with states, it is quite apparent that many local and state systems are underfunded. Unless a serious attempt is made to fund these programs at actuarially sound levels, there is a possibility for default at a later date. At the very least, a continuation of the current funding approach means that residents in future generations will pay the .pension costs of current employees. Switching to a program coordinated at the state level would not necessarily end the pension problem, but it could be a significant improvement.

Consolidation of Local Governments

At the local level, efforts should be undertaken to reduce the competition among governments for property taxes and to encourage better coordination in local services. Whenever possible, incentives should be developed to encourage a reduction in the number of governments with taxing powers. In Illinois, for example, township services in urban areas should be examined to determine whether an alternative governmental arrangement could provide the service more effectively. Likewise, when a special district has outlived its usefulness, a method should be devised for dissolving it without a long and involved legal process. Although the constitution encourages consolidation of services and cooperation among governments, much more effort is needed to accomplish this objective.

State Revenue Allocation

In the late 1970s, Illinois municipalities found that the state revenue sharing programs did not increase as rapidly as the costs of providing the services that they were financing. This was particularly true in the motor fuel tax reimbursement program. The revenues received by cities were declining in real terms, while the costs of constructing and repairing streets were rising more rapidly than the general inflation rate.

An attempt must be made to protect local governments that depend on the state intergovernmental revenue sharing programs to finance services. This means that the state motor fuel tax should be based on something other than the number of gallons sold. Switching to a tax based on the amount of sales would be of considerable assistance in protecting local governments from a reoccurence of the present situation.

Within the state, some thought might be given to basing the allocation process of state intergovernmental aid on factors in addition to population. Large cities suffering population declines are still required to maintain the same street mileage. Inevitably, their receipts will decline significantly, which will place even greater fiscal strain on them. In many instances, population serves as a reasonable allocator of revenues. An additional adjustment may be needed for streets, however, especially if the population losses persist in the large central cities.

Within the suburban areas, attention may have to be given to the growth of regional shopping centers since they can have a major impact on the sales tax receipts of surrounding cities. Developing a reasonable solution will be difficult, given the numerous cities that will be affected. However, a continued growth and concentration of sales will certainly widen the disparity in revenue-raising abilities among suburban communities.

Federal Intergovernmental Revenues

The growing importance of federal assistance, especially to independent cities, was described earlier. The future of municipal finance will certainly be affected by the direction these programs take. The current prospects for a continuation of federal assistance at existing levels are not bright. If cutbacks are forthcoming, cities will have to make corresponding adjustments. Cutbacks may affect independent cities more than the suburbs. If cutbacks occur, cities would have to rely more heavily on the state government for support, and the importance of a realignment of fiscal responsibilities would increase.

SUMMARY

This study has attempted a careful review of the manner in which middle-size cities are financed in an urban industrial state. While most of the analysis deals in detail with Illinois cities, the experiences of these cities are, for many reasons, meaningful for those in other states. Though the analyses are presented to highlight similarities or differences between the suburbs or independents, one cannot help but gain a strong impression of the highly complex nature of local finance.

At the beginning of this project, we noted a need for improved understanding of municipal finance practices before far-reaching policy changes are adopted. The current climate of tax limitation, many times without reform, can lead to outcomes other than those intended by proponents and may even limit services to urban residents in the future. If this book adds insight into the complexities of financing cities and offers some direction for improving the financing of city governments, our efforts will have been well rewarded.

NOTE

1. *Illinois Population Projections 1970–*2025, rev. ed. (Springfield: Illinois Bureau of the Budget), pp. 5–11.

Appendix

Note on Statistical Methodology

Throughout this book we have used two statistical techniques. The first is a test of significant difference between means for two city groups, suburbs and independent cities. The second is the multiple-correlation-and-regression technique used to identify the association of independent variables with a dependent variable. Because of space limitations, we cannot provide a complete analysis of the techniques; for an in-depth treatment, refer to an elementary statistics text.

TEST OF SIGNIFICANT DIFFERENCE

A common statistical technique is the test of significant difference between sample means. When cities have been grouped by type, it is important to know whether differences in the averages for each variable are statistically significant from zero at a generally accepted level of confidence. A comparison of means, without a test of significance, has limited use because of variations within the samples. The test of significant difference adjusts the difference in means for the variations with each city group. The following formula is used:

$$Z = \frac{\overline{X}_1 - \overline{X}_2}{\sqrt{S_d}}$$

where

$$S_d = \frac{\sigma_1^2}{n_1} + \frac{\sigma_2^2}{n_2}$$

$\overline{X}_1, \overline{X}_2$ = the means of the two samples

S_d = the standard deviation

$\sigma_{1,2}^2$ = the variance of the two samples

n_1, n_2 = the sample sizes

To conclude that a difference between sample means does not result from random variations (null hypothesis), the *Z*-statistic must exceed a certain level. For example, if one finds a *Z*-statistic of 1.96, one can be reasonably certain that if the test of significant difference were conducted repeatedly, one would accept the null hypothesis when, in fact, it was incorrect only 5 times in 100(95-percent confidence level). The traditional test is 95-percent confidence, but in the text, we have shown both 90-percent and 95-percent levels, permitting readers to make their own determination of significance.

In using this test to compare the groups, it is obvious that in cases where there are wide variations within the samples the standard deviations (variances) will be larger, lowering the *Z*-statistic and lessening the likelihood that a significant difference will be found. This means that to find a significant difference the absolute difference must be greater.

MULTIPLE-REGRESSION ANALYSIS

In some cases it is important to determine whether variations among socioeconomic characteristics are related to variations in expenditures or revenues. In these instances a *Z*-statistic might be significant, but this simple test cannot identify which factors are most closely associated with variations in the dependent variable. The common method for examining these relationships is multiple-regression analysis. In multiple-regression analysis, variations in a set of independent variables are compared with variations in a dependent variable in order to test a hypothesis or set of hypotheses about an expected relationship. The analysis yields several measures that can be used to evaluate the association.

A linear regression equation of the following form is usually estimated:

$$Y = a + b_1X_1 + b_2X_2 + b_3X_3 + \ldots + b_nX_n + u$$

where
- Y = the dependent variable
- a = the constant
- $b_1, \ldots, b_n$ = the regression coefficients
- $X_1, \ldots, X_n$ = the independent variables
- u = random variation in the dependent variable

With results received from computer programs, one is able to test the significance of the associations between the independent and dependent variables. The traditional test of the significance between, say, X_1 and Y when all other variables have been held constant statistically, it to compare the size of the regression coefficients with their variations about the mean. This involves dividing the regression coefficient by its standard error. If the ratio (*t*-ratio) is at least 1.96 in absolute terms, one can conclude that if this regression were estimated many times, only 5 times out of 100 would the researcher accept the hypothesis that a relationship is significantly different from zero when, in fact, it is not. Several levels of confidence are used. The 1-percent level (an incorrect hypothesis is accepted 1 time in 100) requires a *t*-value of 2.58; the 5-percent level of confidence requires a *t*-value of 1.96, as noted above.

The regression coefficient shows the extent to which variations in a dependent variable are associated with unit changes in an independent variable. For example, a regression coefficient of 1.45 when Y is regressed on X_1 would mean that for this sample a one-unit increase in X_1 is associated, on the average, with a 1.45-unit increase in Y. If the *t*-value exceeds 1.96, one can accept the hypothesis that the relationship is significantly different from zero.

The size of the partial regression coefficient is determined by units of the independent variable, which makes it difficult to compare the magnitude of the coefficients to determine their relative importance. If a comparison of the relative importance of the coefficients is desired, one can divide each coefficient by its standard deviation to obtain a beta (standardized) regression coefficient. The result is now a pure number and not affected by original units. The larger the beta coefficient, the greater the relative importance of the variable in the regression equation.

A second statistic is the coefficient of multiple determination, R^2, which measures the proportion of variation in the dependent variable which is associated with changes in the independent variables in the regression equation. This statistic provides information about the ability of the independent variables, taken together, to predict values of the dependent variable. The higher the coefficient of multiple determination, the greater the predictive ability of the variables.

The F-value can be used to determine whether the variation accounted for by the independent variables is due to other than random chance—in other words, whether the same proportion of variation could have been "explained" by the inclusion of a set of random variables. The greater the F-value, the less likely that a set of random numbers would have accounted for this proportion of variation. Statistical tests can be used to determine whether the explained variation is significantly different from zero at various confidence levels.

LIMITATIONS OF REGRESSION ANALYSIS

Whereas regression analysis is a powerful technique for identifying and testing relations among strategic variables and the resulting outcomes, it does have several inherent limitations. These problems should be recognized in interpreting the results shown in the text so that greater significance than is warranted is not attributed to the results.

Correlation Is Not Causation. Perhaps the most significant limitation of regression analysis is the temptation to assign causation to a statistical relationship. The fact that X_1 is significantly associated with Y does not mean that X_1 causes Y. Actually, since the association runs in both directions, it may well be that Y causes X_1. For this reason, the use of good theory in selecting variables and in establishing hypotheses is critical. If, after sound political and economic reasoning, a relationship can be posited, a regression analysis can help determine whether this theory is consistent with the facts. However, the regression analysis cannot prove the theory, and the researcher is never sure that an alternative theory might not offer a better explanation.

Results Are Limited to the Sample. A second limitation of regression analyses results is that they are based only on the observations in the analysis. In our study, the results are based on Illinois municipalities with populations of 25,000 and over, excluding Chicago. It is hoped that they are meaningful for similar-size cities in other states with broad home rule authority. However, the usefulness of the results for purposes of generalization is related to the comparability of the cities in the two samples. The regression results should be viewed as summarizing the relationships in the middle-size Illinois cities, and extension of the results should be undertaken with care.

Regressions Are Only as Good as the Data. The regression results are only as good as the data on which they are based. The fact that regression analysis is high-powered and can be very useful in describing relationships is of limited use unless the basic data accurately describe the cities, residents, or other variables under study. Unfortunately, in the social sciences, researchers have sparse data and are forced to use proxies or indirect measures of the variables in which they are interested. Each time the relationship is estimated by a proxy, there is a loss in the confidence that can be attached to the results. The regression technique cannot differentiate between good and poor data and will yield statistical results based on either. It is left to the researcher to be sure that the data used in the analysis accurately represent what is being measured.

A NOTE ABOUT DATA SOURCES

A major difficulty in conducting a statistical analysis of local government finance is to obtain data that are reasonably current and that accurately measure the characteristics in which a researcher is interested. This is particularly troublesome when studies are undertaken at the city government level, because a single statistic for a city may disguise a whole host of other factors. Likewise, decisions about government finance will be affected to a considerable extent by factors in neighboring cities or influences outside the city limits. These difficulties go a long way toward explaining the lack of significant empirical results common in many studies. With existing data bases, one simply is not able to capture the essential factors involved in the decision-making processes. Even if factors involved in determining levels of service or other outcomes could be measured, adequate funds to collect the data are usually not available. Thus a majority of research endeavors use existing data with suitable recognition of its weaknesses. We now turn to a brief discussion of the major data sources used in this project.

Census of Governments Survey. At five-year intervals the

Bureau of the Census, Governments Division, conducts a massive nationwide data-gathering effort based on a survey of local and state governments. The information is compiled into the Census and organized by states, counties, municipalities, townships, and other governments. We used the 1977 Census covering the fiscal year ending in 1977 as the basis for our analysis.

Illinois Comptroller's Annual Survey. By law each city in Illinois, excluding Chicago, must file with the Comptroller's Office a copy of the annual audit and complete a supplemental report. Data from these reports are compiled and published in the *Statewide Summary of Municipal Finance in Illinois*. In recent years the Census Bureau, as part of its effort to collect general revenue sharing data, has contracted with state organizations to collect data. Illinois is one of the states in which this cooperative effort has been undertaken. Thus, the two data series should be reasonably comparable. For the larger governments, the Census Bureau reviews the data by comparing cash flows, and may reconstruct portions of the data based on its analysis to assure comparability between governments.

Illinois Property Tax Statistics. The most comprehensive information on property taxes available on an annual basis is from the Illinois Department of Revenue. County officials provide information that contains detailed data on taxes, assessed valuations, and extensions for each taxing unit in Illinois. The greatest limitation of this data source is that it is not published until several years after the information is collected. This lag occurs mainly because appeals must be heard and adjustments to the tax base must be made, but also because much of the data compilation effort is undertaken manually. Even with its limitations, however, this data series is the best available.

Census of Population. The major source of information about the socioeconomic characteristics of city populations is the 1970 Census of Population. While few would dispute that the data is outdated, there is very little that a researcher can do unless funds are available for a major data-gathering effort. In a few instances more recent information is available, such as 1975 population estimates and 1975 per capita income estimates needed for updating the revenue sharing data.

Personal Interviews. The published information on Illinois cities was supplemented by personal interviews with officials in 20 of the 61 cities. Usually we interviewed the city manager, finance officer, or mayor, and sometimes we interviewed all three in a general session. In most instances we tried to interview personnel at the departmental level—such as the police, fire, or street department head. We selected the cities to achieve a balance of large and small cities, close-in and far-out suburbs, and free-standing cities with differing economic bases. The information we obtained was invaluable in helping us learn of unique experiences and in helping us gain a perspective on decision-making practices at the municipal level.

Index

A

B

C

H

I

Q

R

S

T

U

W

About the Authors

Norman Walzer earned a B.S. in business administration from Illinois State University and a Ph.D. in economics from the University of Illinois at Urbana-Champaign. Since then, he has actively researched urban poverty, housing, and public finance. For the past seven years, Professor Walzer has served as a consultant to state and local governments and as research director for a state government commission studying problems facing cities. Currently professor of economics at Western Illinois University, he has published articles in *Review of Economics and Statistics, Land Economics,* and *National Tax Journal*, among others.

Glenn W. Fisher received his B.A. from the University of Iowa, his M.A. from the University of North Carolina, and his Ph.D. from the University of Wisconsin at Madison. He is Regents Professor of Urban Affairs at Wichita State University, where he has been on the faculty since 1970. Previously, he was a professor in the Institute of Government at the University of Illinois at Urbana-Champaign. Professor Fisher is the author of *Taxes and Politics: A Study of Illinois Public Finance* (1969) and the coauthor of *Illinois Municipal Finance* (with Robert Fairbanks, 1968) and of *Politics of the Purse: Revenue and Finance in the Sixth Illinois Constitutional Convention* (with Joyce Fishbane, (1974). His current research is in the field of property tax administration and the relationship of property taxation to local government structure.

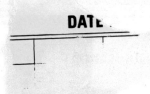